THE THIRTEENTH TURN

THE
THIRTEENTH TURN
A History of the Noose

JACK SHULER

PublicAffairs
NEW YORK

Published in the United States by PublicAffairs™,
a Member of the Perseus Books Group

Printed in the United States of America.

PublicAffairs books are available at special discounts for bulk purchases in the U.S. by corporations, institutions, and other organizations. For more information, please contact the Special Markets Department at the Perseus Books Group, 2300 Chestnut Street, Suite 200, Philadelphia, PA 19103, call (800) 810-4145, ext. 5000, or e-mail special.markets@perseusbooks.com.

Book Design by Pauline Brown

Typeset in 12.5 pt Adobe Garamond Pro by the Perseus Books Group

Library of Congress Cataloging-in-Publication Data

Shuler, Jack.
    The thirteenth turn : a history of the noose / Jack Shuler.—First edition.
        pages   cm
    Includes bibliographical references and index.
    ISBN 978-1-61039-136-8 (hardback)—ISBN 978-1-61039-137-5 (electronic) 1. Hanging—United States—History. 2. Lynching—United States—History. 3. Violence—United States—History. I. Title.
    HV8579.S58 2014
    364.1'34—dc23

                                                                    2014007475

First Edition

10   9   8   7   6   5   4   3   2   1

Contents

A GOOD DEATH

Acknowledgments

I WOULD LIKE TO FIRST THANK the amazing individuals who let me interview them and shared their hearts and minds and time. I am grateful.

Writing this book made me aware of the many limits to my intellectual abilities. If not for the help of countless librarians and fellow researchers, it wouldn't have happened. One person who was a constant touchstone for research was the ever-exceptional Joshua Finnell. I was ably assisted by four gifted scholars—Holly Burdorff, Olivia Nienaber, Cecilia Salomone, and Elisabeth Halse—and a treasure trove of Denison librarians past and present, including Lareese Hall, Michael DeNotto, Pam Magalaner, and, especially, Susan Rice, who tracked down many obscure sources for me.

Many wonderful people read parts or all of the manuscript. I appreciate their efforts on my behalf. The flaws that may appear in this book are my fault alone. Thank you, Gene Shaw, Jon-Christian Suggs, Mark Noonan, Bill Munn, Walter Hoover, Mitchell Snay, Paul Thompson, Katharine Jager, Benjamin Gessner, Toni "The Enforcer" Lisska, Dennis Read, Keir Bickerstaffe, Jim Davis, James Weaver, and Mike Croley.

Linda Krumholz and Fred Porcheddu were my first and last readers. You two are gems.

Many thank yous to all my talented colleagues in the Denison English Department and its fearless organizer and captain, Anneliese Davis. Thank y'all for giving me a home and a sounding board.

Generous funding from the Denison University Research Foundation helped support my research. A special thank you also to Denison faculty who offered assistance along the way, including Laurel Kennedy, Toni King, Sylvia Brown, Ann Townsend, Erin Henshaw, Isis Nusair, Andrew McCall, David Baker, Stephen Kershner, Harold Von Broekhoven, David Busan, Sandy Runzo, and Jess Clawson.

The amazing folks at Sandra Dijkstra Literary Agency, including Sandy and my friend and champion, Elise Capron, helped make this book a book. Thank you, Elise, for believing in this project.

Thank you to all of the inspired folks at PublicAffairs including Benjamin Adams, Brandon Proia, Clara Platter, Josephine Mariea, and Melissa Raymond.

Many thank yous to the curators, librarians, and volunteers in all the archives, museums, and historical/genealogical societies I visited, phoned, or e-mailed. Y'all are the front line, the guardians of history and story in this country, and your work is key to our future.

Countless people looked up random facts/tidbits, helped me make contact with people to interview, and offered advice along the way: Craig Keeney, Chris Johnson, Rabbi Robert Kaplan, Peter Hawes, Anna Connor, Becky Michaels Anderson, Heidi Beirich, Lloyd Bourgeois, Terry Bradford, Fred Counts, Bill Munn, Sheri Sharlow, Crys Armbrust, Susan Thoms, Lee Morgan, Betsy Blake, James Burgess, David S. Reynolds, Jane Rissler, Bill Barker, Doug Perks, Chris Evans, Elizabeth Baer, Rick Lybeck, Nic Butler, Leo Riegert, Joan Hunstiger, Mo Stemen, Niels Lynerup, Markil Gregerson, Ole Nielson, Anne E. Bentley, Kalki Winter, the Brothers Snyder, Lin Fredericksen, Blair Tarr, Laura L. Phillippi, Bruce Elleman, Patricia Schaefer, Chuck Haddix, Edward J. Akins, Theodore Miles, Rico Ainslie, Alan Bean, Trina Seitz, Marva Felchlin, Katy Klettlinger, Richard Graves, Neal Coil, David Turk, Todd A. Cox, Hayes Oakley, and Rick Williams. I'm sure I'm leaving someone(s) out, and I do apologize.

To the craftsmen and women of the International Guild of Knot Tyers, thank you for letting me join and participate in your annual guild meeting. Thanks especially to Glenn Dickey, Colin Byfleet, Lindsey Philpott, and Owen K. Nuttall.

To Ceciel, Amelie, and Frankie—thank you for tolerating my absences and for anchoring me. I love you all.

Lastly I would like to acknowledge the response and activism of Denison University students during the fall semester of 2007, my first semester on campus. Their reaction to seeing the noose and their ways of understanding this powerful symbol inspired the writing of this book. My colleagues across the campus and, in particular, my friend and fellow CUNY Graduate Center alum Nida Bikmen deepened my knowledge and encouraged me to write this book. That experience reinforced something my parents taught me long ago—violence must be met with examination and dialogue, not with more violence.

Preface

An oak tree stands in the center of the campus commons at Jena High School in Jena, Louisiana. It's an imposing oak with stretching limbs ringed by sidewalks and the kind of well-trodden grass one finds at many American high schools—sandy spots here, a discarded potato chip bag there. A tree whose limbs offer shade at lunchtime and underneath which, rumor had it, only white students could sit.[1] But it was August, and a few black students wondered whether they could sit there too; they'd also heard the rumors but didn't believe them. They asked the principal, who said they could sit wherever they pleased.

The next day two nooses, or, more specifically, hangman's knots, fashioned from nylon rope, were found hanging from that oak tree. It was already Louisiana sticky-hot in the early morning, and the nooses hung like dead weights in the thick air—immovable reminders of a past that's not even past, to borrow from William Faulkner. A school administrator cut them down, but the message had already been delivered.

A day later a group of black students held a sit-in beneath that tree, and the school launched an investigation to identify the culprits. It didn't take long to find them—three white students did it, they said, as a joke. Those students spent nine days away from the school and two weeks at in-school suspension, and then were required to undergo psychological evaluations. The local school superintendent claimed that "many persons of authority" interviewed the three students and that "the result of those interviews showed that the students were not motivated by hate and there was no indication from any of the students that they had any inclination to do any violence."[2]

1

The school's child welfare supervisor, Melinda Edwards, noted that it was very clear to her that these students had no understanding of the history of lynchings in their home state nor elsewhere, nor did they understand what the noose symbolized for many African Americans. She claimed, "We discussed this in great detail with the students. They honestly had no knowledge of the history concerning nooses and black citizens. This may seem hard to believe for some people, but this is exactly what everyone on the committee determined."[3]

Jena's noose incident was followed by several violent encounters between black students and white students on and off campus. When a group of black students apparently beat up a white student, the accused were brought up on charges of attempted murder and conspiracy to commit murder. News of those charges spread nationally, and Jena's noose incident became part of a national conversation. On September 20, 2007, this little Louisiana town played host to one of the largest civil rights demonstrations in recent years. Jena was in the news and in the public consciousness, and soon nooses started showing up everywhere—at workplaces, in front of private homes, or dangling from trees at schools across the country. These "noose incidents"—a clunky but widely used term used to describe a range of events— involve one or more persons using a noose in order to intimidate another. The noose referred to here is usually a particular kind of noose, the hangman's knot or hangman's noose, a knot consisting of somewhere between six and thirteen loops or wrapping turns. These nooses are often fashioned from rope or sometimes drawn on a piece of paper, but recently nooses also have been sent as text messaged photos, in faxes, or in e-mails. In many cases a noose incident is considered a hate crime.

On November 25, 2007, the *New York Times* published an editorial graphic depicting forty-seven noose incidents across the eastern half of the United States, incidents that the Southern Poverty Law Center (SPLC) and Diversity Inc. had culled from news reports or from individuals. Their research revealed that noose incidents were happening not just in major East Coast cities and the rural South but also in California and Oregon and Colorado. This wasn't a new phenomenon, though. At an NAACP (National Association for the Advancement of Colored People) meeting in July 2000, Ida L. Castro, chair of the Equal Employment Opportunity Commission (EEOC), acknowledged a spike in noose-related workplace harassment suits. "These cases," she said, "are not confined to a particular geographic area or region of the country. Rather, they are occurring from coast to coast and border to border."[4]

As news of the Jena controversy dissipated, the nooses remained with us. They have, it seems, become a new version of the burning cross. I've been tracking noose incidents since September 2010 and, since then, can account for at least eighty-two incidents in which the noose was used in order to intimidate some minority group or person.[5] This number includes several incidents in which white children put a noose around the neck of a black child and then either beat or taunted them.[6]

But it was the incident in Jena, with its chilling overtones and national publicity, that compelled me to write this book. Kids do all kinds of nasty things to each other, especially young teenagers. Yet I knew, as most people know, that hanging those nooses is over the line. Why is that? How and when did the noose acquire so much symbolic importance? It's almost like a collective family secret: feared, assiduously hidden, never spoken about until our kids stumble upon it. And then we have some hard thinking and explaining ahead of us.

WHEN I FIRST CAME ACROSS THE JENA STORY I wondered how it could be that the noose hangers didn't understand the significance of that object. Though lynching was more common in southern Louisiana, Jena and its neighboring central Louisiana parishes had their share, so it seemed surprising that those high school students claimed ignorance of this history.[7] Today Jena is the parish seat of La Salle Parish and is surrounded by Grant, Winn, Caldwell, Catahoula, Avoyelles, and Rapides Parishes. But until 1908 Jena was part of Catahoula Parish, no stranger to extrajudicial killings. On July 16, 1908, three black men in Catahoula—Miller Gaines, Sam Gaines, and Albert Godlin—were accused of torching a cotton gin and then were lynched by persons unknown. In the same parish sixteen years earlier another black man, John Hastings, was accused of murder and lynched. His son and daughter met the same fate three days before, presumably because they wouldn't give their father up to the mob. And in the parishes that surround present-day La Salle—Avoyelles, Rapides, Grant, Caldwell—there were at least fourteen lynchings between 1885 and 1928.

There was a history of lynching in Jena's backyard, but these young people claimed no knowledge of it. Was it mere chance that they chose this particular symbol to display? Surely they knew something about this history? Maybe not.

My last book, *Blood and Bone*, explored the Orangeburg Massacre, the killing of three black college students and wounding of many others by South Carolina highway patrolmen in 1968. This happened just a few miles from my childhood home, and yet it was a topic most white folks wished to avoid discussing. It wasn't until I was much older that I learned what really happened. I understand the noose-hangers' ignorance because I lived it. In researching the Orangeburg Massacre I also learned how the noose had been a part of my community's history, something I didn't know about until I was in my thirties.

There are reasons for this, of course. Lynching isn't something many wish to discuss, let alone bring up in a classroom. It's a nasty part of American history; the stories produce discomfort, especially for white people like myself. And well they should: the violence and the numbers are staggering. According to one estimate, from 1882 to 1968 there may have been at least 4,743 *recorded* lynchings in the United States.[8] Lynching served as a method to reinforce and maintain a white supremacist social order, especially in the South in the years following Reconstruction. Black men made up the majority of those lynched, but black women, recent immigrants, Native Americans, and white men were as well. Researchers meeting at the Tuskegee Institute in 1940 asserted that a lynching occurs when three or more people kill someone illegally and when the killers claim they are serving justice, race, or tradition.[9] Lynching is not the same as private murder. There must be some evidence that a community supported the act, either actively or through their collective indifference.

As practiced during its heyday, lynching was brutal, vicious, and routine. More often than not, to be lynched was to be hanged. Not only were people hanged, but they were often beaten, burned, and bludgeoned before or after and their bodies left on display. The rope helped facilitate this display, holding the body high off the ground for all to see. Sometimes body parts—fingers, toes, genitalia—were kept as mementos. Sometimes photos were snapped of a smiling young girl standing by a hanging corpse or of hanging bodies in the background and a crowd of onlookers in the fore, gazing solemnly into the camera as if to say, "We did this. This is our work. This is our routine."

LYNCHING AND CAPITAL PUNISHMENT are a central part of American history. Hanging is a part of American history, our history. So the noose can teach us a lot about the underside of our progressive narratives of freedom, justice, and the rule of law. We love to praise the strides we've made as a nation, but those notes ring hollow if we lack an appreciation for what life looked like before them.

In *Regarding the Pain of Others* Susan Sontag addressed the controversy over an exhibit of lynching photographs and postcards called *Without Sanctuary*. Sontag writes,

> Some people, it was said, might dispute the need for this grisly photographic display, lest it cater to voyeuristic appetites and perpetuate images of black victimization—or simply numb the mind. Nevertheless, it was argued, there is an obligation to "examine"—the more clinical "examine" is substituted for "look at"—the pictures. It was further argued that submitting to the ordeal should help us to understand such atrocities not as the acts of "barbarians" but as the reflection of a belief system, racism, that by defining one people as less human than another legitimates torture and murder. But maybe they

were barbarians. Maybe this is what most barbarians look like. (They look like everybody else.).[10]

Including, of course, all of us.

What do those deep and violent roots say about American culture today? When writing of the St. Bartholomew's Day Massacres in sixteenth-century France, Natalie Zemon Davis argues that the ease, the regularity of that violence indicates that these are behaviors passed on from generation to generation, that massacre is a kind of *cultural technology*, that it is taught and learned.[11]

Could we also think of the noose as a cultural technology? This book tells the story of this cultural technology and its manifestations across time as part of a conscious and complicated routine for killing human beings. This book offers a story of the noose—from method of execution to symbol of intimidation. Although numerous and important scholars have explored the history and role of public hangings in Europe and America as well as the history of mob-led lynchings, this book takes a different approach and brings together many hanging stories in order to help us understand how the noose has both a material and symbolic presence in contemporary United States. I will blur the lines between legal and extralegal executions because my focus is on the noose, on the technology, and on telling the stories of the lives it affected—lives that ended by the verdict of some government or the whim of some mob.

In telling the history of the noose, I have chosen stories that I think demonstrate what it meant and how we have—slowly, more slowly than we or any of the schoolteachers in Jena, Louisiana, would care to remember—learned not to use it. It's that lack of memory, that nervous secrecy, that motivated me to write this book. So much history and so much progress live in those thirteen turns that we have to do more than look at it through the spaces between our fingers if we want to understand it. This book is a sketch of the life, a biography of sorts, of an object whose meaning goes far beyond its look and feel.

That biography is a story, I believe, about how we come to under-stand the things that make us wince. In some cases we will travel far from home and into the wilds, so to speak, of the human experience. That journey is important because it puts us in the place of the vio-lent act and reminds us that these things happened in specific places, in our communities, in our backyards, and in our (mostly European) ancestral homes.[12] The noose has served as weapon, spectacle, ritual, artifact, relic, symbol of ultimate state justice, and symbol of igno-miny, as a way of defining victims as inferiors. And throughout I will remain loyal to the questions that stirred me to write this book: why is the hangman's knot being used to intimidate Americans (of many races and backgrounds) in the twenty-first century? Why has the noose become a symbol of intimidation surpassing the burning cross, a tool for radical racists at a moment when some pundits insist that we live in a postracial America? Why does this thing have so much potency as a symbol? To truly understand the American story, these are answers we need.

ORIGINS

CHAPTER 1

The Thirteenth Turn: Origins of the Noose

THIS IS A STORY ABOUT A KNOT. A knot made from a rope. Any rope will do; they are all made by combining smaller strands, the way many narratives combine to create a larger story. And like stories, they can be simple and straight, twisted and complex, useful, or entangling.

As a tool, knots have served humans well. Rope and knot-tying expert Cyrus Day claims that "except for sticks and stones they may be man's oldest tool," though he says there's little archaeological evidence for this in part because ropes are made of organic and, therefore, deteriorating material.[1] For the most part knots have been a technology used for obtaining food—to make snares and nets and to bind things. One of the earliest knots discovered is a fragment from a Mesolithic fishnet found in 1913 on the Karelian Isthmus in what is now Russia. In the nineteenth century discoveries in the Swiss lakes region revealed that textiles and ropework were central to the lives of the Lake Dwellers of the Paleolithic era.[2] Many of the knots archaeologists discovered are still tied by human beings around the world today and are, perhaps, "culturally universal."[3]

I want to better understand this technology, so I take a walk to the hardware store in town to buy a length of rope. A paunchy man with few words, a ruddy face, and a dark green baseball cap rolls some half-inch-thick nylon rope on the store floor from an enormous spool. To measure, he eagle-eyes the rope next to the floor tiles. When he has what looks like ten feet, the ruddy-faced man whips out a large hunter's knife, with a portrait of a golden retriever, bird in mouth, on the handle, from his back pocket and slices the rope, balls it up, and drops it in my hands.

Back in my office the rope rests on my desk, nylon and modern, and the fluorescent bulbs burning above reflect off its slick, white surface—luminescent, radiant. With a YouTube video and several knot-tying books at the ready, I attempt to tie a hangman's knot. After several tries I give up. For a knot-tying amateur and Cub Scout dropout—I never even got my Bear badge—it's a complicated knot to tie well. Besides, tying knots takes patience and practice. I don't have much of the former, which makes the latter almost impossible. So I need help.

Poking around online, I stumble upon a website for the International Guild of Knot Tyers (IGKT), and I shoot off an e-mail in hopes that there will be a member in close proximity to Granville, Ohio, where I live. A few days later I get an e-mail from Glenn Dickey. He tells me he'd be happy to help me with this project—before even knowing what I was up to—and signed the e-mail, "Happy Knotting!" A few days later, as I'm reviewing class notes in my office at 8:30 A.M., my phone rings. It's Glenn.

In what ended up being a forty-minute conversation, Glenn introduces me to the curious world of knot-tying hobbyists. Before he called me, I had no idea that such a world existed. When I tell him about my project, he doesn't seem to wince, and he doesn't hang up. He's intrigued, in part, because my subject is a knot. I ask him if we can meet, stating that I'd like to interview him in person. We talk dates and times and places, and finally he says, "Listen, I'm retired. I don't mind driving to you."

A month later Glenn arrives at my office with no directions from me, a task some students find quite difficult. "You found me," I exclaim, when he walks in. "I'm good at finding things and figuring things out," he replies. He fits the cliché of a guy who can figure things out, a guy interested in knots. Glenn is wearing blue jeans and shiny white

Newbies, a tan expedition shirt, and a thin tan jacket with a "Santa Maria, Columbus, Ohio" emblem on the front. His blue ball cap has the same logo. Glenn, I soon learn, is a longtime volunteer with the Santa Maria replica, a ship moored on the Scioto River in downtown Columbus. Two pins just above the "Santa Maria" emblem on his jacket note his six hundred hours of volunteer service on the project. With all the Santa Maria regalia alone, Glenn would be a character, but the whole ensemble is brought together by two thin pieces of cord hanging around his neck, tied, he tells me later, in a "Carrick bend-on-the-bight" knot.

Born and raised in Ohio, Glenn learned knots by watching his father, a sailor in the US Navy during World War II, make animal halters for local farmers. They lived out in the country, surrounded by farms, and his father had a skill that was in demand. Glenn's father would take hemp rope and make custom-fitted rope halters for horses, cows, sheep, and goats. He was a craftsman from the old school.

Technology and mass-produced imports eventually made his father's knot-tying skills obsolete. When cheaper commercial halters could be made for pennies with cheap nylon webbing and rivets, why pay a neighbor to make them? Cheap imports and new technologies, Glenn explains, have created a world in which most folks today can only tie one or two knots. Some can't even do that; they can't even tie their own shoe-laces correctly. Instead, we live in a world reliant on buttons and zippers, snaps and Velcro to secure and fasten and hold. "In the 1800s most folks could tie five or six knots," Glenn said. "They'd go in to the butcher, and the butcher would tie up a package with string or cord; now things are prepackaged and heat-sealed or taped. Christmas presents are taped up. There's a bit of reflexive nostalgia among knotters for a time when people could use knots: taking string or rope—a flexible tool—and turning it into something useful. Glenn was chasing this nostalgia when he signed on to be the knot expert for his son's Cub Scout troop. He says he volunteered not only because no one else was interested but also because he could remember what it was like watching his father practice his skill and wanting to learn from him; he wanted to share this experience. Glenn quickly realized that he knew only a few knots—not enough to teach the kids in the troop. A friend mentioned the International Guild of Knot Tyers, and he contacted them. They, in turn, put him in touch with the American head of the organization, who gave Glenn great advice on teaching knotting to kids. Glenn soon discovered that he had a gift for knotting. Knots were a problem to be solved and a skill to be gained; he developed what can only be described as a passion for them. Glenn began to live and breathe knots. Before he retired, Glenn was a computer engineer keeping several hundred computers running for an insurance company. Every day there was a different problem and a different solution. It all makes sense: knotters are engineers at their core, people who obsess over complex problems. Not surprisingly, there are a lot of engineers in the IGKT.

The IGKT's raison d'être is straightforward: "We are an educational non-profit making organization dedicated to furthering interest in practical, recreational and theoretical aspects of knotting. Our aim is to preserve traditional knotting techniques and promote the development of new techniques for new material and applications."[4] Despite calling itself a guild, which implies exclusiveness and maybe secrecy, the IGKT is open to anyone. Today it has members in about fifty countries, though these members are few (about a thousand worldwide) and far between (there are just six in Ohio, including Glenn and his brother). This Guild has no secret ceremonies or handshakes, and yet Glenn said there are some members, himself included, who will not share all of their knot-tying secrets openly. Learning to tie knots well takes time and effort; there are some things he just won't share. Glenn tells me, "I learned how to do it—if you get to my skill level, you will too." And he's got skill. "If you walked up to me and asked me if I could do a sheet bend, a square knot, a bowline, any one of these roughly one hundred knots, I could do them without looking at a book. Average people," he says, "know about two or three knots." That makes me average at best.

The knots he lists off mechanically have origins and stories, magic and power. And as I get to know Glenn, I begin to better understand those who believed and still believe there is something magical about can also provoke mysteries. A few years ago at a meeting of the North American branch of the IGKT held in New Bedford, Massachusetts, a guild member brought with him an interesting problem for meeting attendees to solve. There had been a murder somewhere near Detroit. Police found the body of a woman dumped in a body of water; they weren't told if it was a pond, a ditch, a river, or a lake. The woman was found bound with rope, arms fastened tight across her chest with what looked like an old clothesline. And the knots the killer had used were most unusual. The detectives heard about the IGKT and contacted one of its members in hopes that they might be able to identify the knots. Guild members were each shown a series of forensics pictures separately. They took notes and proffered theories. The photos were a handicap—the lighting was poor, the angles were all wrong. And yet every guild member who looked at them, Glenn included, was able to say something about the rope, the knots used, and the handedness of the killer. "We knew that the person who did it was right-handed," he narrates. "We knew that the person had possibly been in a profession in which knotting was used. We knew that the person was dead before they were tied up. We knew that the killer was in a hurry, which makes sense because he'd just killed somebody and he wanted to get rid of the evidence. It wasn't preplanned; it was on the spur of the moment."

In an intense situation human beings are often not creative; they act in ways that come naturally or in ways that have been practiced, rehearsed. Glenn thinks that it's the same way with knots. When the average person has to tie a knot in a stressful situation, they'll tie the easiest one they know, usually an overhand knot or a granny knot, which results from an incorrect overhand knot. The man who had killed this woman used a modified packer's knot, a knot used only by individuals in certain professions, like butchers. In the Tape-Button-Velcro Age few people can tie the knot, let alone identify it. Separately and together, each Guild member noted the uniqueness of the knot, that only someone who tied such a knot on a regular basis would use it in a stressful situation (like, for example, after murdering someone). They re-created the knot and noted that the person tying it was likely right-handed. The important thing, though, was the knot itself, the packer's knot. "So we took that information to the police, and they brought forward two suspects," Glenn explains. "One was, I can't remember, I think an auto mechanic. But the other was a butcher. We said, 'The butcher did it.' The butcher would have to know how to tie up a carcass, to bundle it." The police interrogated the butcher, and he confessed to the murder. As he tells me this story, Glenn is burning the ends of some rope I had in my office. Over the course of the interview he did this to all my rope, almost like it was a compulsion. He cut and burned, cut and burned the ropes, a meditative process, taking something fraying and chaotic and bringing about a kind of order.

Forensic expert Rodger Ide asserts that knots often "provide very good interpretive evidence, helping to reconstruct how the crime or incident occurred."[7] Indeed, he says, "murders by hanging and strangulation are not normally pre-planned in sufficient detail to mislead pathologists and forensic scientists."[8] Therefore, investigators can learn a lot from the trace evidence found on the ropes, medical evidence from the damaged body, and information from the knots themselves. What was the ligature made of—rope, cloth, wire, chain? What kind of knot was tied, and what can that tell the investigator about the knot-tying skills of the murderer or victim? Can those skills link them to any sort of trade or hobby?

Glenn reaches into the knapsack he brought with him and riffles through some books, pulling out a book called *The Black Book* and opening it to a marked page.[9] It's a photograph of the 1908 lynching of four African American men—Virgil Jones, Robert Jones, Thomas Jones, and Joseph Riley—in Russellville, Kentucky, over an apparent labor dispute. I'd seen the image in numerous guises, as photograph and postcard. It's horrific. Four lifeless bodies, each with his hands bound behind his back, dangling from a tree off a desolate country road. One of the men was found with a note pinned to his body that read, "Let this be a warning to you niggers to let white people alone or you will go the same way."

I ask Glenn, "You mean to tell me that you can say something about the knots tied and the people who tied them just by looking at a photograph of a lynching or of a hanging?"

It turned out that he could.

THE THIRTEENTH TURN

On October 28, 2010, a volunteer, Mel Distel, arrived at the Santa Ana office of gay rights organization California Equality Now and found a hangman's noose on the doorknob. She called the police.[10] The officer who responded to her call told her, after observing the noose, that "what it is, is a string on a door." Distel said she couldn't believe what she had heard. She asked him whether he didn't see the relationship between the noose and the threat that it represents. The officer replied, "Sometimes you just have to live with being a victim" and told her that his car was once broken into, somehow equating the two events.

That string on the door was a perfectly tied hangman's noose, with thirteen turns around a black nylon rope. The hangman's noose is a knot, a sliding knot to be exact. Clifford Ashley writes in his *Ashley Book of Knots* (essentially the knot-tying bible) that "a Noose is just one thing: a knot at the end of a rope that tightens when hauled on. Any loop becomes a Noose if a bight is rove a short distance through it."[11] Translation: any loop becomes a noose if the slack part of the rope is curved and one end of the rope can be pulled through it and tightened. Functionally, a noose is a simple slip knot.

The word "noose" has uncertain origins. Its Latin origins are most likely the word *nodus*, which could have meant a knot or tied mass of strings and, thus, is related to the word "node." In the theater a node can be a "predicament" or "entangling complication." Sometime before the Norman Conquest of England the "d" disappeared. Today the word shows up in colloquialisms—"slip the noose" or "tighten the noose." Marriage is often described as a noose. Ties are often described as nooses. In a 2012 article in the *London Evening Standard* Richard Godwin wrote that power-dressing "marks a clear line between our different selves, too. I am happy to wear a tie to work—and also to un-noose myself at the end of the day."[12] I've heard the word used more directly as a verb on National Public Radio's *Talk of the Nation* when a guest from the *Wall Street Journal* was discussing a piece she wrote about the burden of being given the mantle of "most likely to succeed" in high school.[13] One person she interviewed claimed that he had been "noosed" by that title. Neal Conan opines, "Noosed—that's an interesting verb." (Awkward laughter from guest and host.)

Unlike the word "noose," the origins of the knot itself are fairly certain. In fact, it was probably one of the earliest knots because it could be used to capture small animals and birds; it was a tool used for the maintenance of human life.[14] But the noose hanging from that office's doorknob was a hangman's noose, which is more than just a simple sliding knot, more than just a word with possible Latin origins, more than just "a string on a door." A hangman's noose or hangman's knot—sometimes called Jack Ketch's knot after a seventeenth-century English Hangman—is a specific kind of noose, and it must be made in a particular fashion. The hangman's knot is a tool for killing—it is a very deliberate knot. In *The Ashley Book of Knots*, the hangman's noose is Knot #1119; it is part of a family of knots that also includes the Scaffold Knot (#1120), Gallows Knot (#1121), Newgate Knot (#1122), Ichabod Knot (#1123), and Gibbet Knot (#1124).

The hangman's knot binds tightly. The coils or turns are there to add friction to the knot and to make it more difficult to open once placed around a victim's head. There's a debate about how many turns a proper hangman's noose should have; some suggest that it has nine turns because, Ashley writes, "even if a man has as many lives as a cat, there shall be a full turn for each one of them."[15] Others suggest that it should have thirteen turns because of the bad luck such a knot brings. If ever there were an ominous twist of rope, surely it is the thirteenth turn in a hangman's noose.

Glenn Dickey thinks that the exact origins of the hangman's noose might be hard to pinpoint. Finding an originator of this knot would be a bit like trying to find the person who invented the wheel. Other than the Hunter's Bend, there's only one knot named after its supposed originator—the Matthew Walker.[16] Knot #1119 might have been adopted or developed by hangmen from fishing, equestrian, or sailing knots. It looks a lot like a heaving line knot, used to give a rope extra weight so it will reach a dock when a sailor tosses it from on board.[17] Such a knot is formed with wrapping turns around the rope, akin to the turns of hangman's knot. What's certain is that in its popular manifestations the hangman's knot looks formidable, almost elegant, like it would go over well on the big screen. (One guild member I talked to named Don Burrhus called it a "tuxedo.") And yet there's no reason to believe that the thousands of people who have been hanged over time were killed with #1119. A simple slip knot could do the same work.[18]

Like other knots, the hangman's knot likely developed over time for the specific purpose of killing someone quickly. The turns around the rope might have developed so as to better position the neck in order that it might break. "We do know," Glenn explained to me, "that it's a constricting knot, so that if you didn't break the neck, you went into the constricting phase, cutting off circulation to the brain and air to the lungs, which would result in death." It's no exact science; it's just that this particular knot might have worked better than another knot.

So I ask him to show me how to tie one, if possible.

"I don't do this knot very often," he replies. It's not that he's never been asked to demonstrate how to make one—some of the Cub Scouts pester him about it endlessly—but it means a lot of things to a lot of people. Besides, the hangman's knot is a deadly tool, he said; it's not a joke. In September 2010 a tourist visiting the Boot Hill Museum in Dodge City, Kansas, stuck his head in a hangman's noose that was on display, apparently to take a photo.[19] Somehow he lost consciousness, fell forward, and nearly hanged himself before museum staff rescued him. And in October 2011 a teenage girl working at a Missouri haunted house accidentally fell with a noose around her neck, again almost killing herself.[20]

"To start," Glenn explains, "you make a Z in the rope. You leave a longer working end or wend down there below the Z. You contract your parts of the Z together, and you start wrapping the knot around the parts of the Z. There's a lot of folklore about the number of times you go around. One is that you go eight turns for optimum—that it gives you the maximum friction with maximum pulling. Other folklore says that on ships you give it seven turns for the seven seas. I've heard nine. I've heard thirteen—bad luck. After you wrap your turns, there's a loop left up at the top. You run your working end up through the loop, pull one part of your knot down. Make these wrappings as tight as you can, and you end up with a hangman's noose. The idea is that this piece here helps you tighten and loosen that loop."

"As you were doing that," I say, taking a deep breath, "I was thinking about how different tying this knot seems from tying other kinds of knots. It just seems different."

"Because of the wrapping turns . . ."

"No, because of the use. What it's used for. Does it feel different to make this knot?"

"Yeah, this is a different knot. It has a specific purpose. There are few places you run into a knot like this." He tells me that you might see a version of a hangman's knot on a ship's rigging, like when ropes are pulled through deadeyes, round discs with three holes that make them look face-like. You might see a hangman's knot when fishing, like when tackle is attached to fishing line. But these are rare instances.

THE KIND OF ROPE USED TO MAKE THE KNOT makes a big difference. Today, there's a lot of nylon braided rope, and the knot can be produced by a right- or left-handed person fairly quickly. But before the advent of nylon rope, people would have used hemp, linen, or manilla rope. These ropes were typically right-laid, meaning that the strands turn right—a complicating factor for a left-handed person. Glenn picks up a piece of manilla rope and starts the process all over again, tying the knot with his right hand. It's clearly more difficult with this rope. The knot tyer has to pay attention, be precise.

"You have to figure out where everything's going to come out as you're tying your hangman's noose because when you start to wrap

this—see, I've done six turns, almost seven, and I'm out of rope."
He starts over. This situation, a knot expert making a mistake and
having to start over, raises an important question: Could someone
tie such a precise knot quickly, with an angry mob demanding immediate death?

"Listen," Glenn says as he makes his wraps, "if you see a well-made
hangman's noose, you can pretty well figure that it was made ahead
of time."

"That it was premeditated."

"Right. The person couldn't stand in front of the judge and say,
'We just got mad at him and did it on the spur of the moment.'" He
holds up the hangman's knot. "There you go."

"Now can you teach me?" I ask.

I place the rope on the flat surface of my desk and make a six-
to-eight-inch-wide Z with the middle of the rope. Because I'm right-
handed, the left-hand part of the rope is loose—the standing end or
nonworking end. Then I compress the three loops that I formed with
my left hand and start wrapping the rope around these loops. I make
nine wrapping turns, stick the working end through the loop jutting
out from the bottom of the turns, and then adjust the turns to make
sure they're tight. I pull the working end tight. It's done. It has become
a structured form, a potential killing machine made by my own hands.

But I'm working with modern rope, not one made of hemp or jute
or some other natural fiber, but rather rope that's smooth and easy to
manipulate with my unlearned hands. Under pressure it would be even
more difficult to orchestrate. If I wasn't in a climate-controlled office
with excellent lighting, plenty of time on my hands, knot-tying books
and knot guru at the ready, and three different kinds of rope—if all
these conditions didn't exist, I'm not sure I could do it.

CAUSE OF DEATH

In the best of circumstances a modern judicial hanging execution will
follow strict protocols. First the victim is weighed and measured to

determine the exact distance he should be dropped in order to ensure a quick death. At the time of execution the condemned walks onto a platform with his hands tied behind his back. The legs are then bound, and a hood is placed over the head. The noose of seven to thirteen turns is placed around the neck and tightened. At a signal, a trapdoor is released, and the condemned falls below the scaffold to his death. If all goes well, the noose and drop will do the work of quickly dispensing the condemned via what's often called a "hangman's fracture": "the violent breaking of the C-2 vertebra just below the base of the skull."[21] This will fracture the spinal cord and compress the arteries in the neck. If the drop isn't precise, the victim will die of strangulation or decapitation.

The protocols and accoutrements of the hanging execution were developed over centuries; they are the result of technological progress, if you want to call it that. But no matter how "scientific" the process becomes, the hanged person can endure a range of experiences that eventually will lead to his or her death. The hanged may struggle for many minutes while trying to get air. His bowels and bladder may evacuate, either because a lack of oxygen will relax the requisite muscles or simply as a result of fear-induced adrenaline rush.[22] Limbs might twitch for some time afterward. The noose itself can rip flesh from the neck and side of face. The body becomes a grotesque figure, as eyes "bug out," tongues protrude, and necks stretch. A heartbeat may be detected in that body for up to twenty minutes after the trapdoor is released.[23] Finally an over-drop can lead to decapitation; an under-drop can lead to a repetition of the process.

An important thing to understand about hanging executions is that they do not always lead to an instantaneous death. A doctor of anatomy at the University of Washington School of Medicine named Cornelius Rosse believes that instantaneous death from the fracture of the spinal cord happens in only a few such executions.[24] He believes that "the weight of the prisoner's body causes tearing of the cervical muscles, skin, and blood vessels. The upper cervical vertebrae are dislocated, and the spinal cord is separated from the brain, which causes death." Although hanging *may* cause the spine to break, strangulation or suffocation is usually the cause of death.

After a thorough study of a number of hangings, British physiologist Harold Hillman offers a few insights to support Rosse's claims. Hillman asserts that rapid "fracture-dislocation" doesn't always happen, especially if the condemned "has strong neck muscles, is very light, the 'drop' is too short, or the noose has been wrongly positioned."[25] There are simply too many variables. And, Hillman adds, "If the fracture-dislocation is not rapid, death results from asphyxia." In such a case death is prolonged and painful. When asphyxiation occurs, the noose closes off "the jugular veins and carotid arteries but the vertebrae protect the vertebral and spinal arteries which also supply blood to the brain." In other words, the hanged person is still aware and hasn't lost all sensation. Even if fracture-dislocation occurs quickly, the hanged person doesn't lose sensation. Hillman writes that "the sensory signals from the skin above the noose and from the trigeminal nerve probably continue to reach the brain until hypoxia blocks them." Thus, it's tough to say when a hanged person no longer feels pain.

The cap or hood as well as physical restraints around arms and sometimes legs obscure manifestations of pain and further complicate our ability to gauge the amount of pain a hanged person experiences.[26] We know, for example, that dislocations and fractures cause pain, but for obvious reasons signs of pain like shouting or screams cannot be heard when someone is hanged.[27] However, other signs like "violent movements," "contraction of facial muscles," urination, and defecation can be observed.[28] The source of the pain, Hillman writes, is from stretching skin, the fracture-dislocation of the vertebrae, and the often long process of asphyxiation. Hillman argues that the pain experienced by the hanged is severe. He points out, though, that although most contemporary judicial hanging executions occur under the best of circumstances, some do not.

Forensic scientists note that the literature on the physiology of hanging is still sparse. One of the central questions about hangings—how long does the hanged person live after they are dropped?—still lacks a definitive answer. In 2010 a group of forensic pathologists, part of the Working Group on Human Asphyxia, published a review of animal models of hangings as part of concerted effort to begin addressing this gap in knowledge.[29] Based on this research, they believe that "cessation of cerebral blood flow, rather than airway obstruction" causes the victim to cease breathing. Muscles stop moving after one to three and half minutes, and then a generalized seizure occurs. In another study, also by members of the Working Group, researchers analyzed a filmed suicide and noted that although the victim lost consciousness after thirteen seconds, he then began to convulse, the last muscular movement happening four minutes and ten seconds later.[30]

The Lynching of Virgil Jones, Robert Jones, Thomas Jones, and Joseph Riley.

But most of these studies have been done on hangings that, like judicial executions, occur under controlled conditions. In the worst of circumstances, like when someone is lynched, the victim would endure significantly more pain and would, most likely, die as the result of asphyxia. The knots used can tell us a lot about why and how that pain came about. In the photograph of the lynching of Virgil Jones, Robert Jones, Thomas Jones, and Joseph Riley in Kentucky, the knots are inelegant, to say the least. More importantly, the nooses that killed them were not hangman's nooses.

Even though it's a poor image—from a bad angle, poor resolution in spots—Glenn Dickey says that it is obvious to him that the person who tied the knots was right-handed. The lay of the rope is his first clue. Using his hands to demonstrate, he says that if you are tying the knots in the photo with right-laid rope, the rope would go right. "You'd use your left hand to bring the rope around and bring that loop down. If you were left-handed, it would go the other way because you'd be using your left hand to pull it through and your right hand to shove the loop down." The photo also reveals that all of the men have their hands tied behind their backs. Pointing to one man in the photo (left of center, back to the viewer) Glenn adds that the rope is wrapped low around his wrists. "He was likely alive when this knot was tied. It's a binding knot—you're trying to restrict this person's movements. The knot goes up and around his wrists. It's a form of handcuff knot. They just looped it around his wrists a number of times and then tied what you'd consider to be a bowtie knot or square knot."

"It's not an elegant knot," I note.

"No, it's not elegant. Whoever tied it was in a hurry, and they used whatever rope was at hand. You can tell that most of the rope is three-stranded right-laid rope. And this was a rural area, so it was probably used on the farm. This was probably manila rope—half-inch to three-quarter inch."

"Thinking about the intensity of the moment—the lyncher must go with what they know. The most basic knots they can use. What they can do quickly."

"Not to mention," Glenn interjects, "that the person probably isn't sitting there obediently saying, 'Go ahead and do this.'"

We quietly stare at the photo. There is no hangman's noose. No gallows. No hood to cover their faces. Those four men were strung up, quite literally lifted off of the ground and left to slowly strangle. There was no clean "hangman's fracture." Their deaths were slow and painful.

Glenn breaks the silence, "It's amazing what people are taught and learn, isn't it?"

CHAPTER 2

Rope, Ritual, Roots:
The Iron Age Hanging
of Tollund Man

I'M ON A TRAIN TRAVELING from Copenhagen, Denmark, to Silkeborg, a small city in Jutland and home to Tollund Man, an Iron Age (circa fourth century BC) body discovered in a Danish bog with a noose around his neck. I have an appointment with a Danish archaeologist named Ole Nielson to talk about this bog body and how he might have died. But I'm especially curious about this noose, in part because it is so ancient but also because it takes this story to Europe, where so much of America begins.

The train heads east through a tunnel and over a bridge crossing the Storebælt, the great strait connecting the Kattegat and Baltic Seas. Out the window, I spy a beach where a man with a fluttering black scarf walks his dog as the waves crash on rocks covered in a layer of thick white ice. In the distance wind turbines spin above the water. After Odense, the train eventually arrives in Jutland and passes frozen, snow-dusted fields anxious for spring. A hint of sun soon disappears, and it's all gray sky and field again. I could be back in sunless Ohio where, two days before on the way to the airport, my daughter asked, "Daddy, when will the sun come back?"

"I hope by the time I come home," I told her.

I press my face against the glass and think of the small towns I whoosh past and the lives led in them. I see farms with haystacks resembling teepees and then a small herd of red deer run across the snow. The train zips through a stand of evergreens, a dark swatch of forest, and quickly back to gray sky, white field, and, suddenly, to my right I spy a herd of American Buffalo.

I get off the train at Silkeborg and walk out of the station onto an empty and wind-blown street. It is late Sunday morning, and there are few folks around. Nothing but the station looks open. I don't have a map and am a little nervous. I've heard the Danish are serious about being on time. So I go with my gut, turn right out of the station, and just start walking. Ahead of me I spot a woman with a stroller turning a corner, and I catch her eye.

"Do you speak English?" I ask with the biggest "I'm-a-lost-American" grin I can muster.

"A little," she says.

"I'm trying to find the Silkeborg Museum."

She thinks for a moment. "Art or old stuff?"

"Old stuff!" I laugh.

"Keep going straight and then turn left and walk some more. You will see it on the right—big yellow building."

"Thank you," and I'm on my way.

Ole Nielson's office is on the second floor of the big yellow building. It's an ample-windowed corner affair with a large desk, home to an enormous computer screen (with one of the busiest desktops I've seen in some time: multiple files and folders cover the screen). Nielson has close-cropped salt-and-pepper hair. He's about my height, thin, with bright eyes and smile, and wears jeans and shiny black leather shoes, a dark purple collared shirt that's half sticking out of his black sweater. He's half-rumpled, half-put-together. This could be stereotypical scientist-chic or it could also be the result of parenting young children. We sit down at a circular table, and he offers me a cup of dark coffee. It's windy outside, and the windows shake as he pours.

Nielson is an archaeologist with a background in prehistoric and medieval archaeology. Most of his life's work has been about presenting complicated research for public consumption. He has worked at a reenactment park, other museums, and now he's in Silkeborg. "All the work archaeologists do is of little worth if the people don't know about it," he says. The public has to get something out of it, in part, he says, because they fund the research. But they also have the right to know why you're digging where you are and what you're learning from it. This is their history.

"By the Malta Convention," he tells me, "we have obligated ourselves to preserve the remains where they are, *in situ*, actually. But if that's not possible, we have to keep it for research." Prior to the twentieth century some bog bodies were left in the bogs where they were discovered; others were given "Christian" burials. More recently, though, bog bodies have become important resources for scientific study, and rather than be reburied, curators and researchers alike are giving them a lot of attention.

Tollund Man was discovered on May 8, 1950, by a local family digging for peat, a common source of heating fuel. They were in Tollund Fen in Bjaeldskov Dal, only six miles from the museum. When those diggers saw what looked like a face buried in the peat, they called the police. One of the police officers who arrived happened to be a volunteer at the Silkeborg Museum. He could see immediately that it wasn't a recent crime—that it was a bog body—and he summoned an archaeologist named Peter Glob from Aarhus to help dig the body out. A team of volunteers constructed a wooden crate to carry the body, encased in an enormous piece of peat. Then the body and peat were lifted by hand ten feet up onto a horse-drawn cart for transport to the train station and on to the National Museum in Copenhagen. It was quite an effort—one volunteer, a local policeman with heart trouble, died from overexertion a few days later.

Once it was at the museum, researchers began the process of cleaning and studying the body. Meanwhile the folks from Silkeborg

Tollund Man. Photo by Ole Nielson. *Used with permssion of Silkeborg Museum*

wrote to the National Museum, wondering whether the body would one day be returned so they could display it. The museum replied that such a display might not be a "good idea," that it would be a little "macabre."[1]

Nielson disagrees, though. "First and foremost I'm a scientist, and I'd like to have the most information from the material." He stops himself and notes, "I even use the word 'material.' And I want that information because of the people who live today." By studying bodies and bones, he says, we can compare and contrast and actually discover quite a bit about what it was like to live in the past that might help us understand how we live now. But sometimes what's best for you isn't always best for others, he says. Sometimes beliefs or feelings get in the way.[2]

"But he could be your relative," I say.

"I'm from the northern part of Jutland originally. So, sure, yes, Tollund Man might be my ancestor," Nielson replies.

"But you don't look a thing like him—there's more red in your cheeks!"

"Yes, but I do say hello to him every time I see him."

"You do?"

"Yes, I say, 'Hello, old friend!' I really do. He's beautiful. He looks very human-like. I think many people feel that connection. I know I do."

In 1950, when Nielson's "old friend" was first examined, some might have questioned that positive description. He measured about five feet three inches and was estimated to be between thirty and forty years old when he died, sometime around 350 BC. Images of his body when he was first completely exposed revealed a man in the fetal position who looked asleep. His eyes were barely shut, his lips pursed. The flesh from his arms and legs had disappeared, but his rumpled feet were whole. You could still see the stubble on his chin, eye lashes, eye brows, fingernails, the lines on his fingers, and the soles of his feet. An autopsy revealed intact organs, including the stomach, whose contents revealed his last meal, eaten twelve to twenty-four hours before his death.[3] It was a simple repast, gruel really: barley, linseed, oats, and then ground-up seeds of weeds—persicaria, fat hen, corn spurry, gold of pleasure, field pansy, and, possibly, hemp nettle—likely all part of a normal Iron Age diet.[4] It's curious that he was preserved at all. That he was preserved so well, organs intact, is somewhat of a miracle. The conditions had to be perfect. Tollund Man had to be placed in the bog in the winter. If the bog was warmer than 4 degrees centigrade, his body would have deteriorated rather quickly.

When he was first discovered, Tollund Man was naked except for a sheepskin cap and a belt. But there was another piece of material on his body—a plaited leather rope formed into a simple slipknot. The fact that the rope was fashioned into a noose and tied around Tollund Man's neck has led to the assertion that he was hanged. There is other evidence too. First of all, the rope was positioned behind his neck and not in front.[5] Also, there were marks in the skin beneath the chin and on the sides of the neck suggesting hanging.[6] There was no complete fracture of the vertebra column, but that's not unusual for a hanging, especially one that likely didn't involve a substantial drop. And so because of the location of the knot, the marks on his neck, and X-rays performed by pathologists in 1950, the consensus has long been that

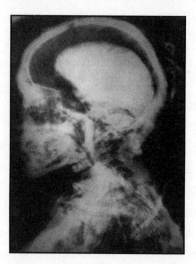

X-Ray of Tollund Man. Image by Bispebjerg Hospital. *Used with permission of Silkeborg Museum*

he was hanged rather than strangled. CT scans in 2002 further support this consensus.

Nielson ushers me over to his computer and opens a file with a picture of one X-ray of Tollund Man's head and neck. "The knot was behind his neck," he says and points to it. "Here in the front you can see the groove from it. It was cut off at a certain length, and he was put in the bog with it. It was still very tight. It was not a hanging in the English sense, where you drop from a point and then you snap your neck. He was choked to death by this noose but not strangulated, because the rope would be further down on his neck."

Why he was hanged, though, is an open question: we don't have any written records from the Iron Age, so there's almost nothing to go on. A first theory, though, is that Tollund Man was a criminal or undesirable, executed and tossed into the bog. Many bog bodies show visible signs that they were brutally beaten, some were strangled, and a few of them hanged—signs of punishment or retribution.

Hanging has deep roots in Northern Europe. Arab travel writer Ahmad ibn Fadhlan commented on the customs—including hanging executions—of the peoples of the Volga Bulgaria he encountered during his travels from 921 to 922; these were probably what are today called Rus', and probably at least partly of Viking descent.[7] Fadhlan wrote that "if they catch a thief or a robber, they lead him to a thick tree, throw a trusty rope around his neck and hang him to the tree, and he remains hanging until with the wind and rain he falls to pieces."[8] Hanging on gallows is mentioned in *Beowulf* as well as in the *Edda* and the *Sagas* of Iceland. Perhaps the most often cited source regarding the roots of hanging in Northern Europe is Roman Senator Tacitus, who, in synthesizing reports of the Germanic tribes in the second century, mentions that traitors or deserters are hanged on trees.[9] Though based on oral accounts and not a true history per se, Tacitus claimed that some tribes also punished people by throwing them in the bogs. He wrote that "cowards, dastards, and those guilty of unnatural practices, are suffocated in mud under a hurdle."[10] The Nazis took a particular interest in the bog bodies and tried to link them to the early Germans in order to make the case that these early Germans populated all of Northern Europe and, therefore, Scandinavia was actually German territory.[11] But they were especially interested in Tacitus's assertion that the bog bodies were "cowards, dastards, and those guilty of unnatural practices" (a.k.a. homosexuals) who early Germans sacrificed for angering the gods. This could open the door for persecution of those the Third Reich deemed to fit in those categories.

These days, though, the leading theory is that bog bodies were not executed criminals per se but were actually sacrificial offerings to the gods. Cremation and burial in a small urn or pot and placement in a barrow was the common Iron Age burial practice.[12] So the fact that these mostly intact bodies have been found in bogs is striking, especially as bogs were considered sacred spaces—home to the gods or the place where one could communicate with the gods. Peter Glob argues that Tollund Man was sacrificed to Nerthus, the goddess of fertility, also known as Mother Earth.[13] Nielson's predecessor, archaeologist Christian Fischer, believes he was a "thank offering" to the god Odin (or a forerunner of Odin), who the Icelandic skalds called the god of the hanged. Fischer notes that, in addition to Tollund Man, other bog bodies show signs of hanging, including Elling Woman and possibly Borremose Man.[14] Others were found with ropes around their necks and the cause of death more ambiguous.

Fischer traces the relationship of hanging and religion from the Middle Ages backward, beginning with two accounts of groves of trees with multiple sacrifices to Odin, the god of the hanged.[15] A tapestry from circa 800 AD, placed in a ship burial at Oseberg by Oslo Fjord, shows a hanging grove (grove of trees used for hangings), perhaps also sacrifices to Odin. That tapestry is similar to a picture stone from circa 700 AD found near Gotland.[16] Lastly, Fischer mentions gold fogeys (gold figures from the sixth and seventh centuries) that look like hanged bodies.[17] It's hard to get much closer than that time frame, and Fischer concludes that we can't say definitively that the bog bodies were sacrifices to Odin because there's no clear link.[18] Clearly, though, Tollund Man was part of some shared ritual involving hanging or strangling, given how many of the bog bodies that were found had been hanged or strangled.

Nielson underscores Fischer's argument. "Just because we can't see any positive signs that Odin was a god at that time doesn't mean that he or the forerunner of Odin didn't exist. At some point this belief must have worked its way in. Elling Woman, the other bog body in our museum, was hanged too. We have the noose, a different type of noose than the one Tollund Man was hanged with, but also made of leather. He and Elling Woman are not the only ones. He is part of a group from that period, all found in the bogs, and more or less they may have the same faith. They were killed some way or another, with a slit throat or hanged or maybe were strangled, and thrown into the bog, from a period when people were cremated properly. So he's part of a system, you might say."

But why? That's totally another question.

Nielson tells me we have to pay attention to the care given to Tollund Man because that bolsters the sacrifice theory. "When he was found he looked very, very peaceful. He had his mouth and eyes closed.

Noose on Tollund Man. Photo by Arrne Mikkelson. *Used with permission of Silkeborg Museum*

He was laid down in the fetal position. He looked like he was asleep. He was put in an old peat pit and rather quickly he must have been covered or he would have been eaten by scavengers. This shows me that there was a certain care for him and about him. It wasn't like he was an awful criminal that you would hang until he fell off the tree himself. I think the way that he was laid down, the tranquility of his face and features, show that somebody closed his mouth and eyes. Somebody cared for him and put him down like that." We'll never know, of course, whether Tollund Man was a willing participant in this process.

In 1950 the researchers at the National Museum were only able to preserve the head, which was sent back to the good people of Silkeborg. So for many years only the head, hat, and noose were on display. The rest of Tollund Man was scattered about the country in several research institutions—a foot here, a thumb there. Christian Fischer worked tirelessly to bring Tollund Man back to his native ground. Some of the recovered body parts had deteriorated a great deal, so Fischer made a replica of the rest of his body, and this is what is on display today and what attracted me along with thousands of others to Silkeborg every year.

"Why are people fascinated by Tollund Man?" I ask Nielson.

"Because you can literally stand face to face with a prehistoric man. He looks like a person who could wake up at any moment. . . . He looks like just a normal man with some wrinkles and stubble on his chin, the imperfections—the nose is bent a bit. An image from the Iron Age is one thing because we can see that it's a reflection from them. But this is different. This is a *person* from the Iron Age—a person that's two thousand three hundred, two thousand four hundred years old. And I think he's really beautiful."

Nielson is almost lost in this reverie—it's strangely endearing. Smiling, eyes wide, and clearly delighted that this is his job, that he gets paid to work with Tollund Man. There's a genuine respect and care in his approach to his work with this body, this person.

"Let's go have a look at him," he says. "Okay?"

We walk through the central museum building and outside though a courtyard to the building that houses Tollund Man. I hear peals of laughter from children and smell coffee. It was warm and cozy, or *hygge*, as the Danish say. As we enter, Nielson is greeted by his children, who are participating in a special kid's day at the museum. They're making crafts and are ably assisted by volunteers dressed in what appears to be period costume.

After chatting up his children, we walk through the Iron Age hall to see Tollund Man. He's in a dimly lit room off the back of the main hall, resting in the center of the room on a raised platform. The platform is partially circumscribed by a bronze railing. Nielson walks up to the display, leans down, and whispers in English, for my sake, "Hello, old friend."

I do see what Nielson is saying: even though he is over two thousand years old—even though he is a hanged corpse—there is a placid, handsome quality to this man. His pursed lips, closed eyes, his prominent but awkwardly bent nose. He's just resting, I think. He could wake up at any moment. I ask Nielson what he'd say to him if he did wake up.

He laughs, "I'd have quite a few questions! Hah. That would be something." He pauses and thinks. "You know, his brain is well preserved. And I often wish I could take a USB stick and plug it in to download his last thoughts! This probably will never happen, but when I started studying archaeology thirty years ago I had no idea that there would be something in DNA that could tell us so much about people and migrations, how people evolved." And DNA testing of Tollund Man is in the works—an exciting prospect, says Nielson, because it could tell us so much about this man, his background, his tribe. And maybe whether he's related to Elling Woman, a find that could further support the sacrifice theory.

This man from Tollund Fen represents two meanings of the noose: ritual and spectacle. The noose is part of a ritual central to his culture, and he was hanged in order to realize the desires, be they religious or disciplinary or both, of the community he lived in. Rituals *are* community; they demonstrate community and reinforce values, create solidarity. Modern executions are rituals of sorts: we kill to rid our communities of those we deem evil or those who have broken the social contract. But the noose can also be part of a spectacle—a hanging execution that serves political and social purposes, a visual performance with pedagogical intentions.

Yet Tollund Man's death does not fit neatly into either category. He was perhaps both ritual and spectacle when he was killed, and in many ways he is ritual and spectacle still. When we look at him we are looking into the past. The bog preserved a man from one age for view in the present. And, in the noose, because hanging is still a ritual we recognize, we can also see the past in the present.

CHAPTER 3

An Ignoble Death:
Hanging from the Roman Empire
to Medieval Europe

MOST ARCHIVES RESTRICT ACCESS or at least require some hoop-jumping in order to deter casual researchers. But the process itself isn't terribly complicated. In order to view manuscripts in the Sherman Fairchild Reading Room at the Pierpont Morgan Library, I fill out an online form with detailed information about myself, my project, and the manuscripts I want to view, set up an appointment, exchange a few e-mails with the librarians, and then, on a bright Manhattan morning, stroll down East 37th Street to the side entrance of the Morgan. After signing in, I take an elevator to a special access floor and walk across a space bridge to the reading room entrance. I place my coat, backpack, and computer case in a locker and then wash my hands, as directed, at a special sink in the foyer to the reading room. I'm buzzed into the windowless reading room, where I am told to read the researcher guidelines and sign my name, acknowledging that I will not touch what can't be touched or handled and that I will not trace, rub, tear, rip, dismantle, or destroy any of the materials.

The librarians are kind and curious, rechecking the catalog to see whether there was something I might have missed in my own search. They bring out a number of manuscripts. The first one I look at takes my breath away.[1] It is Manuscript.M.390, a Catholic Book of Hours from sixteenth-century Belgium, with gorgeous illuminated leaves. The first page I see is a Nativity scene, and the pages seem to glow golden, the edges dotted by tiny flowers and insects—moths and snails. Stunning.

I slowly turn the pages of the manuscript, reading the images as they trace the life of Jesus Christ from birth to crucifixion. One image of the crucifixion is itself quite striking: a pale Christ crucified on a deep brown cross, with bloody wounds in the hands and feet and Mary Magdalene crying at the base. Jerusalem is in the background looking a lot like a medieval city, with spires that remind me of the castle at Segovia, Spain (on which the Disney Castle is modeled). To the right of Christ is a group of men and soldiers, and on the hills beyond—just part of the scenery—are two tiny gallows (with people hanging on them), two Catherine wheels, and a tree from which hangs the limp body of, I assume, Judas.

There's no money shot of the noose around Judas's neck; it's too small. Regardless, the noose is quite present. In subtle ways Christ and Judas are being compared and contrasted here, and it is through images like this that the practice of hanging enters the cultural lexicon of the Western world. Here all eyes, including those of the Virgin Mary, are on Christ. And there's visible sorrow in the eyes of both Marys. Christ is mourned and martyred; he is cared for. In contrast, Judas and the other hanged bodies are left to rot in ignominy.

But most obvious to me as I sit in this reading room is the color— the ecstatic palate used for Christ shows the copiers' position on this matter quite clearly, something I never could have understood by viewing this image on a computer screen or in a book. Christ's crucifixion is all magnificent colors—vivid blues and reds, bright green grass below the cross, and golden rays emanating from Christ's crown. Conversely, there is the darkness of those pedestrian punishments beyond, the hanged men suspended between heaven and earth.

ANCIENT HANGINGS

References to hanging found in ancient Greece as well as in the Bible suggest that some have long viewed hanging as a dishonorable way to

die. In ancient Greece especially it was considered dishonorable because it was associated with female suicides; a woman, it was believed,
committed suicide by hanging because hanging was thought to be a
bloodless death (though it is often not). For example, in Sophocles's
Oedipus Rex Jocasta, upon learning the truth about her son-husband
Oedipus, hangs herself from a "dangling noose."[2] Classicist Eva Cantarella writes that in ancient Greece, "the noose was not only the privileged instrument of female suicide, but also, very often that with which
women were killed."[3]

In Homer's *Odyssey* the noose is used to punish women. After
his long absence spent warring and wandering, Odysseus returns to
Ithaka and murders the men who have been pestering his wife, Pe-
nelope, for years. After the bloodbath he orders his wife's disloyal servant women to clean up the mess and then tells his son, Telemachus,
to "hack them with your swordblades till you cut / the life out of
them."[4] But Telemachus has other plans: "I would not give the clean
death of a beast / To trulls who made a mockery of my mother / And
of me too—you sluts, who lay with suitors." And then he performs a
bit of rope work:

> *He tied one end of a hawser to a pillar*
> *And passed the other about the roundhouse top,*
> *Taking the slack up, so that no one's toes*
> *Could touch the ground. They would be hung like doves*
> *Or larks in springès triggered in a thicket,*
> *Where the birds think to rest—a cruel nesting.*
> *So now in turn each woman thrust her head*
> *Into a noose and swung, yanked in air,*
> *To perish there most piteously.*
> *Their feet danced for a little, but not long.*

As the maidens swung in their cruel and ultimate nests, the men went
to Melánthios (Odysseus's turncoat goatherd), who was also hanging
from a beam by rope. They cut him down, sliced off his nose, ears, and

genitals, and then tossed them to the dogs. Only then, Homer tells us, "Their work was done."

In ancient Rome punishments were also spectacles, but they rarely involved hanging by rope.[5] Executions were more likely to involve shoving the accused off the Tarpeian Rock, decapitation, crucifixion, or being thrown to wild animals. The Romans also had a clever punishment for parricides—the condemned was sewn into a sack, at times with animals, including snakes and dogs, and tossed into a body of water.[6] Strangulation, perhaps by rope, was one possible punishment, but as with the Greeks, it was strongly associated with women. All those executed were stripped naked beforehand, so executed women were shielded from the public's view by curtains; thus, their death by strangulation could be heard but not seen. Fourth-century writer Pacatus writes that hanging "is a feminine death, unworthy of a man," and the Roman historian Livy describes the death of one man who hanged himself, Quintus Flavius Flaccus, as "the most disgraceful death imaginable."[7] Men were not supposed to dangle from a rope; they were to throw themselves onto their swords.

Hanging may have been a punishment among the Assyrians, and some historians point to two examples from the Book of Esther to support this argument. The first comes from Esther 2:23, when two men accused of attempting to kill the king are "both hanged on a tree." In Esther 7:9–10 King Ahasuerus's Prime Minister Haman is put to death on a "gallows fifty cubits high" that Haman himself had built in order to execute Mordecai. In the King James Version of events Haman is "hanged," and in the New International Version he is "impaled." It's likely that he endured the latter punishment of impalement first and then had his body hanged on display for the public to gaze upon, a postmortem display intended to further disgrace the executed. This manner of punishment would be supported by Mosaic Law in Deuteronomy 21:22–23 (NIV): "If someone guilty of a capital offense is put to death and their body is exposed on a pole [or tree], you must not leave the body hanging on the pole overnight. Be sure to bury it that same day, because anyone who is hung on a pole is under God's curse. You must not desecrate the land the Lord your God is giving you as an inheritance." Joshua was a fan of hanging bodies, putting them on display in order to further disgrace the dead—he does so with the bodies of the King of Ai and the five anti-Gibeonite Kings.[8] And yet none of these examples fully supports the idea that hanging by the neck until death occurs was a form of judicial or extrajudicial punishment in the Old Testament.

But there are, in fact, two perhaps more significant examples of people hanging by rope until they die in the Bible—one in the Old and one in the New Testament. Although both are suicides, how they are remembered and discussed shapes, I believe, how hanging is subsequently viewed in medieval Europe—the next destination in our journey. The first example of suicide by rope occurs in II Samuel when Ahithophel, a counselor of David, joins David's son Absalom when he rebels against his father, trying to take David's kingdom. After the initial rebellion Ahithophel counsels Absalom to attack David again before David's forces are able to regroup. Absalom ignores his advice. Foreseeing Absalom's future demise and, therefore, his own, Ahihtophel takes his leave. What he does next is explained tersely in II Samuel (NIV): "When Ahithophel saw that his advice had not been followed, he saddled his donkey and set out for his house in his hometown. He put his house in order and then hanged himself."[9]

There are other suicides in the Old Testament—Abimelech, son of Gideon; Samson; Saul and his squire; and Zimri—but Ahithophel's is the only one involving a rope. The other suicides involve either swords or fire. In some ways Ahithophel's hanging death foreshadows Absalom's own death, as he is ultimately killed after his hair gets caught in a tree. But the importance of his story, for this book at least, is that Ahithophel was a turncoat, and therefore, his death was viewed as disgraceful. In Psalms 41:9 (KJV) David writes of his former counselor: "Yea, mine own familiar friend, / in whom I trusted, / which did eat of my bread, / hath lifted up his heel against me." In other words, Ahithophel betrayed David, a move that has led some to refer to him as "the Old Testament Judas."[10] Theologians would eventually say quite

a bit about Ahithophel, in part because his betrayal of David typolog-
ically anticipates that of Jesus and Judas.

JUDAS AND THE NOOSE

The story of Judas Iscariot is, of course, better known, but it shares a
prophetic connection with the story of Ahithophel. In the Gospel of
John Jesus declares during the Passover meal, presaging his own demise, "I speak not of you all: I know whom I have chosen: but that the
scripture may be fulfilled, He that eateth bread with me hath lifted up
his heel against me" (KJV, 13:18). Jesus echoes Psalms 41, David's lam-
entation about those who have turned against him, asserting that his
imminent betrayal will be, in a sense, a fulfillment of prophecy. This
story of betrayal is part of a long literary tradition. Some critics argue
that gospel writers like Matthew may have been aware of this trope and
that some may have been aware of Homer's *Odyssey* (and, therefore, the
story of the treacherous goatherd Melánthios mentioned earlier).[11] In
each of these stories the betrayer dies an outcast, a disgrace.

Indeed, Jesus is ultimately betrayed by "He that eateth bread"
with him, and his betrayer dies shortly thereafter. But of the various
versions of Judas's death, Matthew 27:5 is the only one to mention suicide by hanging. "Throwing down the pieces of silver in the temple,"
the author writes, Judas "went and hanged himself."[12] In Latin this
reads *recessit et abiens laqueo se suspendit*, or he "went away and hanged
himself with a noose."[13] This line from Matthew is a simple, almost
casual line, and of the various descriptions of his death, it's the least
gruesome. In the Acts of the Apostles he buys a field with the money
and then "his body burst open and all his intestines spilled out."[14] If
that weren't dramatic enough, in the apocryphal Gospel of Judas, Judas
has a vision that the other disciples stone him to death.[15]

Throughout medieval Europe it was common for Judas's death
to be associated with the noose. And even though the Bible doesn't
indicate where Judas hanged, his death is often (like Jesus Christ's)
associated with a tree in visual representations.[16] In an early portrayal

Panel from an ivory casket, circa 420 AD. *Used with permission of the Trustees of the British Museum*

of Christ's crucifixion, a relief panel housed in the British Museum and dating from around 420 AD, Judas is depicted hanging from a tree, a noose around his neck.[17] This depiction of Judas has a clear message: Judas is a dastardly Christ-killer. The tree bends down from the weight of Judas, but the other figures all focus on Christ. Alongside the noble death of Jesus Christ (who looks directly at the viewer) is the ignoble death of Judas, who looks away in shame. The simple noose around his neck holds him forever fixed between heaven and hell. This panel also draws a relationship between death by hanging and death on the cross. The cross is, perhaps, a heroic death and the noose a shameful one, a message underscored by the work of Christian theologians across millennia.

Tracing commentaries on Judas's death across the centuries reveals a critical mass of opinions that reinforce this message. In the fourth century St. Jerome wrote that Judas's suicide by hanging was more offensive to God than his betrayal of Christ—it was his greatest sin.[18] St. Ambrose, Jerome's contemporary, writes that Judas "strangled himself with the cord of his own wickedness . . . O the unseemly cord of the betrayer."[19] Writing in the fifth century, Pope Leo the Great notes that Judas's death was all the more horrendous because he did not seek repentance for betraying Christ: "despair dragged thee to the halter. Thou shouldest have awaited the completion of thy crime, and have put off thy ghastly death by hanging, until Christ's Blood was shed for all sinners."[20] These and other statements by the Fathers of the Church were recopied and corroborated throughout the subsequent thousand years. But in the thirteenth century Thomas Aquinas, in his *Catena Aurea* (a collection of biblical glosses), cites Origen (c. 184–253) as saying that Judas was, essentially, possessed by the devil and gave into despair. He writes that Judas "received that more abundant sorrow supplied to him by the Devil, who sought to swallow him up, as it follows. And he went out, and hanged himself."[21]

In general, though, people were fascinated by Judas in the Middle Ages, in part because the Bible leaves so much out of the story—what were his motivations? What was his background? Who was this man so central to the narrative of Jesus Christ? His story of betrayal and suicide inspired paintings and sculptures, folklore and creative literature. And as the story was told across the Mediterranean world and into Europe, differing opinions emerged about which kind of tree Judas hanged himself on.[22] Early legends claim the fig tree was Judas's gallows; later versions say it was the elder, the aspen, the tamarind, wild carob, or the Judas tree. In each version, though, the tree deteriorates and/or dies after he hangs himself from its limbs. For example, a Sicilian tradition has it that the fig tree has not flowered since Judas hanged himself upon it; in Greece the tradition has it that the same tree was once tall but has bent low since his suicide.[23] In England, France, and Germany some believed that Judas hanged himself on an elder—a legend that is referenced by Marlowe, Ben Jonson, and Shakespeare—and according to some, this explains the tree's bitter fruit.[24] What's interesting about these arboreal legends is that they reinforce the belief that Judas hanged himself and that, like Christ, he died on a "tree."

As a literary character, Judas appeared in many apocryphal stories. In Middle English Judas appears in Jacobus de Voraigine's *Legenda Aurea* or *Golden Legend* (c. 1270), the South English Legendary (c. 1300), and the Towneley Manuscript's *Suspencio Iudae* play, among others.[25] These stories are concerned with Judas's motivations—why he did what he did—and opinions on his motivations run the gamut from inexplicable maliciousness to necessary plot device in the Christ narrative. In the *Golden Legend*, for example, after his death by hanging, Judas's soul erupts from his belly in a horrible fashion.

Thus, by the late Middle Ages, Judas's death by hanging is often depicted as not only ignoble but sinister. In a fourteenth-century image from Italy Judas is hanging from a gallows with feet dangling above the ground and the silver in a bag in his hand.[26] A string running from the bag wraps around his neck, and a little black devil sits on his left shoulder. (It's interesting to note that in the twelfth century Bernard of Clairvaux referred to Judas's noose as the "noose of avarice" or *avaritiae laqueo*.)[27] In other works Judas's hanging is associated with Hell and its punishments. Art historian Lee R. Sullivan suggests that in the late Middle Ages the image of Judas served as an icon of avarice, treachery, and contempt for authority and Christianity. Sullivan examines a glass panel of Judas's hanging produced in either Alsace or southern Germany sometime between 1520 and 1530, claiming that it is meant as a warning to rebellious German peasants in the wake of the Peasants' War (1524–1525).[28] Sullivan asserts that "an independent representation of Judas's suicide . . . makes a perfect statement about the inevitable result of such a transgression."[29] Judas is a traitor, and traitors will hang—and the Devil will receive their souls.

It's significant (and perhaps goes without saying) that Judas's hanging death is intimately connected to Christ's crucifixion. As noted above in the fourth-century panel, Judas's tree and Christ's cross are depicted in the same moment, in the same image. They are meant to be viewed together, to be compared and contrasted. Often when Christ's crucifixion is depicted we also bear witness to the crucifixion, on either side of him, of the two thieves. But this is not always so: curiously, in a Book of Hours from the thirteenth century that I saw in the Morgan Library the thieves are not crucified—they are hanged.

From a Catholic Church Book of Hours (MS M.739,
fol 23 r), Germany, possibly Bamberg, 1204–1219.
Used by permission of Pierpont Morgan Library

TURNED OFF

Judas's death by rope might have affected how hanging to death as judicial punishment was viewed and understood during the Middle Ages.
In Christian cultures Judas's supposed hanging could have contributed
to a belief that such a death was nefarious and despicable, a death for
thieves and traitors. Depictions of Judas's hanging death may have
shaped how some viewed hanging executions in medieval Europe, but
the belief that hanging was an ignoble death may also have originated
from the actual method and practice of hanging itself.[30] It was a painful
and potentially gruesome way to die in public.

When crucifixions were banned—most likely in the fourth century under the newly Christian emperor Constantine—hanging executions became more common.[31] And by the eleventh century *The
Vocabulary of Archbishop Alfric* indicates that hanging executions had
become common and public. In our popular imagination we think of
medieval punishment as drawn from a hodge-podge from gruesome
to gruesomer—mutilations, beheadings, boiling,
drowning, breaking on the wheel—but the reality
is that during this period hanging was the most
common form of execution. This is true especially
of late medieval Europe (England, Germany, Italy,
and France, for example).[32]

Typically hangings took place outside of
city walls (like at Tyburn outside of London).[33]
Oftentimes a gallows would be on a hill or at a
crossroads. The condemned would have to travel
there, either walking or riding on the back of a
cart, wearing either a tunic or full dress; sometimes
the victim would wear the noose around his neck
during his travel to the site.[34] After arriving at the

Detail from the illu-
mination of Aelfric's
Genesis (c. 1050), BL
MS Cotton Claudius
B.IV f.59r.

execution site the victim climbed a ladder or remained in the cart. His
hands were bound in back or front. A simple noose, a slipknot, was
then tightened around his neck.[35] This noose was typically made of
rope, though sometimes chains were used.[36] The rope was attached to
a rudimentary gallows—two poles with a cross-beam. Then the ladder
or cart was moved away—this was called "turning off"—and he was
left to die by slow strangulation. In some cases the victim was lifted
or pulled up into the air off the ground rather than being turned off.
If the condemned was lucky, his friends would pull down on his legs
in order to hasten death (or he would pass out and be presumed dead
only to revive later on).[37] It was uncommon for a hood or cap to be
placed over the victim's head, so onlookers saw it all—contorted face
and mouth, jerking body, bowels evacuating.[38] Some onlookers took
relics, such as splinters from the gallows, pieces of the rope, or body

parts of the hanged—a tradition that persisted well into the modern era.[39] These relics, they believed, could cure and heal and, perhaps, protect.[40] Often, though, the body remained intact and in place for all to see—until the weather, wind, and birds finished their work.

Hanging was considered a "disgraceful" mode of punishment, reserved for thieves and the lower classes in part because it involved such a prolonged death, while decapitation by the sword was "honourable."[41] This appears to be the general consensus across Europe. C. V. Calvert notes that in medieval Germany "the substitution of the sword for the halter was considered a favour in some cases."[42] The mode of punishment was important because it telegraphed to onlookers the rank or class of the victim—the confined nature of the slow strangulation of the hanging death (and the ignominy of the rotting corpse) was less desirable than the quick cut of the blade—as well as the severity of the crime.[43] But not all hangings were the same; some were more ignoble than others. In thirteenth-century Germany as well as in France a unique process of execution was reserved for Jews, whereby victims were hanged upside down between two dogs or wolves.[44] Those with power and money, however, could escape punishment altogether. Many would claim the "benefit of clergy" by reading a passage from the Bible, thus proving their literacy and status. The passage they read was typically the 51st Psalm (which became known as "the neck verse"), and, thus, they would be exempt from the harshest secular courts' penalties.[45]

During the Middle Ages a hanging execution was a public spectacle, a community gathering that took place in front of hundreds of onlookers. So pervasive were these spectacles that, as art historian Mitchell Merback notes, many late-medieval painters based their paintings of Christ and the two thieves on their own experiences with public executions.[46] They painted what they saw, and what they saw, from the most mundane hanging to burning at the stake or drawing and quartering, was often brutal by today's standards.

But Esther Cohen notes that "one cannot dismiss public executions as expressions of sadism and barbarity alone. The deliberate causation of physical suffering can qualify as barbarism only if one accepts modern perceptions of and attitudes towards pain."[47] Cohen rightly points out too that people suffered more in the Middle Ages—there was no anesthesia to speak of—and most experienced some intense pain "absolutely intolerable to modern sensitivities" at least once in a lifetime.[48] The notion that pain should be avoided is a modern invention. For the condemned, suffering was viewed as necessary for receiving grace and salvation.[49] Jesus Christ provided an excellent model for such behavior.

A public hanging was also an expression of state power. Before the advent of the press, governments had to assert their authority via processions, festivals, and, of course, public executions.[50] Executions sent a strong message to the people about the church and/or state's ultimate authority and about who (or what) would be protected or not. In *Discipline and Punish* Michel Foucault notes that "the public execution . . . is a ceremonial by which a momentarily injured sovereignty is reconstituted. It restores that sovereignty by manifesting it at its most spectacular."[51] Hanging was just such a spectacular demonstration of power. It was, Foucault writes, a kind of performance: "In the ceremonies of the public execution, the main character was the people, whose real and immediate presence was required for the performance. An execution that was known to be taking place, but which did so in secret, would scarcely have had any meaning. The aim was to make an example, not only by making people aware that the slightest offence was likely to be punished, but by arousing feelings of terror by the spectacle of power letting its anger fall upon the guilty person."[52] The noose, of course, was central to this spectacle.

As hanging executions developed throughout the Middle Ages they gathered with them the requisite customs and accoutrements that shape the popular imagination of the practice—the gallows, the crowd, the victim (penitent or otherwise), the hangman, and the rope knotted about the neck. There need be little more for a hanging to take place. It is an act requiring simple technologies, so simple that all those "accoutrements" are not technically necessary for a hanging to occur—Judas did it alone. But by the end of the Middle Ages those accoutrements are unquestionably there. They too are part of the spectacle and ritual, part of the pattern of humans creating a space for other humans to die, and in a way that seems different from the ritualistic Iron Age hanging of Tollund Man.

Yet it also feels universal: there is something elemental about depriving a human of oxygen. A living person has a rope placed around her neck and is left to hang by that rope until she strangles to death, her legs kicking at the air, seeking support, some solid ground upon which to stand and perhaps save herself. She is drowning on dry land. This image of the jerking body of the hanged human signifies justice for some and tragedy for others. It is also an essential moment during which the human body grasps for the most basic need—breath. Dangling bodies kicking for life are at the center of medieval poet Dante Alighieri's version of hell. After pilgrim Dante and guide Virgil pass through all the circles of hell, bearing witness to unimaginable suffering, they reach the last circle, where a three-faced Lucifer is frozen with the bodies of three traitors (Brutus, Cassius, and Judas Iscariot) hanging out of his three mouths, forever struggling to get free, forever suffering the pain of Lucifer's moving jaws. This is the center of hell, a place for history's most dastardly traitors. But as Virgil explains to Dante, "'That soul up there who suffers most of all / . . . is Judas Iscariot: / the one with head inside and legs out kicking."[53] The two travelers must then climb down the body of Lucifer, who is fixed forever in ice. Dante writes, "We climbed, he first and I behind, until, / through a small round opening ahead of us / I saw the lovely things the heavens hold, / and we came out to see once more the stars."[54]

REVOLUTIONS

CHAPTER 4

At the Crossroads:
The Spectacle of Hanging
in Colonial New York

WHEN EUROPEANS EXPLORED AND COLONIZED the so-called New World, they carried their histories and cultures with them. On ships, sailors perfected their knot-tying skills in order to ensure safety in difficult weather and rough seas. When they arrived in port some tossed to shore heaving lines made from wrapping turns like those used in a hangman's knot. Travelers on ships brought their languages, foodways, religions, politics, and even their punishments. Hanging executions were common enough in Europe. In the period of England's "Bloody Code" (roughly 1688–1815) there were 222 crimes (including murder, rape, robbery, arson, and counterfeiting) that could potentially lead to the noose, though they might also lead to "transportation" to one of the colonies or a stint in the military.[1] The first European-administered hanging in North America may have been that of eight Native Americans in August 1572 by the Spanish in retribution for killing a group of Jesuit missionaries.[2] In British North America hanging executions were around from the earliest days of settlement: the first was likely Daniel Frank, hanged in 1623 for stealing a calf in Virginia. And the first in Massachusetts Bay Colony was John Billington, a *Mayflower* passenger, hanged on September 30, 1630, for murder.

The noose traveled on board immigrant ships across the rolling Atlantic as both a cultural technology and an icon of brutal memories. In her 2008 novel *A Mercy* Toni Morrison imagines how this memory shaped the lives of colonists. The noose is a ghostly presence for a "mail-order bride" named Rebekkah, who witnessed many hangings in seventeenth-century England. Rebekkah thinks she has left these experiences behind but hasn't—the memory of what she has witnessed is ever-present. Rebekkah remembers,

> The first hangings she saw in the square amid a happy crowd attending. She was probably two years old, and the death faces would have frightened her if the crowd had not mocked and enjoyed them so. With the rest of her family and most of their neighbors, she was present at a drawing and quartering and, although she was too young to remember details, her night-mares were made permanently vivid by years of retelling and redescribing by her parents . . . it was clear in her household that execution was a festivity as exciting as a king's parade.[3]

Morrison's fiction depicts one reality for many colonists—that they carried memories of public hangings with them to the cities and towns of the New World.

Indeed, immigrants always bring the ideas of their old world into their new one. They foster confrontation and collaboration, collision and contact at the crossroads. Manhattan Island is perhaps America's greatest crossroads and has, from its inception, been so unstable that across centuries those with power on this island have felt compelled to assert themselves and their authority through very public displays: the great skyscraping monuments to capitalism, the New Colossus in the harbor, and, in colonial America (before the people granted their authority to a document, the Constitution) authority asserted itself quite effectively by hanging someone by his neck until he was dead. And usually this was done in a public space, perhaps at a crossroads, where the message would be seen and felt.

The first nonindigenous settler to come to Manhattan Island was Jan Rodrigues, a man born in Santo Domingo to a Portuguese father and Congolese mother—a precursor to the ethnic heterogeneity of the island that persists to this day. Rodrigues lived in Manhattan for over a decade before the Dutch established a permanent settlement in 1624. And when they did, a free black community developed and soon became the largest free black community in the seventeenth-century North. These early African Americans could own property and develop small economic enterprises.[4] In fact, during the 1650s there were free black farms along the Bowery from today's Prince Street up to Astor Place.[5] Free black farmers sold their wares in weekly markets, where the port cities' diverse inhabitants rubbed elbows and competed for economic gain. And yet these free blacks lived alongside an *enslaved* black community.

The slave population was initially small, but as the Dutch colony grew, more farm labor was required. Many white colonists who came to work farms turned to trade, and by the time the English took over the colony in 1664, 20 percent of the population was enslaved.[6] In addition to a new flag, the English brought their laws that required stricter controls on all black people. They also began the process of making white slavery virtually illegal in the colony.[7] This shaped not only the lives of enslaved blacks in New York but also those of free blacks, who became increasingly less free as the seventeenth century bled into the eighteenth. Free blacks weren't allowed to vote, be jurors, testify, serve in the militia, and, in some cases, own property.[8]

And yet slavery in New York City was not like that of the plantation South. First of all, there were far fewer slaves in New England and in the Middle colonies.[9] These people were not, generally, brought from Africa—slave owners made more money further south. In the early eighteenth century about 70 percent of slaves in New York came from other New World colonies in the West Indies or in the South.[10] Most slaves arrived in small groups and weren't crammed into the hulls of ships. They often worked as they traveled on these ships and learned a lot while doing so.[11] The skills they gained at sea were often transferred to work in the ports, where slaves were employed as sailors and related naval industries—ship building, sail making, and rope making.[12]

In the North there were no grand plantations; most slave owners owned only a few slaves, housing them in their attics or cellars. Despite this physical proximity, black slaves and whites lived in separate worlds. But slaves had some freedom of movement, and this helped them develop connections across the city. The urban infrastructure, the many taverns, and simple cover of darkness provided ample possibilities for fostering communication and community.[13] As was the custom in many Atlantic port taverns, white and black people mingled and drank, sometimes fought and sometimes sang.[14] Proprietors weren't supposed to sell alcohol to slaves, but many were willing to overlook legal status when money was being offered.

In general these early African Americans were a cosmopolitan group—some spoke several languages—and had shared maritime experiences with some of their free black and lower-class white tavern-mates.[15] At various times throughout the latter half of the seventeenth and the early years of the eighteenth century authorities tried to regulate such interracial and cross-class gatherings as well as gatherings among slaves themselves. Such laws weren't always effective, but stifling communications among slaves would become paramount after New York's first slave revolt on April 6, 1712.

The revolt began on Maiden Lane, in the present-day financial district. At one time this street was on the edge of the city and it was so named, the story goes, because at one time a stream flowed there, and it was popular for young women to do the washing and for young men to watch. But there was no courting this night, as a group of mostly Coromantine slaves, free blacks, and at least two Native Americans had assembled on the street carrying hatchets and guns and swords—whatever weapon they could muster. They swore a blood oath, and some rubbed their clothes with a powder that was supposed to provide protection.[16] At about two o'clock in the morning two slaves belonging to a baker named Peter Vantilborough set fire to his house while their armed coconspirators waited in the street. When a general panic ensued and white people came out of their houses, the rebels set upon them. Nine were killed and at least seven were wounded.

Gunfire woke up city residents, and shortly thereafter Governor Robert Hunter summoned citizens and troops to take up arms. The rebels ran; some hid in the town, but others raced to the woods north of the city. At least six killed themselves rather than being caught and tortured and/or executed. Perhaps they knew about an incident from a few years earlier when two slaves were convicted of killing a Long Island family of seven and were tortured to death—one was burned alive while the other was hung in chains and then impaled.[17] Or, more likely, they had simply lived long enough in the Atlantic world to have known what was in store for them.

The revolt, according to a report in the *Boston News-Letter*, gave New York "no small consternation."[18] More than seventy slaves were arrested and forty-three brought to quick trials in April and May. In the end fifteen were hanged (one of whom was a pregnant woman whose execution was postponed until she'd given birth).[19] Two were burned alive, and one, according to the record, was burned slowly for eight or more hours. Another slave, named Robin, was hung in chains while still alive. But the most gruesome of all punishments was that meted out to a slave named Claus, who was broken on the wheel, a process that involved stretching the condemned out on a wheel and then breaking his limbs. The victim was left in anguish to a slow and eventual death. In addition to the executions, the memories of some of the executed were further denigrated through the public display of their bodies and heads.

THE RITUAL OF HANGING CROSSES THE ATLANTIC

Such large-scale and brutal punishments were atypical for the American colonies. In general colonists were less likely to reach for the noose than their relatives back in England, despite the fact that there were no prisons to speak of until the late eighteenth century. Actually, prisons were impractical in growing colonies: the entire community had to pay for imprisonment, and a prisoner would be unable to support her family, creating another expenditure for the community. The consensus, then, was that punishment should be public and should humiliate the convicted in an effort to reform. Popular colonial punishments included whipping, sitting in the stocks, clipping ears, or forcing people to wear letters denoting the crime they had committed, such as "D" (drunk), "T" (thief), or "A" (adulteress), made famous by Nathaniel Hawthorne.[20] If none of this worked, there was the noose.

Colonists took executions seriously and believed there must be a pedagogical intent to them. Not only should a public hanging punish the criminal, but it should also warn others and act as a deterrent for future crimes, an argument one still hears from contemporary death penalty advocates.[21] Each colony made its own laws about which crimes warranted the noose, and these laws changed over time. Initially crimes against morality, rather than property, were more likely to receive death sentences in New England.[22] Historian Stuart Banner notes that "blasphemy and idolatry were in principle capital crimes in Connecticut, Massachusetts, and New Hampshire; adultery was capital in early Connecticut, Massachusetts, and New York; sodomy and bestiality were capital throughout the region, even for the animals involved."[23] But such executions became few and far between as New England and the colonies in general focused less on policing morals and more on making money. Concurrently, over the course of the eighteenth century there were more instances of executions for crimes against property.

Protestant communities in colonial America continued, like their European forebears, to observe the ritual of public executions, an event witnessed by most colonial Americans at least once in their lifetime.[24] Executions were held outside and sometimes in front of crowds that numbered into the thousands. In 1701 Esther Rodgers was hanged for infanticide in Boston in front of between four and five thousand spectators.[25] Sarah Bramble was hanged in New London in front of about ten thousand in 1753.[26] Daniel Wilson was executed in Providence for rape in front of more than twelve thousand people two years before the Declaration of Independence was signed. Crowds attending hangings in New York City grew so large that officials moved hangings to islands in the harbor; people then chartered boats and crowded along docks to gain the best vantage points. Hangings were mass gatherings (historian Stuart Banner claims they were the largest gatherings of any sort) for the ritual reenactment of community values and norms.[27] Public hangings also reinforced, as they had in Europe, the values of the state and church. On the one hand, the state had the authority to punish criminals, and on the other, the church had the authority to assist in the criminal's salvation or damnation. A public execution was, then, a grand act of education and, possibly, indoctrination.

Early American execution attendees were mostly serious and solemn, in contrast to their English counterparts.[28] Children were often present at executions, and religious leaders encouraged their parents to bring them. For Christian ministers a scheduled death was an excellent opportunity to teach the central tenets of Christianity—God's punitive and redemptive power. The work of preparing the way for execution day began, sometimes, weeks beforehand, when ministers met with a condemned criminal in hopes of saving him or her. This would be followed by the execution sermon, which was delivered in church on the Sunday before (sometimes with the condemned criminal present) or at the scaffold on execution day.[29]

After the sermon the condemned might speak, and the hope of the minister and the audience was that she would confess her guilt and be saved before dying. Sometimes onlookers would ask questions of (or say a prayer with) the condemned, and the condemned would respond.[30] Thus, just as in medieval Europe, the execution was a place where a criminal could repent, reconnect with God, and die a good death—a result that onlookers desired. It's important to remember that in seventeenth- and eighteenth-century America people did not view condemned criminals as distinctly different from themselves—they were human beings as themselves and had gone astray, like anyone could.[31] Likewise Stuart Banner writes, "Most colonial Americans assigned responsibility for crime to the criminal himself rather than to his environment. Among writers on the subject, humankind was often understood as intrinsically depraved, as having a natural tendency toward evil."[32] So when someone committed a crime it was because they weren't being responsible for their actions, and then the community was obligated to punish them. For some, Puritans in particular, addressing criminal behavior meant keeping the community intact and on course.[33]

And yet the community was also obligated to assist or at least encourage the sinner to repent. Whether this would happen was a source of dramatic tension befitting the greatest theatrical production. If it all went smoothly, then the condemned would offer a heartfelt confession, and the execution would be deemed successful because it fostered "conversion."[34] Conversion might also mean a reassertion or reintegration of morality into a community—a way of fostering community cohesion. John Winthrop famously underscored this belief in his "Modell of Christian Charity" when he claimed that the Puritan community would be one body knitted together by their Christian love, a vision of people from different classes, of different sexes, but with one mission. He wrote, "We must delight in each other, make others' conditions our own, rejoice together, mourn together, labor and suffer together, always having before our eyes our commission and community in the work."[35] They are joined together by love, by mission, and by belief. And public punishment was the hard edge of this love, but it was also a mechanism for the community torn apart to be stitched back together.

The punishments for slave rebellions tested this noble justification, though. There are moments when communities demonstrate no desire whatsoever to reintegrate. I should note that many of the condemned in early America were foreigners, in part because it was easier to get a conviction for such persons.[36] It is also clear, especially in the southern colonies, that the list of executable offenses became especially long for black people, a list that often included conspiracy to commit crimes or rebellion.[37] Slave resistance was met with swift punishment; sometimes slaves were gibbetted, branded, and, for persistent runaways, hamstrung. On September 9, 1739, after white colonists in South Carolina put down the Stono Rebellion, forty accused rebels were summarily executed and their heads placed on posts along the road to Charleston. Cutting up the body of the rebel or criminal and making it visible for public consumption was nothing new, of course, and had long been practiced in public spaces and crossroads throughout Europe.[38]

But violent responses to threats on the community that went beyond singular hanging executions weren't always about slavery. In 1692 nineteen people were hanged (and one pressed) in Salem, Massachusetts, because of "witchcraft" (at least fourteen people had been hanged for the same charges in colonial America prior to that year).[39] Of course, "witch hunt" has become a watchword for an outbreak of hysterical recrimination. The relationship of the communal hysteria in Salem to what the colonists carried with them across the Atlantic is worth noting. Salem had much in common with the pogroms and massacres of medieval and Early Modern Europe, though it integrated the European-style public execution into its rituals. Twenty years later the revolt executions in New York demonstrated again the ways that spectacles could be used to effectively "other" whole classes of people—to attempt to eternally situate them in a lower social location. These executions had much in common with latter-day lynchings; indeed, there was no desire in 1712 to reintegrate black people into the community. In many ways 1712 prepared the way for America's future work in the art of tying knots and hanging people. In many ways 1712 prepared the way for 1741.

NEW YORK'S SECOND SLAVE REBELLION

Between May 11 and August 15, 1741, authorities in the city of New York hanged twenty-one people and burned thirteen others at the stake.[40] One man slit his throat rather than face the torment and humiliation of public execution. Of those executed, four were white and thirty were black; all had been accused of participating in a plan to incite a slave rebellion that would effectively overturn the colonial government.

The executions made an already extraordinary spring in this bus-
tling coastal colony all the more extraordinary. The city was just pulling
out of a brutal winter and was on edge because Great Britain and Spain
were fighting the War of Jenkins' Ear, and hundreds of troops had left
the city to fight; many feared a Spanish invasion while they were away.
The war began, in part, because Spanish coast guards chopped off the
ear of a British merchant ship captain. When he showed said ear to
Parliament, the course was set. But the war wasn't really about an ear;
it was about Atlantic world rivalries, the struggle for prominence in a
growing global economy, setting political limits, establishing allies, and
creating hierarchies. It was the kind of struggle that played out in little
and big ways throughout the North American colonies over the course
of the eighteenth century—a struggle for order within communities
and without.

The crisis that led to those thirty-four executions began on February 28 with a simple case of robbery. Investigators traced the crime
back to three black slaves, named Caesar, Prince, and Cuffee, who, it
turned out, had an ongoing relationship with a white tavern keeper
named John Hughson, in whose basement some of the stolen property
was found. Hughson's hardscrabble waterfront dive stood either in or
just south of what is today called Zuccotti Park at the corner of Liberty
and Trinity Place.[41]

Investigators' main source was Hughson's sixteen-year-old indentured servant, Mary Burton.[42] She claimed that not only did she know
who was involved in the robbery but also that black men spent a lot of
time in the tavern. In fact, she explained, one black man, Caesar, was
in a relationship with a white prostitute named Peggy Kerry, and they
had a child together.[43] Hughson's tavern, investigators learned, was a
place where laws and norms were flaunted. Mary Burton said she could
tell them more but feared for her safety. Shortly thereafter Prince and
Caesar were arrested and John Hughson and his family interrogated.

The information about Hughson's tavern would have piqued the
interest of colonial authorities, for sure, but when the dots were connected to the events that followed, that interest turned into hyste-

ria. What came next was a series of fires that threatened to destroy the entire infrastructure of the colonies. The first fire engulfed Fort George, the city's defense from the sea, on the day after St. Patrick's Day. And then there was another and then another—thirteen fires in all, spanning the course of a few weeks. One Sunday morning during this burning time a white colonist claimed to have overheard a black slave named Quack exclaim, "Fire, Fire, Scorch, Scorch. A little damn it, by-and-by" as he walked along Broadway with a group of friends.[44] Indeed, something strange seemed afoot.

A grand jury began an inquest into the events on April 14. It was led for the most part by a ladder-climbing lawyer named Daniel Horsmanden, who was eager to make a name for himself in the city. Horsmanden was suspicious of the fires and suspected a conspiracy, especially given Quack's statement and the fact that a slave named Cuffee was seen fleeing one of them.[45] Meanwhile officials urged laws to curtail assemblies of black people in the city and stepped up night patrols.[46] And in late April a proclamation was published announcing that any white person who could "discover" anyone involved with the fires would get one hundred pounds if they were convicted. If a slave did so, he would be free and his owner compensated. And a free "Negro, Mulatto, or Indian" who did so would receive forty-five pounds.[47]

Hughson's indentured servant Mary Burton took the stand on April 22 and told tales of miscegenation in Hughson's waterfront tavern, late-night inter-racial carousing, and, most startling of all, a plot to overthrow the colonial government and replace it with one ruled by King John Hughson and Governor Caesar.[48] A city census from around 1737 "counted 8,667 New Yorkers: 6,947 whites and 1,719 blacks"; this meant that about one in five New Yorkers was black, and most were slaves.[49] Black people were in a clear minority, and yet rebellion was still a possibility. The people in New York would have heard about slave rebellions outside of Charleston (1739), in Antigua (1736), and on St. John's (1733). For her testimony Burton was offered her freedom and one hundred pounds. So she kept talking, and over the spring and summer of 1741, 20 white people and 142 black people were arrested.

In court defendants weren't allowed attorneys, and much of the evidence—or all of it, really—was based on confessions from folks stuffed into the basement prison at City Hall. In this uncommon case the courts relied on an uncommon tool—evidence from black people. Slaves and free blacks were told that if they offered evidence against another slave or free black, they could avoid the harshest penalties. Historian Michael Kammen notes that what emerged was "a pattern of terror and intimidation in which blacks were offered pardons only for 'telling the truth,' which really meant confessing and implicating others. Denials and professions of innocence went unheeded."[50] And yet much of what Horsmanden and company were able to wring out of the defendants had roots in Mary Burton's testimony.

In early May Caesar and Prince were convicted and became the first persons implicated in this crisis to hang by their necks until dead.[51] But as spring slipped into summer, the executions began in earnest: generally burnings were held in the afternoons and evenings and hangings in the morning.[52] When Quack and Cuffee were burned near the African Burial Ground, an enormous crowd gathered to watch, anxious to see them executed. After they had been chained to the stake they were questioned, and both began confessing all manner of things—including responsibility for setting fires—and accusing over thirty people in hopes of winning a reprieve or sentence reduction.[53] Neither was in the cards for them: they were engulfed in smoke and flame.

In early June John Hughson, his wife, and Peggy Kerry were convicted and sentenced to death for "confederating with the Negroes . . . and encouraging them to burn the town and kill the inhabitants."[54] The three were carried to their execution in a cart. This was, as with most early American executions, a very public journey from jail to the site of execution, typically a location with few visual obstructions and an ability to accommodate throngs of onlookers. Sometimes executions would take place at the scene of the crime. The condemned were usually told to look down and not make eye contact as they traveled toward their imminent demise—in a sense, underscoring a symbolic break with the community.[55] But John Hughson stood up in the cart on his way to the gallows, gazing upon the crowd as if looking for some sign of possible rescue, and "one hand was lifted up as high as his pinion would admit of, and a finger pointing, as if intending to beckon."[56] Or maybe he was looking at the people who were about to kill him. "At the gallows his wife stood like a lifeless trunk, with the rope around her neck . . . she said not a word and had scarce any visible motion." Peggy apparently was about to say something before they were to be executed, but Mrs. Hughson "gave her a shove."

The hanging proper would have utilized technologies that had changed very little from the Middle Ages. One method was to have the condemned climb a ladder, to bind her hands, and then to place the noose around her neck. The noose used was most likely a traditional slipknot, as there's no clear indication that the hangman's knot was in use yet. The rope was attached either to a simple gallows fashioned out of two poles and a cross bar or to a tree. In colonial America most towns built gallows for specific hangings, though larger towns might have them in place at all times. After the condemned climbed the ladder and the noose was adjusted, the ladder was pulled away, and he or she strangled to death.

The ladder was eventually replaced by a cart, as it seems to have been for the executions of the Hughsons and Peggy Kerry. Their procession would have ended with the cart being pulled up to the gallows, the rope attached, and the beast of burden pulling the cart whipped. The three were then quickly jerked off the cart and hanged. Some reformers thought using a cart would lead to a quicker death; however, the use of the cart required a shorter gallows and, thus, the condemned suffered a short drop and, most likely, still died of prolonged strangulation.[57] Others believed that if you could situate the noose beneath the left or right ear rather than behind the head, it would result in a quicker death—most likely by fracturing the spinal column.[58] The people handling all of this technology, the hangmen, weren't experts but rather locals with little experience; often it was the sheriff or some other known member of the local community.[59]

The execution of Levi Ames from "The dying groans of Levi Ames, who was executed at Boston, the 21st of October, 1773 for burglary." This is a good example of Colonial execution. Note the presence of both the military and the clergy. *Library of Congress*

When the condemned was declared dead, family members could claim the body. But the bodies of the executed were generally never claimed. In London they were often given to surgeons for dissection, but in the colonies they were typically buried in a communal grave, if they were buried at all. Hughson and Caesar suffered the double ignominy of being hanged in chains on an island in the collect pond, just north of the city (and close to today's Federal Courthouse). But a curious thing happened to the bodies of John Hughson and Caesar as they hung in chains. Horsmanden writes that Hughson's "face, hands, neck, and feet, were of a deep shining black, rather blacker than the negro placed by him."[60] His hair, he wrote, began "curling like the wool of a negro's beard and head, and the features of his face were of the symmetry of a negro beauty." His body also began to swell. Conversely, Caesar became "bleached or turned whitish." It seemed as though the two had "changed colors." Hughson became "as black as the devil."[61] Eventually, though, time and nature took its course in the heat of the New York summer, and Hughson's body exploded with "pail fulls of blood and corruption."[62] It's clear that Hughson was gibbeted as

of a "popish" plot and accused a man named John Ury of being a Spanish priest in disguise. They believed Ury had recruited Hughson, whom he had converted, along with many slaves, to Catholicism.[70] But Ury denied all accusations on the scaffold and was the last to hang on August 29.[71] When he "appeared at the gallows with a very composed countenance, he kneeled down and prayed very devoutly. And in his prayer to God he denied the facts witnessed against him, so he prayed that it would please almighty God to cause some visible constraint upon the witnesses to manifest to the world, that they had been witnessed against him was false."[72] According to one newspaper, he then gave a prepared speech: "I am now going to suffer a death attended with ignominy and pain; but it is the cup that my heavenly father has put into my hands, and I drink it with pleasure. It is the cross of my dear redeemer, I bear it with alacrity; knowing, that all that live godly in Christ Jesus must suffer persecution; and we must be made in some degree partakers of his sufferings, before we can share in the glories of his resurrection."[73] Ury claimed his innocence and that he knew nothing of the conspiracy, that he didn't even recognize his courtroom accusers. "I depart this waste, this howling wilderness," he exclaimed, "with a mind serene, free from all malice, with a forgiving spirit." And then he entreated, "No longer delay; seeing the summons may come before you are aware, and you, standing before the bar of a God, who is a consuming fire out of the Lord Jesus Christ, should be hurled, be doomed to the place where their worm dies not, and the fire is never to be quenched." Ury removed his wig and handed it to a friend, who helped him adjust the noose around his neck and the cap over his head.[74] Through it all he remained composed, cool, and calm. And then the cart pulled away, and John Ury likely strangled to death.

The plot, the hysteria, the scare—call it what you will—fell apart as Mary Burton began accusing high-ranking white people and her reputation came into question.[75] Not to mention the fact that many slave owners were losing money as their slaves, their property, were executed. In early August Cadwallader Colden, one of the city's most prominent citizens, received a mysterious letter from an author who claimed to be from Massachusetts and noted the similarities between the Salem witch trials and what was happening in New York. The writer claimed to be a "well-wisher to all human beings and one that ever desires to be of the merciful side."[76] Some wondered if the letter was not from a disgruntled New Yorker.

As summer slipped into fall, the proceedings became increasingly unpopular and would soon come to an end. When all was said and done, thirty-four people had been executed, five white men were pressed into military service, and over seventy people of African descent had been transported out of the colony, most to the brutal slavery of the West Indies, where they could only expect a few more years of life. Pardon wasn't uncommon in the colonies; it was at the governor's discretion. The overall pardon rate in the New York colonies for capital offenses was 51.7 percent, and 72 percent of slaves were pardoned in this case.[77] That more weren't executed was likely due to the fact that they didn't actually kill anyone and so few were actually involved. On November 11 Mary Burton received her last payment and, thus, her freedom from indentured servitude—she was never heard from again.

There is no single agreed-upon narrative of what happened in New York in 1741. Some argue that the trials and executions were the result of the dismantling of an actual scheme devised by slaves and poor whites to rob and pilfer from New York's wealthiest.[78] Peter Linebaugh and Marcus Rediker claim that what happened in New York was a part of a series of revolutions that spread throughout the Atlantic world, what they call "a Caribbean cycle of rebellion," and they cite "more than eighty separate cases of conspiracy, revolt or mutiny, and arson—a figure probably six or seven times greater than the number of similar events that occurred in either the dozen years before 1730 or the dozen after 1742."[79] In New York the organizers were "soldiers, sailors, and slaves from Ireland, the Caribbean and Africa."[80] They argue that the "cooperative nature of work in the port" fostered social relations and rebellious networks.[81] In the end New York authorities tried to regulate the taverns and reinforce racial boundaries—"promoting a white identity that would transcend and unify the city's fractious ethnic divisions."[82] But others argue that the convictions were based on hysteria and that many innocent people died. Winthrop Jordan calls what happened "a classic witch hunt," and Mary Burton, an "imaginative informer."[83] Philip D. Morgan claims that what we really might be looking at is a case of white racism and a desire to see rebellion where there is none.[84] It should be noted too that many of the confessions were gained through the promise of rewards or of the cessation of torture.

Was there an actual conspiracy and was this an example of lower-class collaboration and an attempt to transform a colony in the New World? Was it, perhaps, an attempt to *make* a new world? One thing is certain: many people were hanged, and most of them were people living on the margins of the community—free blacks and enslaved Africans, poor people and immigrants.

Daniel Horsmanden sincerely believed that black slaves and freemen, under the direction of whites, were plotting to destroy New York City, or at least that's what he says in the book he published in 1744 with the lengthy title *A Journal of the Proceedings in the Detection of the Conspiracy formed by Some White People, in Conjunction with Negro and Other Slaves, for Burning the City of New York in America, and Murdering the Inhabitants.* Horsmanden's report of the events of that year is the most thorough extant source on the event and a fascinating contribution to the genre of crime literature, but it must be read with caution. Horsmanden had a lot riding on these prosecutions. First of all, he had been on the losing side of a trial that has become a seminal event in American legal history—the 1735 trial of printer John Peter Zenger, who was accused of libel but found innocent of the charges, a case viewed by many as a foundational event for establishing a free press in America. So for Horsmanden, the prospect of uncovering a grand slave conspiracy offered the possibility of redemption from that loss. He argued for the initial investigations, sat on the Supreme Court, and doled out sentences.[85] Contemporary readers must keep a sharp eye out when reading the pages of this "journal," for it is hard to tell what can be trusted and what cannot; thus, the debate continues about whether there was a plot in the first place. Was it a fabrication? Is this a work of fiction? Was Horsmanden using the convergence of a variety of alarming events to his advantage?

Nonetheless, his book is a dramatic example of gallows literature, and amidst its problematic pages two things stand out to me: the author's relative erasure of the actual executions and his clear attitudes about race. The conspiracy trials are particularly important because they lead to one of the most intense episodes of mass hangings in early America and offer an important case study for examining the ways in which race becomes an important social category in America. One way to read what happened in 1741 is that it is the story of how hysteria turns into scapegoating. But it is also about how racial categories are formed, how blackness is equated with crime and, I will argue, with the noose itself. As historian of American slavery Ira Berlin claims, "Race is not simply a social construction; it is a particular kind of social construction—a historical construction."[86]

And yet the 1741 conspiracy court could not understand "the monstrous ingratitude of this black tribe" whose "slavery among us is generally softened with great indulgence; they live without care, and commonly better fed and clothed, and put to less labor, than the poor of most Christian countries."[87] They could not understand why any enslaved person in their fine city would want to change her circumstances—either through rebellion or robbery. Not only could they not conceive of why she might wish to rebel, at one point during the trial Attorney General Richard Bradley asserted that there was no way any slave could have organized the rebellion herself. As a group they were, he claimed,

> stupid wretches seduced by the instigation of the devil, and Hughson his agent, to undertake so senseless as well as wicked enterprise . . . it cannot be imagined that these silly unthinking creatures . . . could of themselves have contrived and carried on so deep, so direful and destructive a scheme, so that we have seen with our eyes and have heard fully proved, they had prepared for us, without the advice and assistance of such

abandoned wretches as Hughson was—that never to be forgotten Hughson, who is now gone to his place, as did Judas
of old to his.[88]

Hughson, like the Judas of legend, hanged. His memory would be
forever denigrated because he was friends with, conspired with, was
in contact with black people. This was the message sent by New York
authorities: there is no place for "mixing" in this community. They
desired fixed divisions of race and class in the city. But reality is more
complicated, people are more complicated, and this will always lead to
conflicts at the crossroads of cultures and economic interests. Whites
never truly imagined a place for black people in their community; they
could work for them, be near them, live near them, but they would
never be truly integrated into their sense of self or nation. Perhaps,
then, the ethnic and national diversity fostered a sense of white solidarity and black otherness. And in order to do so, and with the help of the
noose, whites fostered a destructive and spectacular violence. Natalie
Zemon Davis writes that rather than fall into such "rites of violence"
as a means for securing safety and community, "we must think less
about pacifying 'deviants' and more about changing central values."[89]
In a sense she says that we should reflect on how we learn to hate and
how we learn to kill. These things do not come out of thin air.

SIGNS AND SYMBOLS

I moved to New York City shortly after I graduated from college in
1999. On my first night in Brooklyn I was trying to fall asleep in the
August heat of my top-floor tenement apartment. Lying on two tow-
els on the floor, the only bed I had at that point, I discovered that if
I raised my head just so, I could see the blinking light of the North
Tower of the World Trade Center. To the right of that light a lone
star and then an airplane headed for a safe landing at LaGuardia.
Two years later I climbed up to the roof for a better view: on that day
there was only smoke and ashes where grand towers once stood. Burnt

pages of computer paper floated on currents, helicopters circled, and, beyond, nothing but blue sky. Those buildings, which once seemed so firm in their push to heaven, had buckled under the weight of too much hate. There was a lot of death in that place, in that moment. And yet that spit of land hugged by the East River and the Hudson is no stranger to violent death.

Today that violent history is mostly paved over, buried beneath skyscrapers and years of living. It's difficult to find it, to find even a glimpse of what was once there. It's almost impossible, like trying to understand why and how humans can be so violent. Lower Manhattan has seen its share of spectacular violence. Situated at the mouth of a river that goes deep into a landscape of great resources, it is and has been for centuries a place where people come together to trade—a commercial crossroads. As such this space, jutting out into one of the finest harbors on the Eastern Seaboard, has also been a crossroads of cultures and politics. Lower Manhattan gathers people together to do both awesome and horrible things—to create culture through the trade of stories and languages, to create empire through the accumulation of wealth, but also to produce very public displays of violence. Not surprisingly there's a conflict over memory at Ground Zero and in Lower Manhattan and how the violence of 9/11 is to be remembered and memorialized. To some, Ground Zero should be a graveyard; to others it should be a testament to American enterprise and ingenuity winning out over evil deeds. To some, Ground Zero is the present; to others, Ground Zero is the past.

If you walk east from Ground Zero and cross the street to Zuccotti Park at Liberty and Trinity Place, you will walk where, in 1741, a group of African slaves and freemen and a smattering of poor white sailors gathered in Hughson's Tavern. Keep walking eastward down Liberty and cross Broadway. Shuffle over to Maiden Lane and Williams Street, about to where the 1712 Rebellion began. Stay eastward and a bit southward as you make your way down to 75 Wall Street, where a slave market once stood. Today it's sophisticated condominiums, a rooftop lounge, and modern amenities.

Turn up Water to Fulton Street and the South Street Seaport area, a manufactured vision of nineteenth-century New York City full of upscale commercial outposts—Guess, Coach, Abercrombie, Superdry, Brookstone. It is a fake space: a far cry from the seafaring past it represents, but then again it is tapped into the global marketplace of our day. And there are alehouses still and many languages spoken. But most of the ships around this "seaport" are museums—history repackaged for easy consumption.

Turn back inland, toward the city, and make your way up Fulton and go north up Broadway, over to City Hall Park. In 1741 most of what is today City Hall Park was the commons; it was also a likely site for the gallows. There's nothing marking that gallows, though there is a prominent statue in honor of Nathan Hale, America's favorite hanged man, who was likely hanged near the present-day United Nations. It's curious how much is remembered about Hale, he of the famous line about having only one life to give for his country.

From City Hall Park, walk over to the corner of Chambers and Centre, where the burnings took place, and look north to where the collect pond stood, just outside the city walls. In the middle of that pond was an island, and on that island Caesar and Hughes were gibbeted. They were served the double ignominy of being gibbeted but also being left to decay outside the city proper. Today this is Thomas Paine Park, just above Foley Square. A sign at the park explains that this would have been a freshwater swamp during Paine's time in New York City and that it was surrounded by several British prisons for Revolutionaries, including the Bridewell, where many died from "wind and cold exposure while waiting for trial."

This park is close to where contemporary justice is dispensed in New York City: One Police Plaza and the New York State Supreme Courthouse, which looms in all its granite glory over this convergence of streets and traffic islands and crosswalks with "The true administration of justice is the firmest pillar of good government" inscribed above its Corinthian columns. There is some justice in this space: the spring that fed the collect pond (where Hughson and Caesar were hanged in chains) today feeds a fountain, part of a sculpture called "Triumph of the Human Spirit," dedicated "to all the unknown and unnamed enslaved Africans brought to this country including the 427 Africans excavated near this site." It is there because in October 1991 construction workers discovered human remains at a building site near Duane and Elk Street, just a stone's throw away. Archaeologists rushed in and soon discovered that this was the site of New York's old African Burial ground, where as many as 20,000 black people had been buried during the seventeenth and eighteenth centuries. Back then the 6.6-acre site was just outside of city limits, a place deemed appropriate for the burial of black people in a majority white city. Archaeologists quickly learned a lot about the people buried there—that some died of disease, many labored strenuously, and many early African Americans were able to retain elements of their cultures. Human remains were found with heads to the west so they would face homeward, buried with objects and with coins covering eyes.

The discovery of this burial ground sparked a tremendous controversy, as many in the African American community saw the potential desecration of the remains as one more example of white racism and just another attempt to ignore a complicated history. It was a tumultuous time for race relations in the city. In the 1980s three black men were killed by mobs—Willie Turks (1982), Michael Griffith (1986), and Yusef Hawkins (1989). And in August 1991, the death of seven-year-old Gavin Cato, son of Guyanese immigrants, by a car in a motorcade for the leader of the Chabad Lubavitch Hasidic sect, sparked three days of unrest in Crown Heights, Brooklyn. The discovery of all those remains was just one more indignity. After much protest, architects for the construction site reworked plans to incorporate a memorial at the site. And in 2003 a group of African American New Yorkers held a traditional burial of some of the remains at the memorial.

The memorial of dark granite is dramatic. To enter, you pass an inscription that reads, "For all those who were lost. For all those who were stolen. For all those who were left behind. For all those who were not forgotten." You then walk down a circular path lined with numerous symbols representing the cultural and religious heritage of the people buried here. On the ground are listed the age and sex of some of those buried: Burial 22, child between 2½ and 4½ years; Burial 348, child between 1 and 2 years; Burial 105, man between 35 and 45 years; Burial 284, man between 21 and 28 years. In the center of the circle a fountain gurgles—the water that brought those men and women to this continent. The water slips into a narrow passage or chamber, which, when you walk through, makes a sound like that of water splashing against a boat, the ghostly sounds of a slave ship.

If those construction workers hadn't paused from their work, those bodies may have been forever lost beneath some glassy skyscraper. They may have been lost beneath the metropolis, rebuilding and rebuilding, growing into something new, leaving the past buried beneath steel and concrete—a bedrock of bones. In fact, in and around the African Burial Ground National Monument there could be some ten to twenty thousand remains. But building and destroying is the lifecycle of the city, so there they rest, I suppose. There is always a frontier, always a new world to explore in a metropolis. It is a space where people come and go and do. And those people coming and going and doing are bringing with them whatever they learned from wherever they came.

Ranger Cyrus Forman of the US National Parks Service, one of the many caretakers of the site, feels a deep responsibility to this history, stating, "My job is to educate or to mitigate the possibility of violence. But education is just one of the things we do. We are also a place for the living to pay respect to the dead. The fact that the burial ground was lost for one hundred ninety-seven years meant that people couldn't have a place to come and ask the oldest ancestors and to speak to them and worship them. The most amazing thing for me is when I'm at the memorial and I see a lawyer on his way to court or a messenger on her way through the day and they stop and nod in such a way that I can tell that it's a pause for their ancestors, for the past."

When Forman speaks about the people buried here he calls them the city's "African founding fathers and mothers." And when he talks about colonial America he notes that these were the people whose skills helped farm the fields, shoe the horses, and build the boats that connected New York to the Atlantic world. These people literally built the city, filling swamplands, shaping its topography. Many retained African cultural practices, as evidenced in the burial ground itself, a sacred and communal space for New York's early Africans. And these people came from as near as Morocco and as far as Kenya—early New York was a melting pot of African cultures. To center this experience, to center this way of viewing history may not be a new idea for some scholars, but for a lot of visitors who take tours with him, it is. Sometimes, Forman says, people cry when he's giving a tour. Some cry out of sadness; children, especially, he's noticed, will cry because of a deeply felt empathy. But others cry out of anger that they are just now learning *and feeling* the story of the first black New Yorkers, some of the earliest African Americans.

There's another memorial in Lower Manhattan that has caused a lot of controversy, tears, reflection, and debate. On September 11, 2010, when right-wing Dutch politician Geert Wilders spoke at a protest to prevent the construction of an Islamic cultural center at Park 51, close to Ground Zero, he said that "no place in the world is as vibrant as New York City."[90] If you live in New York City, he claimed, you can be whatever you want to be. He told the worshipful crowd that his opposition to the construction of the cultural center was rooted in tolerance and "a tolerant society is not a suicidal society. A tolerant society like your New York should defend itself. We should never give a free hand to those who want to subjugate us." For the sake of those who died on 9/11, he said, we should not allow the mosque here. "In the name of freedom," he shouted, "no mosque here!" With his aggressively dyed blond hair and his dogged attacks on Islam, Wilders is an unlikely spokesperson for tolerance. About a year later, at the end of December 2011, a noose was found a block away by a construction foreman at Ground Zero.[91] The noose was hanging on the 64th floor of 1 World Trade Center, the Freedom Tower.

CHAPTER 5

Hanging Hannah Occuish in Post-Revolution America

PERHAPS THE YOUNGEST VICTIM of the noose in the recorded history of the United States was twelve-year-old Hannah Occuish, who was executed on December 20, 1786. Hannah's story begins, in a way, in 1633, when about 80 percent of the Pequot Indians died from disease; at that point the population was reduced to about 3,000. Four short years later disagreements with English colonists threatened to completely destroy the community when a Pequot attack on an English town prompted a violent reply. Before dawn on May 26, 1637, an alliance of English soldiers and Narragansett and Mohegan Indians attacked a Pequot fort along the Mystic River, setting fire to the fort and killing those who fled. Ultimately only 7 were left in the fort, and between 307 women, children, and old men were dead. Captain John Underhill wrote, "Great and doleful was the bloody sight to the view of young soldiers that never had been in war, to see so many souls lie gasping on the ground, so thick, in some places, that you could hardly pass along."[1] The Pequot community lost half of its already diminished population. The rest escaped and blended in with other tribes, but some were sold into servitude in Bermuda, and many were parceled out to tribes allied with the English, such as the Mohegan and Narragansett. Puritans saw it as divine retribution, but contemporaries have likened the massacre and aftermath to genocide.[2]

Hannah's story is the residue this genocide, if we can call it that. In many ways this loss shaped her social identity; her body was an archive of tragic community trauma, a history that she may have known little about but nonetheless affected her greatly. One sociologist, Ron Eyerman, defines cultural trauma as "a dramatic loss of identity and meaning, a tear in the social fabric affecting a group of people that has achieved some degree of cohesion."[3] It's not necessary for everyone in the group to have experienced the trauma for it to affect the group, especially if the event is often rehashed and retold; it then becomes an integral part of a collective memory. By the time Hannah was born in Groton, Connecticut, to a Pequot mother and black father, this collective trauma would have been sewn deep into the fabric of what was left of the Pequots.[4]

We know little of Hannah's early life save that she was raised by her mother, Sarah, who was an alcoholic.[5] Hannah's entry into the public record, though, was rather auspicious. When she was about six years old, along with her brother Charles, she was accused of assaulting a young girl in order to steal "her clothes and a gold necklace which she had on."[6] The girl, covered in blood, escaped to tell her parents. Town leaders investigated the incident and thought it best that they "bind them both out."[7] In other words, Hannah and her brother may have been forced into indentured servitude. This was a common punishment for misbehaving children in eighteenth-century New England, especially for Native American children.[8] Officials could indenture a child (a girl until age eighteen or a boy until twenty-one) if they thought their parents could not care for them—sometimes a rather arbitrary determination. Hannah's mother didn't like the idea at all and took her daughter to the home of a widow named Mrs. Rogers, who lived just outside of New London.[9] She told the woman and Hannah that she'd return in a few days, apparently after she had figured out her next move. If she went back to Groton, what would happen to Hannah? Where could she take her daughter and son? But months passed before Hannah's mother returned, and when she did, she didn't have a plan except to beg the woman to keep Hannah. The woman agreed, and there's no indication that Hannah ever saw her mother again.

Abandoned by her mother and already stigmatized by a liminal racial identity, Hannah's life would have been tenuous at best. She struggled to form positive relationships—Mrs. Rogers was abusive, and other children were afraid of her, not surprising given the reason she had to leave Groton in the first place.[10] Hannah gained a reputation in the community for lying and thieving.

All of these events and forces led to the crime for which she was condemned to death. On the morning of July 21, 1786, the body of six-year-old Eunice Bolles was found "in the public road leading from New-London to Norwich, lying on its face near to a wall."[11] It appeared that the murderer had tried unsuccessfully to cover her/his tracks, covering the head and arms with some stones. "Upon examining the body the skull appeared to be fractured; the arms and face much bruised, and the prints of finger-nails were very deep on the throat."[12] The *Connecticut Courant* reported that "the head and body were mangled in a shocking manner." Authorities searched for the perpetrator. When they questioned Hannah, she claimed that she'd seen four boys in a garden close to where the body was found, and shortly thereafter she heard the garden wall fall down. That must have killed Eunice, she told them. But the boys were never found, and fingers began pointing in Hannah's direction.

The next day she was questioned again. Despite her youth, none of the adults in Hannah's life were notified of the charges against her, and given her tenuous place in the social hierarchy, one wonders whether it would have mattered or if they would have cared. In the fashion of such investigations at the time, she was taken to where Eunice was killed and told what had happened there. Hannah "burst into tears and confessed that she killed her; saying that if she could be forgiven she would never do it again."[13]

Hannah apparently revealed even more details, claiming that she saw Eunice as she was walking to school and called after her, promising Eunice a piece of calico. Then Hannah "struck her on the head with a stone which she had taken for the purpose, and repeating the blows the child cried out, 'Oh, if you keep beating me so I shall die.'"[14] Soon the child stopped moving for a moment and then stirred. Hannah then choked the girl to death. Her motive, she said, was that the little girl had gotten her in trouble five weeks beforehand. Apparently Hannah had taken some of her fruit when they had picked strawberries together.

Hannah's trial took place in early October in the New London County Superior Court with Judge Richard Law presiding. Judge Law appointed an attorney named Timothy Larrabee to counsel Hannah. She pled not guilty. The magistrate asserted that it was a premeditated crime based on the strawberry dispute.[15] The court claimed that Hannah must have known that killing Eunice was wrong because she tried to make the murder appear to be an accident and then claimed she had committed her crime with "malice aforethought."[16] She was depicted as a depraved human, "marked with almost everything bad," despite the fact that the legal age of discretion at the time was fourteen.[17] When testimony was over, the judge summarized the evidence to the jury, and although he noted that she had been raised poorly, he also acknowledged evidence of premeditation and asserted that to not hang her would be to say that children can murder with impunity.[18] On October 7 the jury returned a guilty verdict.[19]

And then, when the judge read her sentence, he explained, "Nothing remains but to pass the painful sentence of this court—which is, that you should be returned hence to the gaol from whence you came, and from thence be carried to the place of execution—and there be hanged with a rope by the neck, between heaven and earth, until you are dead, dead, dead and may the Lord, of his infinite goodness and sovereign grace, have mercy on your soul."[20] Some in attendance cried upon hearing the sentence, but Hannah, to the shock of all, seemed hardly aware of the significance of the judge's words.[21] Timothy Larrabee petitioned the Connecticut General Assembly for a reprieve on Hannah's behalf; he cited her youth, that she hadn't had a Christian upbringing, that she didn't know her left from her right.[22] Larrabee claimed she hadn't intended to kill Eunice, just to beat her, but when Eunice cried out, Hannah struck her hard to keep her quiet. Lastly, Hannah's pathetic attempt to conceal the body demonstrated that she didn't know right from wrong. But to no avail: his petition was rejected on October 26.

Hannah's apparent ignorance continued during her final days in jail, a sign, perhaps of her stress, her youth, or her ignorance. And then, according to the *Connecticut Courant*, "about a fortnight before her execution, when she seemed to be more anxious, and on being asked by those who went to see her, how long she had to live? She would tell the number of days with manifest agitation. On the day before her execution, she appeared in great distress, saying that she was distressed for her soul; and continued in tears for most of the day, and until her execution."[23]

"FASHIONED OF THE SAME SPIRITS"

It is upsetting to think that a twelve-year-old girl was condemned to death during a period that is often referred to as the Age of Enlightenment. Writers during this period sparked political rhetoric that fostered the American Revolution; they also sparked a conversation about crime and punishment. By the late eighteenth century in the United States and in Europe there was a growing movement to ban public executions. This movement was led by middle- and upper-class people who argued that public punishments were brutal and that they brutalized the viewer, fostering more violence rather than deterring it. This line of reasoning ran parallel to arguments against the use of torture to extract confessions and to punish; instead, enlightened thinkers favored the use of prisons as a way to reform criminals. Steven Pinker writes that in recent decades some writers and scholars have mentioned the Age of Enlightenment with a "sneer," scoff at its naiveté ("We are all rational beings capable of solving any problem!"), and blame the Enlightenment for twentieth-century atrocities.[24] And yet, he notes, we do a disservice to this period of vibrant intellectual growth if we write it off completely. Consider what came before—consider the Salem witch hunt, consider those slaves burned alive and broken on the wheel in New York—all punishments made at the behest of civil governments. Because of the Enlightenment, slowly but surely those governments that practiced such punishments were often publicly condemned.

Out of the Enlightenment milieu were born ideas that many hold dear today; indeed, intellectuals and citizens at the end of the eighteenth century articulated ideas about "human rights" and penned groundbreaking documents like the Declaration of Independence and the Declaration of the Rights of Man and of the Citizen. Also in this period the first organizations combating the Atlantic Slave Trade were formed, the earliest human rights advocacy organizations whose descendants are Human Rights Watch and Amnesty International.

Why and how did these transformations of conceptions of human dignity occur? One argument is that people were becoming more literate. In England, for example, literacy rates were on the rise throughout the eighteenth century and into the nineteenth. Historian Lynn Hunt suggests that this increased literacy spurred a change in sensibilities—that people began to care for individual human beings in ways they had not before. As human beings began recognizing themselves in other human beings, she argues, sentiment and care grew, and this, she claims, fostered the development of Western conceptions of human rights: "reading accounts of torture or epistolary novels had physical effects that translated into brain changes and came back out as new concepts about the organization of social and political life."[25]

These changes would lead to active questioning of time-honored practices: how to educate young people, how to organize governments, and how to punish criminals. In fact, many began to question the punitive nature of justice, acknowledging that public punishments like whippings, the stocks, and even executions granted no possibility for the social transformation of convicts, no opening for them to become productive members of society. Humans who believed in the rights of man confronted the structures that had cemented public executions and public torture.

The Enlightenment also spawned attention to the technologies of executions throughout Europe and America. The guillotine was introduced in France in 1792 and promoted as a humane tool of execution because it resulted in an instantaneous death. The problem of dispatching human beings humanely was more complicated when the ready tools were gallows and noose, but prison officials seem to have worked to improve their methods. In England and in America rudimentary drops were being used. Many early drops were short, collapsible platforms situated on top of an already constructed scaffold.[26] The condemned stood on a piece of wood or drop supported by a beam or two. When the beams were pulled out of the way, either by pushing them by hand or pulling them out with a rope, the drop would fall. Since the sixteenth century most of London's condemned were executed publicly at Tyburn on what was affectionately known as Tyburn's Triple Tree, a simple triangular gallows that utilized the cart method for "turning people off," sometimes several at once. In 1760 a trapdoor drop was used at Tyburn for the execution of Earl Ferrers. The trapdoor didn't work well, and Ferrers didn't drop far enough and, thus, was subjected to a prolonged strangling death.[27] *That* trapdoor was never used again. In 1783 a sophisticated new gallows with drop was unveiled at London's Newgate prison, and an image of it appeared in *Gentleman's Magazine* along with an explanation.[28] This gallows, readers were told, was meant to "strike serious awe into the hearts of the most obdurate and heartless." Beyond that, the gallows drop was a technological advance—the swiftness of the drop "being much more sudden and regular than that of the cart being drawn away, has the effect of immediate death." The same technology was finding its way to the United States, though most executions were still of the cart and simple gallows variety.

But one of the most significant contributors to the process of transforming seemingly fixed public punishments was an Italian named Cesare Beccaria. Before the turn of the century his short work *Of Crimes and Punishments* was published in at least twenty-eight editions in Italian and nine in French, despite having been banned by the Pope.[29] An English edition appeared in 1767, and soon afterward it was published in Charleston and Philadelphia. Beccaria's thoughts on punishment offered a radical shift from what came before and helped shape the way some Americans understood the role of punishment in the late eighteenth century. Beccaria attacked torture as a mechanism for extracting confessions, noting that torture was essentially judging and punishing the accused before trial—punishment proportional to the crime should only come after there was conclusive proof that the accused was guilty.[30]

He was also critical of the death penalty and believed it should be reserved only for someone who threatens the "security of a nation" and whose continued existence could foster open rebellion; it should also be permitted when there has been a total breakdown of law and social norms.[31] Under a stable government, Beccaria argued, the death penalty was ineffective, serving as a spectacle to some but teaching nothing. He observed that a criminal will weigh the risks involved and choose to commit a crime if she knows that the outcome could be a moment of pain and then death. Conversely, if the criminal knows she could be committed to prison and hard labor for the remainder of her life, another decision might result. More importantly Beccaria argued that it was absurd that a state would kill someone for killing, that it was a savage example at the very best.[32] That the public despises the hangman should indicate something—that we know it is wrong. To those who argue that the death penalty has always existed, Beccaria notes that history is a "vast sea of errors."[33]

Beccaria's treatise, which urges humans to evolve beyond death as punishment, led to reforms throughout Europe. Leopold, Grand Duke of Tuscany, abolished capital punishment entirely in 1789 largely due to Beccaria's influence. His essay traversed the Atlantic and had a profound effect on punishments in the new nation. But Historian Louis P. Masur notes that it wasn't just Beccaria who sparked the debate after the Revolution but rather that it was emerging on its own. He writes, "The experience of the Revolution and the problem of how to make punishments consistent with the objects of republican, Christian institutions sparked the initial opposition to the death penalty in the early Republic."[34] The noose looms over the early days of the nation as it did over the signers of the Declaration of Independence, who were, in a sense, signing their own death warrants—for if the Revolutionaries had lost, they may have faced the gallows. Executions were common on both sides of the Revolutionary War. There is, of course, Nathan Hale (hanged by the British on September 22, 1776), but General Washington signed off on the deaths of both British and continental soldiers, retribution for one and discipline for the other.[35] Later, the postwar crime wave (often involving former soldiers) gave many leaders pause as they struggled with a burdened legal system and an attempt to legitimize capital punishment in the new republic.[36] Ironically, over the period of March 2 to May 11, 1786 (just months before the Bolles murder and the Occuish trial) the *New Haven Gazette* serially published a translation of Beccarria's treatise on the dubious benefits of capital punishment.[37]

EXECUTION DAY

On December 20, 1786, the day of her execution, Hannah Occuish, like many condemned men and women before her, was the center of the public performance of an execution sermon. The sermon was delivered by a young Yale tutor with a Unitarian background named Henry Channing, who was also a candidate for a job at New London's First Congregational Church. This would have been a significant moment in his early career. And that makes the sermon all the more interesting: Channing's sermon seems crafted not only for Hannah but also for her audience. As I've said, most execution sermons were meant to instruct listeners to stay on the right path (and Channing does this), but he also admonishes the congregation, claiming it is their duty to take care that others do as well, to support them. Hannah, he says, was a clear failure in this duty. This is striking. So too is the fact that he chose Jeremiah 6:8 as the passage on which he would be preaching—Jeremiah, that gnarly prophet of the sixth century BCE who annoyed all of Jerusalem with his insistence that they repent from their wicked ways (I once heard a preacher liken him to a fly buzzing in your ear). In chapter 6 Jeremiah shouts that if his listeners didn't repent, they would be destroyed by Babylonian invaders—which did happen in his lifetime. Verse 8 reads, "Be thou instructed, O Jerusalem, lest my soul depart from thee; lest I make thee desolate, a land not inhabited." Three verses later Jeremiah continues, "I am full of the fury of the LORD; I am weary with holding in: I will pour it out upon the children abroad, and upon the assembly of young men together: for even the husband with the wife shall be taken, the aged with *him that is* full of days."

Hannah, Channing claimed, is a member of "our guilty race" and committed a crime that "freezes the mind with horror."[38] The root cause, he suggested, was her "uninstructed mind."[39] She was a girl who "repeatedly declared to me, that she did not know that there was a God, before she was told it after her imprisonment."[40] This was shameful, he claimed, and thus he attempted to educate the audience so there would be no more Hannahs. God was using this event, he asserted, to instruct the community—to hold family devotions, to teach their servants to read, to bring them to church, to encourage good behavior and discipline bad, and to be a good example.[41] Channing stressed the significance of what is learned early in life, that it has the potential to shape the future and that it is the duty of parents and masters to direct a young person's education.[42] He suggested that a community is responsible for everyone in their midst and that, as a community, they had neglected Hannah. Invoking Jeremiah's admonition to the people of Israel, he said that a "Nation, a family, or an individual" who doesn't pay attention to the obvious instruction this horrible circumstance presents, "their national blessings will be bitterness in the latter end."[43] Adults are responsible to their families and their children but also to all children in their community.[44]

Channing, of course, admonished Hannah as well, telling her directly, "the time for you to die is come . . . in about two hours, your eyes will be shut by death . . . you will soon see that there is a GOD who loveth goodness and good people; *but is angry with the wicked every day,* and will punish forever those whose sins are not pardoned before they die."[45] And then, "You are now going to be hanged until you are dead." He called on her to repent and ask for forgiveness, saying that this was her last chance. "Remember, if he has mercy upon you, it will be from his own goodness; not from any good thing which he sees in you: —He sees nothing in you but wickedness."[46] Despite his critique, the Congregationalists hired him.

Historian Katherine Grandjean suggests that Channing's sermon was a challenge to racial categories and assumptions. He presents Hannah as capable of redemption, one of the rhetorical methods that many religious people in New England sought in order to shape public thought about racial categories.[47] Grandjean points to a moment in his sermon when Channing proclaims, "Think not that crimes are peculiar to the *complexion* of the prisoner, and that ours is pure from these stains. Surely an idea so illiberal . . . cannot find a place in the breast of a generous youth.—Know, my brothers, that *that* casket, not withstanding its color, contains an immortal soul, a Jewel of inestimable value."[48] Here, Grandjean writes, Channing seems to challenge "the notion that skin color determined mental ability or interior worth."[49]

God's vengeance and grace, it seems, are equal opportunity. Over a decade before Occuish was executed, a teenaged enslaved African in Boston named Phillis Wheatley wrote a now-famous poem entitled "On Being Brought from Africa to America" (1773):

> *'Twas mercy brought me from my Pagan land,*
> *Taught my benighted soul to understand*
> *That there's a God, that there's a Saviour too:*
> *Once I redemption neither sought nor knew.*
> *Some view our sable race with scornful eye,*
> *"Their colour is a diabolic die."*
> *Remember, Christians, Negros, black as Cain,*
> *May be refin'd and join th'angelic train.*

Wheatley's poem suggests to some critics a kind of apology for slavery. But this poem is also a searing attack on racist attitudes many whites held. She is not inherently evil because of her skin color; indeed, she is just like any other human being capable of religious awakening. Like Hannah, she is not condemned from birth.

This was, though, an increasingly unusual concept. The Enlightenment desire to "improve" everything from social ills to execution technologies also seemed to foster a desire to organize and categorize life—from plants to rocks, from animals to humans. This taxonomic impulse led to the development of racial categories that were becoming engrained in American popular culture by the end of the eighteenth century. In *Notes on the State of Virginia* (1785) Thomas Jefferson drew sharp distinctions between Native Americans, blacks, and whites. He presented America's original inhabitants as culture creators and excellent orators, but—in a dig at Wheatley—he claimed black people have no culture and said that "their existence appears to participate more of sensation than reflection."[50] Jefferson posited a kind of great chain being that is informed by race. As he saw it, black people are less rational, less intelligent than whites or even Native Americans; this lack of intelligence, he claimed, was the main reason that if slaves are ever emancipated, they must be separated from whites.[51] He wrote all of this in the context of describing the legal code of Virginia, which conferred the punishment of death by hanging for treason and murder (rape and sodomy being crimes that would lead to dismemberment).

These attitudes about race found their way into gallows literature, a genre growing ever the more popular. As the eighteenth century wore on, printers published fewer sermons like Channing's and more stories about condemned criminals.[52] Evidence of this trend can be found in an appendix to Channing's sermon—a lengthy biography of the life and crimes of Hannah Occuish. Salacious crime narratives had greater cultural cache than execution sermons in a diverse and democratic republic. Readers in late-eighteenth-century America wanted stories of thieves and rapscallions rather than pious penitents.[53] At the same time there was a greater focus on criminals who were outsiders, foreigners, and racial others.[54] In particular, there were more depictions of African American males as "brutes" and "rapists," a stereotype that comes into its own after the American Revolution.

Literary critic Jeannine Lombard points out that from the late eighteenth century to the heyday of the movement to abolish slavery, black people were most frequently read about as human chattel (in advertisements for slave sales or runaway notices) or as condemned criminals.[55] In other words, in popular depictions black people were either chained or noosed. There were notable exceptions, of course— writers like Phillis Wheatley or great orators like Prince Hall and Lemuel Haynes—but most published texts about people of color in this period were negative. And yet the over sixty portrayals of black men as condemned criminals (which comprised about one-third of the published gallows texts from 1674 to 1800) also allowed them an opportunity to craft a voice in the public sphere, even if they weren't the actual authors of the texts.[56] The problem was that this voice associated black people with crime and vice. For example, "The Last Words and Dying Speech of Edmund Fortis" (1795) was published a year after the execution of Fortis, a black man convicted of rape and murder. Like earlier execution sermons, these last words were published in an effort to educate. Fortis (the narrator) offers details of his life—his birth into slavery, his escape, and his life on the road. He was an itinerant thief, and his petty crimes led to bigger crimes and, ultimately, the crime for which he was to be hanged. In prison he had a miraculous conversion and greeted death as one who has been saved.

Over ten years later the dying words of John Joyce, convicted for murdering one Mrs. Cross, offers a similar message, though directed at a black audience. He claims that to "People of Colour . . . the murder of Mrs. Cross, speaks as with a voice of thunder."[57] And then he enumerates a list of stereotypes about "People of Colour": they are sinful, alcoholic, dishonest, lustful, and enjoy too many "mid-night dances and frolics." Joyce urges other "People of Colour" to change their ways before it is too late. Curiously, the impetus for publishing this text was to assuage the fears of white people in the community and to combat stereotypes.[58] The confession—if these were his actual words—was meant to support the idea that the cause of the crime was the moral limitation of an individual rather than the innate characteristic of a group.

But did readers receive that message? And did they comprehend Channing's chastising? Lynn Hunt's suggestion that a rise in literacy rates and the popularity of the novel in the late eighteenth and early nineteenth centuries also gave rise to Western conceptions of human rights is worth reconsidering here. Indeed, creative literature elicited sympathies and educated people about the intricate lives of others; such reading may have fostered common cause and concern. So what happened to people who read gallows literature in the late eighteenth century? Did the same sense of camaraderie or humanitarian impulse occur, or did these texts work against the appeal to human sentiment of creative literature? Perhaps readers sympathized with a criminal's fate, but the text may have also done the subconscious work of categorizing other human beings.

Grandjean notes that sermons like Channing's demonstrate that in early America "race was neither monolithic nor inevitable. It was not unquestioned. It was the product of a thousand choices, made silently by a quite ordinary public."[59] But choices were made, and therein lies the problem. What Henry Channing was saying, in a nutshell, was that Hannah Occuish never received the attention she deserved as a human being until she completely ruptured the social contract by killing another human being. He suggests another version of the role of communities in the early days of the United States of America, that the community is a body "knitted together," as John Winthrop, one of the first "New-Englanders," wrote years before. But law and social reality butted up against these particular Christian interventions. Hannah Occuish, though, was a poor outcast and likely mentally ill or developmentally delayed. Poverty and powerlessness exacerbated these circumstances. Thus, by virtue of her age, class, and race, she was an especially vulnerable human being in New England culture.

A few hours after listening to Channing's sermon young Hannah Occuish and members of the New London community processed from the church to the gallows, which had been built behind the town meetinghouse. They walked uphill and through a port town still recovering from the ravages of the Revolution. This, of course, was the town where Nathan Hale taught before giving one of his lives to America. And it was nearly destroyed, with help from none other than Benedict Arnold, during the 1781 Battle of Groton Heights. From the Meeting House Green, where the gallows was erected and where their walk ended, Hannah and the spectators would have been able to see down to Winthrop's Cove and the Thames River beyond. Hannah said very little at the gallows; one account claims she appeared afraid and seemed to want somebody to help her.[60] But just before the noose was placed around her neck, she thanked the sheriff for being kind to her while she was in prison. Shortly thereafter Hannah Occuish's brief life came to an end. As it was throughout her life, there was no one there to help her.

There may have been some dissent in Connecticut about the execution of a twelve-year-old girl and perhaps about whether capital punishment was a just punishment at all. The *Connecticut Courant* concluded their report with lines that seem to echo Channing's sermon: "The unhappy fate of this young girl is particularly to be lamented, as it is to be charged principally to a want of early instruction and government.—'Train up a child in the way he should go, and when he is old he will not depart from it.'"[61]

A year later Dr. Benjamin Rush, one of the signers of the Declaration of Independence, wrote a landmark statement on the practice of public punishments and executions in America, asserting that public punishments like hangings have a negative effect on society, that they promote rather than deter crime.[62] They make witnesses less sympathetic to human suffering and destroy the sympathetic feelings that could lead people to do good and to care for others.[63] Rush argued that we must "love the whole human race," despite the choices of the guilty, because those who are being executed are just as human as the witnesses: "They are bone of their bone, and were originally fashioned of the same spirits."[64] Rush favored private punishments: penitentiaries where criminals would receive physical punishments, hard labor, and the cleansing power of lonely and silent reflection.[65] He argued that the penitentiary could be life affirming, the opposite of capital punishment.[66] Rush predicted that public punishments like whipping, stocks, clipping ears, and, potentially, executions would one day be considered "as marks of the barbarity of ages and countries, and as melancholy proofs of the feeble operation of reason, and religion, upon the human mind."[67]

After the Revolution laws began changing, and the number of capital offenses dropped. In the 1780s and 1790s robbery, rape, and counterfeiting were less likely to be treated as capital crimes.[68] Rush's home state was ahead of the curve: in 1786 robbery, burglary, and sodomy were no longer capital crimes in Pennsylvania; those convicted of such crimes would get ten years hard labor. In 1794 Pennsylvania banned capital punishment for all crimes save first-degree murder. What's more, the solitude of the penitentiary—of the kind, more or less, that Rush imagined—began to replace some public punishments. By the end of the century many states had some form of penitentiary, and opposition to public hangings mounted.[69] What's more, overall rates of executions in the United States had dropped significantly— from about 1.5 per 100,000 people per year in 1700 to about 0.5 per 100,000 in 1800.[70]

So how was it that a twelve-year-old was executed in public in the early moments of the new republic amidst the rhetoric of the Enlightenment and changing opinions about the death penalty, especially in the Northeast? Nancy Steenburg, an historian of juveniles in Connecticut's eighteenth- and nineteenth-century judicial system, told me that "it's a disturbing case because in most others when the accused is that young they either found them *non compes mentis* or they didn't execute them." Steenburg added that it was typical for officials to take into consideration the age of a white child caught up in the judicial system but to severely punish African American, Native American, or Irish immigrant children.

"There was that so-called questionable period or gray area between seven and fourteen," she said. "Hannah was in that period. Look, around the same time of the Hannah case a nine-year-old boy committed what certainly looked like murder, but they didn't charge him with murder. He had been to church. Certainly knew the difference between right and wrong, and they didn't charge him with anything. And then there's Hannah."

"It's a strange moment for the new nation," I said. "Who gets to be in and who doesn't."

"She would never have been in. No one tried to teach Hannah— that's the thing, Jack. She was either mentally disabled by fetal alcohol syndrome or it was because she'd been treated slightly better than the cows and the pigs and the chickens."

One thing that troubled me was Hannah Occuish's apparent moment of recognition, her delayed realization that she was going to die and that death is a permanent state. It troubled me because the available record does little to explain her actions and do little for me as a writer two hundred years later. How could she do what she did? How did she get to the place where she would react so violently to a young girl who apparently took her strawberries? Beyond the social history of the Pequot community in Connecticut and the obvious difficulties faced by an abandoned mixed-race child in eighteenth-century America, what other factors may have shaped her life?

Steenburg mentioned fetal alcohol syndrome as one of many possibilities. If we can believe what the record tells us about Hannah's mother, then Hannah may have had a condition that would fall under the contemporary umbrella term of Fetal Alcohol Spectrum Disorder (FASD).[71] This term covers everything from the most severe cases to the least. FASD can lead to behavioral issues like aggressiveness and impulsivity and even a lower developmental age. Magnetic resonance imaging (MRI) research from 2011 indicates that the brain structure of children of mothers who abuse alcohol actually look different; their shape and thickness are unlike "normal" brains.[72] The effects of these changes to the brain can be found in children with visible (facial) abnormalities and those with only cognitive/behavioral symptoms. Each year about eighty thousand women in United States drink regularly throughout their pregnancies; many of these woman engage in other risky behaviors and often get little prenatal care.[73] The result is that after birth there are increased risks for both mother (postpartum depression) and child (developmental delays, behavior issues, and, just as in Hannah's case, foster care placement).[74] Notably, research has also shown that individuals with FASD are disproportionately represented in correctional systems.[75] The study focused on data from Canada and found that the number of undiagnosed cases is quite high and that "youths with FASD were nineteen times more likely to be in prison than youths without FASD on any given day in 2008/2009." Hannah's struggles are still with us, we who are "fashioned of the same spirits."

This point was driven home when, as I was writing about Hannah, something interesting happened: because Connecticut repealed the death penalty in April 2012 as a punishment in future trials, a group of death row inmates are now trying to have their sentences overturned, arguing that death sentences are arbitrary and that there is significant evidence that they are racially biased. A key witness for these defendants, a Stanford University professor named Jon Donahue, noted that minority defendants who kill white people are three times as likely to get the death penalty as are whites who do the same.[76] Hannah Occuish—or maybe it's Henry Channing—is telling me to pay attention across time and space.

CHAPTER 6

Meteors of War: Death by Hanging and the End of Slavery

BY THE MIDDLE OF THE NINETEENTH CENTURY, judicial executions in the Northeast had become mostly routinized and private. Indeed, as of 1835 New Jersey, New York, Massachusetts, Pennsylvania, and Rhode Island executions were being held inside jails with a select few witnesses. As rates of execution declined overall, there was also a seemingly progressive movement to move executions behind closed doors. Louis P. Masur writes that "by instituting private executions, legislators eliminated an occasion for public gathering, imposed control over public space, and precluded the open expression of certain passions and emotions. They also fashioned a new illusion of an ordered, consensual society that replaced an earlier depiction of hanging day as a ritual that affirmed communally shared civil and religious values."[1]

But public hangings were not a thing of the past in other states, especially in the South. Though uncommon affairs in the nineteenth century, when public executions did happen they were well publicized and well attended. A Pendleton, South Carolina, newspaper noted that at three hangings that took place in the mid-1820s crowds were larger than for any other public event they had ever witnessed.[2] People traveled from afar, sometimes on special trains, to the site of execution, where they could buy food and drink as well as literature about the condemned. Young and old, rich and poor, slave and free rubbed elbows and shared this public space.[3] And when it was all over, some even took home relics. As they had in medieval and premodern Europe, some people still believed a piece of hanging rope contained magical properties, that it could cure a toothache or calm a horse or nagging wife.[4]

In the South public executions were still considered an important way to maintain discipline among slaves. It was common for masters to encourage—or force—slaves to attend hangings of other slaves.[5] One spring a South Carolina slave named Charles Ball was encouraged by his master to attend the double hanging of a black slave named Frank and a mulatto woman named Lucy who had killed a white man.[6] The gallows was a large tree in the middle of a field, providing multiple vantage points. Before the execution a white man preached a sermon, and then a black man delivered what was called an "exhortation."[7] Then a cart moved forward, leaving the two people to commence their slow deaths. After about half an hour they were cut down and buried on the spot. Ball explained that the hanging he witnessed took place on a Thursday but that attendees stayed on afterward for a weekend of "music, dancing, trading in horses, gambling, drinking, fighting."[8]

As seen in Chapter 4, when threats were made to a slavery-supported economy, public hangings ensued—the years just before the American Civil War were littered with nooses. In the early nineteenth century, slave revolt was on the minds of many white Americans because time and again slaves would use violence as a means to end slavery.[9] In 1800 Virginia slave Gabriel Prosser had organized what would have been a widespread rebellion. He collected swords and planned to set Richmond on fire, raid the state armory, take the governor hostage, kill white citizens, and demand an end to slavery.[10] But someone revealed the conspiracy to officials and Virginia Governor Monroe, who called in troops while whites organized special courts to investigate the conspiracy. Gabriel was captured and hanged alone on October 10 at the Richmond gallows; other conspirators were hanged via the cart and tree gallows method.[11] In all, twenty-seven slaves were hanged for their roles in the Prosser conspiracy.[12] Two years later another conspiracy scare (again involving slaves in Virginia as well as North Carolina) would lead to the hanging deaths of at least another twenty-five slaves.[13]

Divinely inspired slave Nat Turner led a rebellion in Southampton County, Virginia, in 1831, leading to the deaths of approximately 60 whites. In the aftermath state and federal troops killed at least 120 black people, both slave and free.[14] In some instances the heads of suspected rebels were cut off and displayed on pikes.[15] And then what can only be described as a general hysteria of lynching erupted as whites sought retribution on any person of color they encountered. In her *Incidents in the Life of a Slave Girl* (1861), Harriet Jacobs wrote that "drunken mobs of white men roamed the countryside," and slave dwellings, including Jacobs's own, were raided and plundered, and men and women were whipped in the streets "till the blood stood in puddles at their feet."[16] Nat Turner was hanged from a tree in Jerusalem (now Cortland), Virginia, and his body then turned over for dissection, but he was readily fetishized. Historian John W. Cromwell asserts that "he was skinned to supply such souvenirs as purses, his flesh made into grease, and his bones divided as trophies to be handed down as heirlooms."[17] Ultimately eighteen slaves and one free black were hanged.

In June of 1822 Ball's fellow South Carolinian, a free black named Denmark Vesey who bought his freedom after winning a local lottery, was implicated as the ringleader of a rebellion conspiracy in Charleston, South Carolina. The rebellion was supposedly planned for Bastille Day, when slaves and free blacks would take over the city arsenals, gather slaves from nearby low-country plantations, and slay the white people, thereby taking control of Charleston. A slave named John confessed that every black man had a role to play and was to meet in certain places but that there was no predetermined signal for revolt, only that they were supposed to meet up at midnight.[18] Vesey and others planned to eventually lead slaves to Haiti, where they would presumably be free. John also claimed they had communication with slaves all the way up to Columbia and that there were also poor whites who would join the revolt.[19] Ultimately they were sold out by two slaves, Peter Desverneys and George Wilson, who were offered freedom and money.[20]

Charleston, a city built by and on the backs of enslaved Africans, was a fitting place for such a conspiracy to foment. Slaves in nineteenth-century Charleston had a certain degree of social mobility not unlike slaves in eighteenth-century New York City. Urban servitude provided more opportunities for geographic movement than their rural counterparts had; many Charleston slaves were "hired out" by their masters and spent time working away from the owner's supervision.[21] For example, ringleader Denmark Vesey had once belonged to a Captain Joseph Vesey, who bought young Denmark (whom he first named Telemaque) while trading slaves in the West Indies. Denmark Vesey had years of maritime experience while enslaved, was a skilled worker, and was literate. Others involved in the conspiracy shared similar experiences and skills, and several were members of Charleston's African Church. This urban mobility had serious cultural ramifications as well. Peter Linebaugh and Marcus Rediker note that it spawned a multicultural community and a multicultural plot, a kind of Pan-Africanness or racial identity in Charleston, similar to that observed in early New York City.[22]

But Charleston's slaves did not have free rein. There was always the possibility of the rude discipline of the city's workhouse, or "House of Correction." Masters sent their unruly slaves there, carrying notes telling the men in charge of "correction" how many lashes they were to receive.[23] Masters paid 25 cents for the services the workhouse provided. In fact, slaves and free blacks in nineteenth-century Charleston had much to complain about and much to rebel against. And yet, as with the New York Conspiracy of 1741, some historians believe there was no plot during the summer of 1822 and that it was a product of white fear and paranoia, a result of the racism of the empowered populace.[24] Whether it was real or imagined, the results were similar to what happened in New York—Charleston officials held two courts, arresting over 131 slaves and free blacks, releasing 30, transporting 37 outside the United States, and acquitting 23.[25] Two people died while in custody, and the courts carried out sentences of death on 35—more blacks were executed in Charleston that summer than "in any other Southern slave conspiracy."

Vesey and five others (Rolla Bennett, Batteau Bennett, Ned Bennett, Peter Poyas, and Jake Blackwood) were hanged on July 2 at a place called Blake's Lands just beyond the city limits. The condemned traveled in a cart up King Street to this remote spot along the Cooper River, chosen, perhaps, so there wouldn't be many witnesses. But many people, black and white, did attend the execution.[26] The apparent co-conspirators were likely all hanged from trees at Blake's Lands, and their bodies were given over to the surgeons.[27] An oral history claimed Vesey wasn't hanged along with others at Blake's Lands but rather alone from an oak tree on Ashley Avenue and that he was hastily buried in the nearby potter's field.[28] David Robertson says that those in charge weren't above intentionally "misidentifying Vesey's execution site" so he wouldn't be made a martyr or his burial site become a site of mourning or pilgrimage.[29]

On July 12 two more conspirators were hanged at the Lines, the northern city limits, a place of crumbling War of 1812–era fortifications that had been built across the Charleston Peninsula from the Ashley to the Cooper River. This was the same site chosen for the most spectacular hanging to result from the Vesey conspiracy trials, the public hanging of twenty-two condemned men on July 26. An enormous crowd gathered to watch this mass hanging (the hordes of people spooked a horse before the execution began, trampling a young boy).[30] One witness, John Adger, wrote that one could say "the whole city turned out on this occasion."[31] Adger believed that the extraordinary event of so many people set to be executed at once was "a sight calculated to strike terror into the heart of every slave."[32] And it *was* a terrifying sight, but not in the ways city officials had imagined it would be. The condemned men were to stand on one of three long benches placed against the walls of the Lines, where nooses had been thrown over from the other side; it was a most basic gallows.[33] But the drops were short, perhaps only inches, and the men gasped for air and kicked their feet—a ghastly scene. Captain William P. Dove of the city guard was forced to shoot each one.

What was meant to be a quick demonstration of the government's ultimate authority was instead a poorly managed affair that didn't take into consideration the gruesome spectacle of the simultaneous strangulations of twenty-two human beings. There was opportunity to correct these mistakes, though, when, four days later, four more were hanged and then, on August 9, the last, William Garner, was executed. Some city officials patted themselves on the back for a job well done. One claimed, "It is consoling to every individual . . . to be able to say that, within the limits of the city of Charleston, in a period of great and unprecedented excitement, the laws, without even one violation, have ruled with uninterrupted sway; that no cruel, vindictive, or barbarous modes of punishment have been resorted to; that justice has blended with an enlightened humanity."[34]

But not every white citizen of Charleston concurred. A series of letters from Charlestonian Mary Lamboll Beach to her sister Elizabeth Gilchrist in Philadelphia offer a unique and private perspective on the events of the summer of 1822. Beach strikes a level-headed tone and notes that there were many rumors about the conspiracy, including one that "the black women were to be put to death that the men might have white wives, some say all the young ones to be spared and the old women and children put to death."[35] After the large execution Beach appeared upset and confused by the state of affairs in Charleston. She claimed that at first she felt like the executions were necessary but then wondered whether freeing her own slaves would ensure "safety to us and themselves . . . but this can never be done in my day."[36] She continued, "I understand they behaved with great firmness—they all died on one or rather a continuation of three gallows in one—A deathlike silence reigned over the city at the time. Oh! That God in his mercy may have enabled them as the thief on the cross by faith to look to that blood which alone can save us." Her tone insinuates a sense of forgiveness and quite possibly an understanding of why these men may have wished to rebel. In an earlier letter Beach lamented, "Ah! Slavery is a hard business, and I am afraid we shall in this country have it to our bitter cost some day or other."[37]

What does the noose represent to those witnessing the executions of Denmark Vesey or to Gabriel or to Nat? It seemed to be reinforcing ultimate control over black human beings but also over an egalitarian vision of human rights that threatened the slave regime. In each situation it was a fearful response to the possibility of black people asserting their humanity and their rights as human beings. Historian Bertram Wyatt-Brown likens these responses to a religious ritual, with dubious court trials and convicted men and women serving as "sacrifices to a sacred concept of white supremacy,"[38] as if the fickle gods might imprison white people if not for these offerings. He claims these scares—real or otherwise—are also akin to the heresy trials of the Reformation era and antipeasant backlashes in medieval England.[39] Wyatt-Brown notes that "perceptions of social imbalance led to frantic demands for group conformity to the traditional moral values." For those in power, these scares helped them reassert their authority or "heroism," and in some cases they were able to capitalize on scares by gaining valuable resources—like more guns (or the establishment of a military college), for example.[40] In a sense, he says, whether the insurrections were real or imaginary doesn't matter; what matters is that white people responded to the possibility of black people overturning slavery with fear and with the noose.

HANGING JOHN BROWN

Where does John Brown fit onto this continuum? His December 2, 1859, execution turned a once-maligned abolitionist into a martyr for a cause and heightened tensions between the North and the South that never waned—not until over 750,000 soldiers had died. Depending on your perspective, John Brown's plan was bold, courageous, treasonous, foolhardy, or insane: launch a nighttime raid on a federal munitions depot in Harpers Ferry, Virginia, head for the hills with a mobile maroon army, and launch raids into the South, using the rough terrain of the Appalachian Mountains to escape all pursuers.

Around midnight on October 16, 1859, Brown and his army of twenty-one men began a raid on that tiny mountain town, nestled on a slim peninsula skirted by the Shenandoah and Potomac Rivers. Save for walls surrounding the armory and arsenal, the place was virtually unguarded. They rolled out, well-armed, from their gathering place, a small farmhouse in Maryland, and made their way across the Potomac and into the town. Brown and company quickly took over the two bridges leading into the town and seized the US armory, arsenal, and rifle works. He sent a small party out to neighboring plantations in an attempt to free and arm slaves and began to gather a hodgepodge of hostages. The word got out that something was going down in Harpers Ferry, and ragtag militias and armed men came to town, taking pot-shots at the abolitionists. Then things began to fall apart. Eventually Brown, along with a few of his men and several key hostages, moved into a small engine house within the armory grounds. The building had high windows and was fairly secure. But about thirty-six hours after the raid began, federal soldiers under the command of Colonel Robert E. Lee and Lieutenant J. E. B. Stuart surrounded Brown and his men.

And this is the thing that has always made historians wonder: Why did Brown take so long in Harpers Ferry? Why did he wait? And what was he waiting for? Many explanations have been given through the years—that he panicked, that he thought the slaves were going to join in, that he reached a point of debilitating indecision. Or perhaps he realized the only thing he could do at that point was to die well and to do so publicly—to use his day in court to give the United States of America a tongue lashing and then to die a martyr. Did he realize, laying there with bullets whizzing by, that he had an opportunity to use the noose to show the nation that the South would stop at nothing to maintain slavery? Did he realize that the noose was a tool at his disposal, a tool that might start a war that would end slavery?

Maybe—maybe—he was thinking this when about a dozen US marines under the command of Robert E. Lee captured him in that engine house. Or when he said to a group of men interviewing him a day after that capture: "You had better, all you people at the South, prepare yourselves for a settlement of that question. . . . You may dispose of me very easily. I am nearly disposed of now; but this question is still to be settled—this negro question, I mean; the end of that is not yet."[41] Maybe he was thinking this when he was charged with first-degree murder, conspiring to incite slave rebellion, and committing treason against the state of Virginia. Maybe he was thinking this when he pled innocent because he didn't believe he had done anything wrong or when he announced, in his final courtroom speech (really, his gallows speech), that "if it is deemed necessary that I should forfeit my life for the furtherance of the ends of justice, and mingle my blood further with the blood of my children and the blood of millions in this slave country whose rights are disregarded by wicked, cruel and unjust enactments,—I submit; so let it be done!"[42]

And maybe he was thinking this when Judge Richard Parker ordered that "he be hanged by the neck until he be dead."[43] Parker was specific in his directions too: he wanted Brown to hang not in the jailhouse yard but in public. He wanted folks to see him die. Perhaps Brown wanted that as well. He certainly seemed to say as much when he wrote his brother Jeremiah from jail in Charlestown a few weeks before his execution and claimed he was prepared to die and that he realized now that he was "worth inconceivably more to hang than for any other purpose."[44]

The last act in John Brown's Harpers Ferry drama was set to begin.[45] Three states jostled to have the honor of providing the rope that would form Brown's hangman's noose. Missouri, Kentucky, and South Carolina each sent a length of home-state cord.[46] With characteristic hyperbole, Brown biographer (and ardent abolitionist) James Redpath wrote that they longed "to strangle the fearless man who had dared to beard the lion which the nation dreaded in its oldest and strongest den." South Carolina's rope was made from cotton, of course.

Kentucky's offering was sent by Zeb Ward (a former prison director) direct to Virginia Governor Wise. Ward wrote, "I send you . . . this morning a rope made expressly for the use of John Brown & Co. Kentucky will stand pledged for its being an honest rope—I had it made in her behalf and send it to show we are willing and ready to aid our mother state in disposing of those who may attempt to destroy & overthrow her government. . . . The hemp of which it is made was grown in Missouri—a state that Brown had troubled much, and made at Frankfort, Kentucky. I had it made for the express purpose."[47] After testing, or so the story goes, the cordage from South Carolina and Missouri were deemed too weak, and Kentucky's entry won out. The victorious rope was displayed in the sheriff's office the week before the hanging.[48]

A local carpenter named David Cockerell constructed the gallows, finishing it by Wednesday. For the rest of the week it stood in the yard of the new Baptist church. One reporter noted that it was a typical gallows, nothing extraordinary, "uprights, crossbeam, and trap."[49] The trap door was hinged and held up by a taut rope that, when cut, released the drop and killed the condemned. Gawkers gazed upon the immense structure and tried to carry away relics, pieces of wood, splinters.

On the morning of the execution the scaffold and gallows were disassembled and transported to a nearby field on the edge of Charlestown. The contraption was rebuilt on a little rise in the middle of the field that offered a good view of the surrounding countryside. One journalist, David Hunter Strother (a.k.a. Porte Crayon), climbed up on the scaffold and claimed "the view was of surpassing beauty. On every side stretching away into the blue distance were broad and fertile fields dotted with corn shocks and white farm houses glimmering through the leafless trees—emblems of prosperity and peace."[50] Just about seven miles away was the gap in the mountains at Harpers Ferry, carved for centuries by the mighty Shenandoah and Potomac. From up on the scaffold that morning a good eye would have also spied soldiers on the surrounding hills. The area was on heightened alert and encircled by troops for about fifteen miles. Many feared an attack or an attempt to disrupt the state's bidding. Train travel was halted and outsiders sent packing.

It was an unseasonably warm morning, the sky bright and blue and the air crisp. A mountain haze filtered the sunlight but disappeared as the day wore on.[51] Everywhere, it seemed, perceptions were sharpening, things were becoming clear. In the morning edition of the *Boston Daily Advertiser* the editors noted that John Brown's execution "will prove no ordinary occurrence. And, after all, much as we may now regret it, perhaps it will turn out, in its ultimate consequences, to have done more to hasten the extinction of slavery than any other event of the present century."[52] With the rope selected and gallows erected, all John Brown had to do now was die a good death. As he walked out of the jailhouse at 11 A.M. into the light of the forenoon, he passed a note to a guard at the jail named Hiram O'Bannon.[53] It read, "I, John Brown, am now quite certain that the crimes of this guilty land will never be purged away but with blood. I had as I now think vainly flattered myself that without very much bloodshed it might be done."

Brown was escorted out of the front of the jailhouse at the corner of George and Washington Streets by Sheriff Campbell and jailer John Avis. They were his only escorts to the execution grounds; he didn't want a minister. In a letter written from the Charlestown Jail to Reverend James W. McFarland of Wooster, Ohio, Brown wrote, "There are no ministers of Christ here. These ministers who profess to be Christian, and hold slaves or advocate slavery, I cannot abide them. My knees will not bend in prayer with them while their hands are stained with the blood of souls."[54] In another letter he noted that he'd prefer his "religious attendants be poor little, dirty, ragged, bare headed, and barefooted slave boys and girls led by some old grey headed slave mother."[55] This letter may have had something to do with the legend that developed that he bent down to kiss the child of a slave on his way out of the jailhouse. It's a good story but would have been impossible given the circumstances, because no civilians could get anywhere near the man. In another sense, though, Brown broke with gallows traditions. He didn't decline the gallows sermon because he was somehow evil or out of some devil-may-care attitude; rather, it was because he believed himself morally superior to any minister who might pray or preach on his behalf.

But when Brown stepped out of the jailhouse there were no "slave boys and girls" waiting to escort him to the gallows; instead, he was greeted by a number of soldiers under the command of General William Taliaferro. With his arms tied behind his back above the elbows, Brown climbed aboard a long furniture wagon, nothing but a flatbed that carried a large pine shipping box that contained his coffin made of black walnut.[56] He sat upon the box for the short, maybe ten-minute ride to the field of execution. Brown wore a floppy black hat, ratty black coat and pants, and carpet slippers.[57] One observer noted that he looked like the typical "Western farmer."[58] Strother was more explicit, writing, "He wore the same seedy and dilapidated dress he had at Harpers Ferry and during his trial," he wrote, "but his rough boots had given place to a pair of particoloured slippers and he wore a low crowned broad brimmed hat."[59] Another observer claims that hidden beneath that coat was the noose, already positioned around his neck.[60]

Two white horses pulled the long, narrow furniture wagon, a wagon that belonged to a local undertaker and furniture maker named George W. Sadler.[61] John Avis sat next to Brown in the back, and Sadler and his assistant, Louis P. Starry, sat in front. There was a third man, but no one is positive about who that may have been. Some have claimed it was W. W. B. Gallaher, a local man who worked for the *New York Herald*.[62] As they rode along, Brown looked out upon the countryside, all stubble and stick, nature in its early winter dress, lovely when set next to the backdrop of the Blue Ridge Hills rising in the distance. "This is a beautiful country," he said. "I never had the pleasure of seeing it before—that is, while passing through the field."[63]

"Yes," replied Captain Avis.

Brown continued, "It seems the more beautiful to behold because I have so long been shut from it." In this spate of Indian summer the

John Brown riding to the gallows on his coffin, *Frank Les-lie's Illustrated Paper*, December 17, 1859. *Library of Congress*

warm sun cast its rays over rolling hills here at the northern edge of the Shenandoah Valley.

Mr. Sadler spoke up. "You are more cheerful than I am, Captain Brown," he said.

"Yes," Brown answered, "I ought to be."

Mounted soldiers stood in the woods to the left of the gallows, picket guards toward the rear, and troops in the field in front of the scaffold. Colonel John Preston of the Virginia Military Institute, describing the scene in a letter to his wife, said that troops "were distributed over the field, amounting in all to about 800 men. . . . The whole enclosure was lined by cavalry troops posted as sentinels, with their officers—one on a peerless black horse, and another on a remarkable-looking white horse, continually dashing round the enclosure."[64] Seeing all the soldiers, Brown wondered aloud where the "citizens" were. He was told they weren't allowed to be there; Governor Wise had ordered no one be allowed into the field except those with the military, despite Brown saying he'd give no dying speech.

Yet Brown had spent his last days writing countless letters and his now-famous last note that he slipped to the prison guard. He'd already given what amounted to a gallows speech in the courtroom. The citizens had heard from him already, and they were about to hear from him again, in a way. But there were citizens present within the field, quite a few, in addition to those peering in from the streets and from the tops of buildings.[65] There were soldiers on hand and a number of journalists who were granted last-minute permission to enter the field; Brown's execution was witnessed by an uncanny cast of characters, including pro-slavery advocate Edmund Ruffin, who'd told locals he'd be more than happy to serve as hangman. Ruffin would later affirm his place in history by firing a round at Fort Sumter from Cummings Point, just across the harbor from Charleston—and eventually commit suicide rather than submit to Yankee rule.[66] At Brown's execution Ruffin was with a company stationed about fifty yards from the gallows, closest to it.[67] Future Lincoln assassin John Wilkes Booth was also stationed close to the gallows. Booth had volunteered with militia troops out of Richmond just to be on hand to witness Brown's death.

The wagon halted next to the scaffold, and Brown was the first to mount it. He did so with a coolness that one soldier witness remarked made him look like "he had been going to dinner: he did not exhibit the slightest excitement or fear; not a muscle moved, nor was there the slightest nervous excitement."[68] A journalist from a Baltimore newspaper said he looked like he was walking upstairs to go to bed.[69] Thomas Gordon Pollock, who would later serve under General Lee and die during Pickett's Charge at Gettysburg, noted that Brown "stept up the ladder of the scaffold with an almost hurried step—and seemed to think he was giving an important fact to his biographer and was preparing a martyr's crown for himself."[70] Once up on the scaffold, David Strother noted, Brown took a good last look around, perhaps at the distant mountains where his army was to have fought to liberate the enslaved. In a letter to his wife, Mary Ann, eyewitness Thomas L. Jackson (later nicknamed "Stonewall") wrote that John Brown "behaved with unflinching firmness. . . . Brown had his arms tied behind him, & ascended the scaffold with apparent cheerfulness. After reaching the top of the platform, he shook hands with several who were standing around him."

A relative calm and peace had settled upon John Brown while in jail; he noted in several letters that he'd never been happier. In a November 22 letter to his children in North Elba, New York, he wrote, "I feel just as content to die for God's eternal truth and for suffering humanity on the scaffold as in any other way" and then urged his children to be of "good cheer."[71] Apparently he exuded this serenity while awaiting his execution. Even Ruffin commented on Brown's composure in his last moments. He wrote, "His movements & manner gave no evidence of his being either terrified or concerned, & he went through what was required of him apparently with as little agitation as if he had been the willing assistant, instead of the victim."[72] Brown took off his hat and stood firm as the sheriff pulled a white cap over his head and "placed the hangman's noose about his neck, adjusted the knot under the left ear."[73] He was led to the drop, the "halter hooked to the beam," and his ankles secured. Sheriff Campbell asked if he wanted a handkerchief to drop as a signal to cut the rope.[74] "No," he said, "but don't keep me waiting longer than is necessary."[75] These were his last words, "spoken with that sharp nasal twang peculiar to him, but spoken quietly and civilly, without impatience or the slightest apparent emotion."

Brown stood there on the trap door and faced south, the direction of the land of those who wished him dead and those whom he wished to free.[76] The soldiers then paraded around and into their positions for about ten minutes "as if an enemy were in sight," one journalist wrote with mild disdain.[77] Brown remained steady and still throughout these troop movements, this pregnant tension. Someone whispered to Strother that he could see Brown shaking, to which he answered that, no, the scaffold was shaking because of the "footsteps of the officers."[78] And then Colonel F. H. Smith, who was in charge of the military at the execution site, quietly told the sheriff, "We are ready," and the officers left the scaffold.

John Brown ascending the scaffold, *Frank Leslie's Illustrated Paper*, December 17, 1859. *Library of Congress*

The sheriff did his duty and cut the cord with a small hatchet. With that, the trap door fell and Brown dropped—only about two feet.[79] His body swayed, and there was a "slight grasping of hands."[80] And just like that, Colonel Preston wrote his wife, "the man of strong and bloody hand, of fierce passions, of iron will, of wonderful vicissitudes, the terrible partisan of Kansas, the capturer of the United States Arsenal at Harpers Ferry, the would-be Catiline of the South, the demi-god of the abolitionists, the man execrated and lauded, damned and prayed for, the man who in his motives, his means, his plans, and his successes, must ever be a wonder, a puzzle, and a mystery—John Brown—was hanging between heaven and earth."[81] In the quiet after the drop, after his movements ceased, there was only the sound of the rope and wood beam stretching under so much weight. And in that moment John Brown did, perhaps, become more important to the movement to end slavery in the United States, a cause to which he had dedicated his life at an abolitionist meeting in Hudson, Ohio, twenty-two years before.[82]

His pulse was checked several times, and he was finally declared dead after thirty-five minutes. He was cut down and placed in a black walnut coffin, in which he was eventually transported to the train station in Harpers Ferry and escorted by his wife back north. One reporter claimed, "All the arrangements were carried out with a precision and military strictness that was most annoying."[83] Colonel Preston broke the silence: "So perish all such enemies of Virginia! All such enemies of the Union! All such foes of the human race!" "So I felt," he wrote to his wife, "and so I said, with solemnity and without one shade of animosity, as I turned to break the silence, to those around me. Yet, the mystery was awful, to see the human form thus treated by men, to see life suddenly stopped in its current, and to ask one's self the question without answer—'And what then?'"[84] The question suspended in the air and was to be taken up again in that same Shenandoah Valley a few years later.

Others, though, knew the answer to that question: northern abolitionists had already decided what Brown's death meant to them. After his execution meetings were held, sermons given, and church bells tolled in places like Syracuse, Boston, Providence, Albany, and even little Perrysburg, Ohio, where businesses closed early and church bells rang for an hour. In Albany, New York, one hundred guns were fired between noon and one o'clock.[85] Of course, there were other, vastly different opinions of the man. On the day Brown was executed the Great Emancipator, Abraham Lincoln, said, "Old John Brown has been executed for treason against a state. *We cannot object*, even though he agreed with us in thinking slavery wrong. That cannot excuse violence, bloodshed and treason. It could avail him nothing that he might think himself right."[86] A day later an editorial from the Raleigh, North Carolina, *Register* demanded that the gallows be burned because "The Yankees have no objection to mingling money making with their grief, and they will, unless Brown's gallows is known to have been burned, set to work and make all kinds of jimcracks and notions out of what they will call parts of Old John Brown's gallows and, sell them. Let the rope which choked him, too, be burned and the fact advertised, or we shall see vast quantities of breast pins, lockets and bracelets, containing bits of the 'rope which hung Old Brown' for sale."[87]

And yet, on the fiftieth anniversary of his hanging Katherine Mayo wrote that Brown's raid and subsequent execution "had, like a touchstone, suddenly revealed the country to itself."[88] It would take countless more deaths before the majority of the country would recognize the implications of the slave regime—that the only way it would be dismantled was by violence.

JOHN BROWN'S RESURRECTION

She said she trusted me. And just like that, the white-gloved curator of the Jefferson County Museum took a tiny piece of hemp rope out of a glass case and placed it on the table where I was working. I stared at it, awestruck, that this might actually be a piece of Brown's noose but also surprised by how seemingly insignificant the fuzzy little ball of hemp looked. I had to sneeze but desperately held it back. That piece of rope isn't the only *memento mori* in the Jefferson County Museum's collections. There are others, of equal significance but decidedly more substantial. The wide open, white-walled, and windowless space is dominated by the Sadler furniture wagon, the one that carried John Brown, along with the others who were executed, to his death. It's a handsome and sturdy cart built for utilitarian purposes, to deliver furniture and coffins. It was a workhorse, in a sense. Like the pike in the left-hand corner of the museum, made for Brown's raiders to distribute to those who wished to join them, it was made with purpose.

"Just keep it on the table here," she said. "You can get a better photo this way." She places a tiny card next to the rope fragment that explains it was donated by Lucy Ambler.

"Okay, but I know this rope might be valuable, and I just want to be careful with it. Makes me nervous!"

"Well, we're fairly certain it's the real deal, but then again, you could probably circle the equator with the amount of rope purported to have been from the noose that killed John Brown." I heard that old

A rope supposedly used to hang John Brown. *Massachusetts Historical Society*

saw from at least three different people in the Harpers Ferry/Charlestown area. Everyone's sister, brother, cousin, or aunt claims to have a piece of that rope. One writer says that during the war every soldier that passed through the area obtained a piece of the rope or scaffold, "enough to build and rig a large man-of-war."[89] Inevitably there are numerous stories about what happened to the rope, and each teller claims theirs is true.

Today the Massachusetts Historical Society has a rope, with the noose that was used to hang John Brown still intact. It was given to the society by William Roscoe Thayer, president of the American Historical Association in 1918.[90] But the rope that hanged John Brown can also be found in the West Virginia State Museum, and pieces of it can be found elsewhere.[91] A John Brown archive created by West Virginian Boyd B. Stutler is a trove of Brown rope lore: Stutler may have even had a piece of the rope himself.[92] One letter in the Stutler Archive claims that a rope found in the attic of the jailor Avis's home in 1907 could be it.[93] The wife of the assistant to the undertaker who prepared Brown's body for burial in New York City claims that the noose was still around his neck when it arrived.[94] A man who claimed to have accompanied the body north asserted that he had the rope and would do nothing with it until he heard from Brown's wife.[95] He added, "I do not wish to believe in relics, and I have very little superstition—but the rope by which a Christian climbed into heaven is the next best thing to the ladder which Jacob saw."

How did Brown become a martyr to the extent that his execution would be a source of not just relics but also *holy* relics? In the moments after Brown was captured at Harpers Ferry there was talk of lynching him.[96] Instead, though, Brown was given a trial, a death sentence, and then a month to prepare for his death. Governor Wise was able to prepare for Brown an execution befitting a captive king. The area was on lockdown. Fifteen hundred troops were called up, and enough spectators put pen to paper that we have a good idea that what happened that December morning in Charlestown was nothing short of a spectacle meant to send a message to abolitionists that the South's "peculiar institution" would persist. But was that the message that Brown's execution ultimately delivered? Was it a fearsome spectacle that would keep others from getting violent ideas in their heads? Or did the fact of Brown's stoicism and bravery on the scaffold serve to reinforce his potential martyrdom—the simple frumpy farmer, all alone on the scaffold, facing the many troops with a firmness that belied his frame? Henry David Thoreau later wrote, "No theatrical manager could have arranged things so wisely to give effect to his behavior and words."[97] John Brown was hanged for murder and treason in what was meant to be an ignoble death, but instead Brown disrupted the narrative, intentionally or otherwise. His death is now generally remembered not as the ignoble death of a thief in the Middle Ages or of a sexual "deviant" in seventeenth-century New England but rather as something more complicated. For many, John Brown did exactly what

Ralph Waldo Emerson said he would do: "make the gallows glorious, like the cross."[98]

But in the immediate aftermath of his failed raid this was not Brown's reputation. In the weeks immediately following the raid on Harpers Ferry opinions of Brown were uniformly negative. Fiery pro-slavery advocates and lukewarm abolitionists condemned the man and his actions. Notably, the northern press did their best to placate southerners by describing Brown as "mad" and his comrades-in-arms as a "squad of fanatics."[99] Even the antislavery *New York Tribune* wrote that the raid on Harpers Ferry was "the work of a madman."[100] The majority of Brown's financial backers—Thomas Wentworth Higginson and Theodore Parker excepted—distanced themselves from him.[101] But public opinion began to shift, and Brown gained some vocal supporters. One of the first to side with Brown was Thoreau, who, in an October 30 public address in Concord, proclaimed him a martyr following in Jesus Christ's footsteps.[102] "I am here to plead his cause with you," he told the audience. "I plead not for his life, but for . . . his immortal life; and so it becomes your cause wholly, and is not his in the least. Some eighteen hundred years ago Christ was crucified; this morning, perchance, Captain Brown was hung. These are the two ends of a chain which is not without links. He is not Old Brown any longer; he is an Angel of Light."

Thoreau's pronouncement was aided and abetted by the old man himself, who seemed to understand his new and powerful position. Over the course of his last days in jail John Brown met with countless visitors, many of whom wanted to argue with him over slavery and, in the case of some minister, save his soul. Brown met the public in another way—through the pen and page, writing countless letters and, consciously or otherwise, participating in the gallows literary tradition.

Brown offered his own "true confession" of his deeds. But unlike some writers in the gallows literature genre, Brown does not seek forgiveness; instead, he constructs a martyr's narrative in the classic model of his own Christian faith. In a letter to his wife and children on November 8, 1859, he wrote, "Remember, dear wife and children all, that Jesus of Nazareth suffered a most excruciating death on a cross as a felon, under the most aggravating circumstances. Think also of the prophets and apostles and Christians of former days, who went through greater tribulations than you or I, and try to be reconciled."[103] A week later he wrote in another letter that he doesn't feel "degraded by [his] imprisonment, [his] chains or prospect of the Gallows."[104] Indeed, he notes that the method of his death says nothing about his character.[105] In another letter he proclaimed, "Men cannot imprison, or chain; or hang the soul. I go joyfully on behalf of millions that 'have no rights' that this 'great & glorious'; '*this Christian Republic*,' 'is bound to respect.'"[106] In that last clause Brown mocks Supreme Court Justice Roger B. Taney's 1857 decision in *Dred Scott v. Sanford* that African Americans have no rights as US citizens. For Brown, slavery was the "sum of all villainies," and he was proud to die if it would lead to abolition.[107] "Let them hang me. I forgive them," he writes Christ-like, "for they know not what they do."[108]

The transformation of Brown's reputation, at least in the North, continued after his execution. The day after his execution the editors of the *New York Daily Tribune* proclaimed that "Slavery has killed John Brown. . . . John Brown and slavery were foes to the death. Slavery for the moment is the victor."[109] They claimed that his manner of defeating slavery was "unfit" and his raid "utterly mistaken" but that his death would only serve to strengthen his memory. "History will accord an honored niche to Old John Brown." He will, they wrote, "live in a million hearts . . . his memory will be fragrant through generations. It will be easier to die in a good cause, even on the gallows, since John Brown has hallowed that mode of exit from the troubles and temptations of this mortal existence." John Brown had made the gallows noble, for sure. To some, though, he made the gallows holy. At Shiloh Presbyterian in New York City a man stood up and announced that "Christ died on the cross, but his influence lived." Another man made a direct comparison between Brown's execution on the gallows and that of Christ's on the cross. And at a Boston gathering Brown was compared to Jesus and Virginia Governor Wise

Print after painting "The Last Moments of John Brown,"
Thomas Hovenden, 1885. *Library of Congress*

as Pontius Pilate. Brown's narrative had been reinforced through the
typology of Christ.

Brown's resurrection was also assisted by the apocryphal story that
he had kissed a black slave child on his way out of the jail, captured
in an 1863 Louis L. Ransom painting that was copied and widely
published by Currier and Ives, a Thomas Satterwhite Noble painting
called "John Brown's Blessing" (1867) and later in Thomas Hovenden's
"The Last Moments of John Brown" (1884). John Brown, wizened
elder, leans over to kiss the child of, we are to assume, a black slave;
here he is no mad prophet or insane lunatic, as many claimed he was

in the immediate aftermath of his raid on Harpers Ferry. In Hovenden's painting he is a measured man of peace, a martyr about to give up his body for the cause of freedom.

Material manifestations of John Brown's "Christ-ness" in the accoutrement of his execution, like the rope, became relics like those collected and traded among medieval pilgrims. One story floated around that the sheriff sent a piece of the scaffold to James Redpath, labeling it "A Bit of the True Cross, a Chip from the Scaffold of John Brown."[110] P. T. Barnum tried to get his hands on some of Brown's clothes and perhaps even the noose but ultimately only obtained some of the weapons used in the raid.[111] At his American Museum he displayed, along with his wax figure of Brown, a knife used by one of his sons and several of the pikes made for the raid on Harpers Ferry.[112] The scaffold too was a hot item. According to Joseph Barry, who bases his story on "trustworthy sources," David Cockerell, the carpenter who constructed the scaffold, knew that it might be sought after and, thus, he disassembled it shortly after the hanging and used it to build a porch.[113] As such, it escaped the hands of relic hunters for a while. An item ran in the *New York Times* on February 26, 1884, that claimed the hidden scaffold was, in fact, discovered at a Charlestown home, perhaps confirming Cockerell's story.[114] What happened next, though, is uncertain. Barry claims that later on someone from Washington, DC, purchased it and that there was some attempt to rebuild it at the 1893 World's Fair in Chicago (John Brown's Fort was actually rebuilt there).[115] Pieces of the scaffold are floating around still, apparently; a few are on view at the John Brown Museum in Harpers Ferry.

By the war's end the rope that made John Brown's noose had been freighted with meaning, and unlike medieval relics, these meanings were mostly political. Confederate and Union soldiers each wanted to touch the infamous noose, probably for opposing reasons. Indeed, Union soldiers marched to a song that narrated Brown's struggle and death. This was an important reversal; the shame of the ignoble death was erased, and as Emerson claimed, the noose and gallows became sacred relics.

In Brown's case, then, the noose became a positive rather than a negative symbol. It was transformed into a rallying point for abolitionist sentiment and a point of departure for transforming the nation. But in this work, where were the enslaved people? Where was Denmark Vesey, Nat Turner, or Gabriel Prosser? One need only look to what happened to Brown's comrades in arms to get a sense of the value placed on the lives of black Americans. On December 16, 1859, four more men were executed: John Cook, Edwin Coppoc, Shields Green, and John Copeland. The bodies of the two white men, Cook and Coppoc, were surrendered to their families. The same civility was not rendered to Green and Copeland. They were quickly buried, and an hour after burial Winchester Medical College students dug up their bodies for research. Copeland's family appealed to an Ohio senator for help recovering his body; Union soldiers burned the college down three years later. Their bodies were never recovered, and their deaths were given little attention in comparison to that of John Brown.

In one version of "John Brown's Body," a verse exclaims that "They will hang Jeff Davis to a sour apple tree!" The verse, coming as it does after verses celebrating Brown, implies exacting retribution for John Brown's death by hanging the Confederate president. Although Jefferson Davis was in fact guilty of committing crimes that would typically lead to the noose and the gallows, he didn't hang despite being leader of a "government" that facilitated the war and represented the interests of southern planters and slavers. He served two years in jail and was released on a bond posted in part by one of Brown's former supporters, Gerrit Smith. He became a college president (Texas A&M), like his former general and the man who captured John Brown, Robert E. Lee (Washington College).

Herman Melville's poem "The Portent" describes Brown's execution as a foreboding and forbidding moment in American history. Brown hangs "from the beam / Slowly swaying," casting his shadow across the Shenandoah Valley.[116] Beneath the execution hood, Melville writes, is Brown's anguished face, one "portent" of the nation's future pain. Another "portent" is Brown's "streaming beard" peeking out from

Execution of the Lincoln Conspirators, Alexander Gardner. *Library of Congress*

beneath the hood. The hanged man, noose around his neck, is also "The meteor of the war," violence trailing in his wake. Melville's poem paints Brown's hanging as a moment foreshadowing the war. But there were other warnings, weird signs of the violence to come, and these signs could be seen all over the state of Virginia.

And what was Brown's execution a portent for? Remember Brown's words to his captors: "You may dispose of me very easily. I am nearly disposed of now; but this question is still to be settled—this negro question, I mean; the end of that is not yet." The American Civil War didn't settle that question—the Civil War that supposedly began in 1861 but actually began much earlier than that and certainly did not end in 1865. Its years of violence are noose-filled, rough strands of a complicated narrative that could include the slave rebellions and con-spiracies of New York City, Virginia, and South Carolina; the hanging of forty suspected Unionists in Gainesville, Texas; the lynching of black men during New York City's 1863 Draft Riots; the execution of twenty-two Confederate deserters at Kinston, North Carolina; the execution of Andersonville's Henry Wirz; and all the mayhem of the Reconstruction years, including the apparent mass hanging of twenty-four men, women, and children in Pine Bluff, Arkansas. The one most remembered, though, is the grand execution of the Lincoln Conspirators in 1865. That hanging was, once again, an incredible display of political and military power—as well as technological advances. Execution technologies had developed, and this is evident in Alexander Gardner's famous photos of the executions of the Lincoln conspirators. The conspirators were put to death on a large scaffold with what could be described as a platform drop—the drop was held up by two poles that were pushed out simultaneously—and ropes tied into hangman's knots.

But the noose stayed in the picture and played an important role in the racial violence that manifested in the following decades; the war did not resolve the issue at its heart. The noose that was a talisman for Union troops would become a symbol for reasserting white supremacy and undermining the kind of world Brown imagined.

CHAPTER 7

The Noose in the Museum:
Hanging and Native America

"ARE YOU WILLING TO PUT THAT NOOSE AROUND YOUR NECK? Are you willing to go to that place?"

"What do you mean?" I ask.

"You come here to learn about the noose, but this is much bigger than the noose. This is more about you than it is about the noose. But this is a story about the Dakota people."

I'm bewildered, and it isn't just the slot machine's flashing lights and perpetual high-pitched song, the multiple flat-screens projecting the Vikings-Titans game, the smoke, or the bizarre juxtaposition of oxygen-tanked white people on a Dakota reservation in Flandreau, South Dakota. There is something that I don't know or can't understand, something that is bigger than the story I'm researching: a noose used to hang a Dakota man named Caske at the end of the 1862 US-Dakota War is in the archives of the Minnesota State Historical Society.[1] When the Society began putting together objects for an exhibit commemorating the 150th anniversary of the war, they invited representatives of the Dakota community, many of whom responded negatively to the noose. They didn't want it on display, didn't want people to see it. They want it back. And some Dakota want to destroy it. This is not John Brown's noose—not at all.

J. B. Weston looks out in the direction of the slot machines, points at a dark-suited security man walking by, and says, "He's a descendant of Caske. This is very real for us. You come in and get your story and go home. You write your books, but what does it all mean? This is very real to me. I work every day for the Dakota people."

He points to some kids sitting at a bar booth close by. "I'm doing this for those kids because they are lost. Alcoholism is real. Drug use is real. This noose you want to know about, it's much bigger than just the turns and the knot."

"I understand," I tell him, "that's why I'm talking to you. I want to learn. I want to know more."

"You can't just talk about the knot."

"I agree. And I don't think you're listening to me."

"No, you're not listening to me."

There's a pause, and the awkwardness between us settles in like skunk-spray through a window in springtime. *I'm not going to win this battle*, I think to myself. But what am I trying to win? Why am I trying to win? Is it that I want him to trust me?

One time a man I was interviewing accused me of being an operative of one of his longtime rivals, an accusation that said a lot about him. I pulled out my phone and said I was calling my mother and he could talk to her and that my word is my word and that if he didn't believe me, well, my mother could set him straight. He relented.

But this isn't that kind of situation, I was realizing. It's not about trust—J. B. has no reason to trust me, and any phone call to my mama or my grandmamma wouldn't matter. This is about truth. A truth that, for all intents and purposes, I just can't understand because—as he rightly says—I know nothing about the Dakota people that I haven't read in a book. The Vikings score, and J. B. takes a drag on his cigarette.

He looks straight at me. "You're just dabbling. This is every day for me." The violence in the room resonated—the organized violence of the football game, the generational violence of the kids, the ghosts of a violent history walking across the casino floor. As I traveled about Minnesota and into South Dakota, I heard on the radio again and again updates on the trial of a Minnesota man accused of funneling money and men to the Somali militant group al-Shabaab and the arrest of a Bangladeshi man who tried to blow up the Federal Reserve building in Manhattan. The noose is a link in a long chain of violence.

"You need to think about what it means to put that noose around your neck."

I'm listening to J. B., and the Vikings are playing, and the slots and the smoke, but I was also thinking that life is so sad. That this is so intense. That this is an "hour of lead."

"Don't you know it's a long way from your head to your heart?" Weston says, not waiting for me to reply. "All this may be overwhelming for you, but it's the truth."

And the truth is that 1862 is right now for the Dakota people, and what that means for this book, for this symbol, is that for the Dakota people the noose is not only a symbol of racial oppression; it's a symbol of genocide—indeed, it was meant to be a tool of genocide. But the Dakota are still here, and the Dakota have to deal with this symbol in a way that I can't begin to understand. This is not my story, Weston was saying. And yet if I want to be honest, I have no right to tell it from any other perspective than my own.

HOW THE WEST WAS WON

When the 1862 US-Dakota War is spoken of or mentioned in American history books (if it is mentioned at all) the narrative will mostly focus attention on the six-week-long war and perhaps the spectacular executions at its conclusion. But the events begin, in many ways, in 1492 or 1493, when Columbus penned his first letter to the Spanish Court, a letter to Luis de Santángel, and thus initiated centuries of European discourse about who these New World people were and what was to be done about them. Either they were people to be saved—Christianized—or they were to be killed. Any writer lumping Native Americans, American Indians, or the indigenous peoples of North America into a single traceable narrative commits the grave sin of producing reductionist history, and yet the story can be told over and over

again in what we now call the United States of America, a story of col-
onization and violence, of conflict, of treaties made and broken, and of
white folks, missionaries mostly, with imagined good intentions. Pick
most any geographic location, and you'll likely find this narrative. It's
the same story more or less for Algonquin, Zuni, Cheyenne, Cherokee,
Choctaw, or Hannah Occuish's Pequot.

I've reduced this story into a short paragraph as a gentle reminder
because when we talk about 1862, we have to begin with 1492. The
reasons for the war are greater than that one moment would allow.
The immediate reason why many Dakota went to war was because
they were starving and felt they had nothing to lose. They had already
lost much of their homeland.

The Dakota (which means "allies") are often called by a name be-
stowed upon them by whites—"Sioux," a term that may be a bastardiza-
tion of an Ojibwe word that means "snake." Today some use the term,
while others despise it. They call themselves the people of the Seven
Council Fires (Oceti Šakowin). This includes the Dakota in the east
(Mdewakanton, Wahpekute, Sisseton, Wahpeton), the Nakota (Middle Dakota/Yankton and Yanktonais), and the Lakota (Tetons). Today
Dakota people live all over but especially in Minnesota, South Dakota,
Nebraska, and Canada; Nakota in South Dakota; and Lakota in North
and South Dakota. Dakota people believe they are from Minnesota or
Mni Sota Makoce, the land where the water reflects the clouds. They
don't believe they emigrated there but that they are literally from there,
brought down from the stars to Bdote, where the Minnesota and Mississippi Rivers meet.[2] Dakota people put no truck in the Bering Strait
story, that somehow they are descendants of those intrepid pioneers
who crossed over from Asia so long ago.[3]

In a sense, historians Gwen Westerman and Bruce White write,
there are two competing stories about this place called Minnesota.
From the European-American view pioneer settlements are part of the
story of westward expansion, the various gold rushes, the Oregon Trail,
the coming of the railroad and telegraph line, the reach of civilization,
the opening up of new lands. To most white Americans this place is

simply the state of Minnesota, founded in 1858. For Native Americans it is their lost homeland. There's an obvious and serious gap in the telling of those two stories.

Beginning in 1805 these two competing "stories" clashed when the Dakota entered the first of a number of treaties with the US government. The treaties that would have the greatest impact on the Dakota of Minnesota were signed in 1851 at Traverse de Sioux (near modern-day St. Peter) and Mendota. With those two treaties, the Dakota sold about 35 million acres of land. The treaties called for setting up reservations on the north and south sides of the Minnesota River on a swatch of land about ten miles wide and eighty miles long. The Sisseton and Wahpeton bands would move to what was called the Upper Sioux Agency, near the mouth of the Yellow Medicine River, and the Mdewakanton and Wahpekute bands would move to lands near Redwood Falls at the Lower Sioux Agency. In 1858 Dakota leaders were invited on an extended visit to Washington, DC, where they were required to sign another document giving settlers access to the land on the north side of the Minnesota. After these treaties they were left with scraps of Mni Sota Makoce, the seedbed for their community and culture.

The Dakota were told that the treaties stipulated yearly "annuity" payments for the price of the land as well as goods to help them adjust to the change in their economy, culture, and way of life. When Dakota leaders signed the treaty they also signed a document that called for a large sum of money to go directly to white traders. These traders claimed the Dakota owed them monies for goods purchased. Many of these claims, it seems, were false. Traders often charged exorbitant prices for goods, and they had used those prices when the treaties were signed.

This process was part of what some call the "Indian System," begun in the funk of Washington politicking (congressmen horse trading for lucrative positions and land claims) and that fertilized the West with its muck and mire. In theory the federal government was using its power and money to help Native Americans become self-sustaining farmers, but rather than bettering the lives of the Native Americans the Indian System was meant to serve, it only made them worse. The bureaucracy established to work with Native Americas, specifically the Office of Indian Affairs, was essentially set up to benefit whites who wanted to get rich quick.

There were three primary ways money was made from this exploitive system. The first was by people making claims for destruction of property by Native Americans.[4] Many such claims went uninvestigated and, of course, could never be enforced against white men. Contractors also made money from the system, receiving monies for construction, supplying goods to the reservations, and so on. Lastly and most relevant to what happened in Minnesota were the traders who were notorious for claiming for debts that didn't exist. Because of these myriad boondoggling possibilities, jobs and contracts linked to the Indian System were sought-after prizes. Agents of the government would often hire relatives and friends.[5]

In addition to making immediate money off the government, the Indian System was a good long-term investment because agents often had first dibs at land, putting them at the forefront of land speculation in advance of the railroad, obtaining parcels that made them and their families quite wealthy.[6] Nichols notes succinctly that "the Indian System mirrored the basic drives of American society—social mobility, the acquisition of wealth, unrestricted capitalism, and political activism."[7] On the losing end of this system, of course, were the people the system was meant to benefit.

In the fall of 1861 a Washington-appointed investigator named George E. H. Day was sent to Minnesota to investigate allegations of corruption on reservations throughout the state, including the Dakota reservations along the Minnesota River. Day found dishonest traders, people receiving salaries for work they never did, excessive expenditures, and Dakota people living in squalor.[8] He wrote President Lincoln that he had "discovered numerous violations of law & many frauds committed by past agents & a superintendent." Day claimed he could "satisfy any reasonable intelligent man that the Indians whom

I have visited . . . have been defrauded of more than 100 thousand dollars in or during the four years past. . . . The whole system is defective & must be revised," he pleaded, "or, your red children, as they call themselves, will continue to be wronged & outraged & the just vengeance of heaven continue to be poured out & visited upon this nation for its abuses & cruelty to the Indian."

Day was not the first, nor the last, to warn the federal government. Reverend Henry Whipple, Episcopal Bishop of Minnesota, wrote Lincoln three months later about the conditions his "heathen wards" faced.[9] Whipple believed the government had good intentions but that unscrupulous people had stymied them. Prior to signing treaties, the Dakota had access to resources that would have helped them continue their way of life, but now they had been disconnected from those resources. This, Whipple said, had led not only to material losses but also to social and cultural ones—a breakdown of old customs and relations—compounded by whiskey and greedy agents. The remedy, he argued, would be to employ only men "of purity, temperance, industry, and unquestioned integrity," to place Native Americans under US jurisdiction, provide enough resources so that they can live sustainably, offer ample resources to schools, and appoint a commission to investigate the situation. It's not clear whether Lincoln grasped the seriousness of Whipple's letter. He had a lot on his plate—a civil war, of course, as well as preparations for the Homestead Act of 1862, which offered "free land," 160 acres to be exact, to settlers willing to live on and farm it for at least five years.

Things only got worse for the Dakota. After a poor harvest and a harsh winter, the Dakota at Upper and Lower Sioux were near starving and eagerly awaiting their annuity and goods payments that were supposed to arrive by the end of June. They didn't come, in part due to a Washington bureaucracy caught up in the Civil War. On July 14 about five thousand Dakota showed up at the Upper Agency and demanded food from Agent Thomas J. Galbraith. After some hemming and hawing, Galbraith relented and handed out food. At the Lower Agency some goods were dispersed in June, but supplies were running low for the Dakota in August. This time agents refused requests for goods or demands that traders extend credit. Many traders and shop-keepers felt they'd been too kind already. One of them, Andrew J. Myrick, quipped, "If they are hungry, let them eat grass."

On August 17, 1862, four young Wahpeton men traveling home from an unsuccessful hunting trip passed the farm of Robinson Jones near Acton. They saw some hen eggs in the grass near a white farm-stead; one of them picked them up. Another told him not to, that they belonged to the whites. The first man smashed them on the ground, saying that he was a coward, afraid to take eggs from a white man even though he was starving. With that, the second man said that he wasn't a coward; he'd go kill the white man. Another version of the story is that the men requested food but were denied.[10] Regardless, soon after they passed by that house those four Dakota men were racing back to their community on stolen horses, having killed Jones and his wife as well as Howard Baker, Viranus Webster, and fifteen-year-old Clara Wilson. Dakota elders were alarmed by the news, believing the whites would exact harsh retribution for these deaths. Given the sorry state of affairs, some decided the only option was to declare war—they were starving, their lands and way of life had been taken away from them, and they had little to lose at that point. Others appealed for peace, saying that war would make things much worse than they already were. Still others, especially Dakota of mixed heritage, struggled with the competing cultural narratives in their lives. The war party pressed on and sought the support of Chief Taoyateduta (or Little Crow), the one man who, if they were to have any chance at success, had to be swayed.

Several chiefs as well as the four young men woke Taoyateduta from his sleep just before dawn on August 18. They told him what had happened and of their desire to go to war. He blackened his face and covered it in mourning. He knew the outcome would not be good. Someone accused him of being a coward. Years later Taoyateduta's son Wowinape gave an oral account of his reply to this stinging remark. It is telling: "Braves, you are like little children; you know not what you are doing . . . the white men are like locusts when they fly so thick that

Taoyateduta (Little Crow). *Library of Congress*

the whole sky is a snowstorm. You may kill one—two—ten; yes, as many as the leaves in the forest yonder, and their brothers will not miss them. . . . You will die like the rabbits when the hungry wolves hunt them in the Hard Moon (January). Taoyateduta is not a coward: he will die with you."[11] The next day Taoyateduta led a group of Dakota in an attack on the Lower Sioux Agency. Forty-four white people were killed, including a number of US soldiers trying to squelch the uprising. Trader Andrew Myrick was found dead with his mouth stuffed full of grass. Warriors then let loose on white settlers throughout the Minnesota River Valley, murdering men, women, and children. Though it was not all helter skelter massacre—many settlers were simply taken captive, some settler communities closed ranks and fought back, and still others escaped the area as quickly as possible.

Minnesota Governor Alexander Ramsey called on his predecessor, Minnesota's first governor and a former trader, Colonel Henry H. Sibley, to lead forces from St. Paul to the Minnesota River Valley. Sibley had made his fortune from the Indian System; he played a central role in getting the Dakota to sign the 1851 treaties. But Sibley took his time organizing an army and traveling south. The press howled, calling him "the undertaker" because his troops generally showed up after a battle and played clean-up crew. When Sibley finally arrived many Dakota warriors lost the desire to fight against superior numbers and weapons. After a decisive defeat in the Battle at Wood Lake on September 23, 1862, those Dakota warriors most engaged in the fighting, including Taoyateduta, fled westward to Dakota Territory or northward into Canada. In the end between four hundred and six hundred settlers and soldiers and sixty Dakota were killed over the course of about six weeks.[12]

It's important to remember when telling this story that there was never unified support for the war among the Dakota. In some ways the Dakota community had already been disrupted and fractured by the treaties and the traders. So-called Farmer Indians had given up their old economy and culture for the white one. This created tensions between those retaining Dakota lifeways and those abandoning them. To be fair, both choices were likely made in an effort to survive, but the use of violence against the settlers, many of whom the Dakota considered their friends, further exacerbated these tensions. Those with mixed heritages were often torn by competing ideologies and genealogies; some sided with the whites, while some sided with the Dakota. Ultimately many believed that when the fighting was over, to simply have Dakota blood would make one guilty in the eyes of white Minnesotans. If the Dakota who fought against the whites lost, they thought, all the Dakota would suffer.

So when around two thousand Dakota people surrendered on September 26 at a place called Camp Release (near modern-day Montevideo), those surrendering tried to make it clear they wanted peace. One man went so far as to wrap himself in the American flag as the soldiers marched into camp. Whites who had been held hostage were handed over to the American soldiers, and the Dakota men of fighting age were separated from the women, children, and the elderly, who were marched to Fort Snelling. As they marched with military escort they met mobs of angry whites with clubs and scalding water. In Henderson a white woman grabbed a nursing baby from a Dakota woman and smashed the child on the ground.[13] A soldier pulled the woman away, but the baby died shortly thereafter.

Sibley quickly organized a commission to try the Dakota men who were suspected of being involved in the fighting. The five-member military commission tried 392 men in six weeks. Legal scholar Carol Chomsky claims that trials were problematic in many ways: "The evidence was sparse, the tribunal was biased, the defendants were unrepresented in unfamiliar proceedings conducted in a foreign language, and authority for convening the tribunal was lacking."[14] Furthermore, the Dakota on trial weren't treated as members of a sovereign nation. Some of the trials lasted less than five minutes, and all were conducted in English.

Consider the case of Caske.[15] Caske was charged with the murder of a white man named George H. Gleason as well as "sundry hostile acts against the whites between the said eighteenth day of August 1862 and the 28 day of Sept. 1862."[16] Caske pled not guilty and claimed that Hapa, another Dakota man who was also with him, actually killed Gleason and that, on the contrary, he protected as many whites as he could. Caske had taken special care of Sarah Wakefield, the wife of a physician at Upper Agency. He noted that if he had committed any "hostile acts," he wouldn't have given himself up. Wakefield supported Caske's claims and said he saved her life and that of her two children several times. Angus Robertson, another witness for the prosecution, also praised Caske and supported Wakefield's claims. But no matter. The commission—all men who had been involved in the fighting—found Caske guilty as charged and sentenced him "to be hanged by the neck until he is dead."

Clearly something was going on here. Word had spread around the camp that Wakefield and Caske were more than friends, so perhaps this prejudiced the commission.[17] But reading through the trial transcripts one gets the sense that Caske's was not the only problematic case. As they moved through cases, the trials got shorter and shorter; by the end of the six weeks 303 men were sentenced to hang. On November 9 the condemned were moved to a place called Camp Lincoln near Mankato. Along the way they were attacked by a mob in New Ulm, and two were killed.[18]

When word reached President Lincoln that federal troops were about to execute 303 Dakota men in Minnesota, the rush to the gallows came to a halt. Lincoln wanted his lawyers to review all the trial transcripts and to sign the warrant himself. Ultimately he winnowed the list down to thirty-nine men—those who stood accused of attacks on civilians. But even then the guilt of the condemned men was questionable. Lincoln's private opinions of Native Americans are tough to pin down. Carl Sandburg tells the story of Captain Lincoln during the Black Hawk War, protecting an old Indian man who wandered into camp: when soldiers challenged him on it he basically said, "Try me."[19] The reality, though, was that he was very much enmeshed in the Indian System and he benefited politically from its existence.[20] Certainly Lincoln prevented the deaths of many, but Lincoln chose expediency, and as literary historian Bethany Schneider writes, "The only way to produce the benevolent, all-loving antiracist Lincoln who persists in fantasy if not in scholarly histories, is to hide the Indian bodies."[21]

And that's hard to do, considering what an enormous event the 1862 execution was. Rather than hang each man individually or even several at a time, carpenters constructed a large gallows in downtown Mankato, capable of hanging thirty-nine men simultaneously. A Mankato paper reported that "the gallows, constructed of heavy, square white oak timbers, is 24 feet square, and in the form of a diamond. It is about 20 feet high. The drop is held by a large rope, attached to a pole in the center of the frame, and the scaffold is supported by heavy ropes centering at this pole, and attached to the one large rope running down to and fastened at the ground."[22] Henry L. Mills, who was a soldier on duty, wrote years later that many men who had lost family begged for the chance to help build the gallows.[23]

As the execution date drew near, the condemned thirty-nine were separated from the others. Caske was mistakenly among the thirty-nine; he had been exonerated, but his name was confused with that of man named Chaskadon (case number 121), who had been convicted of killing a pregnant woman.[24] These Dakota men, chained two by two, became objects of curiosity for local media and ministers who visited often in the days before the execution. An account from the *St. Paul Press* reads like the gallows literature of the eighteenth century, regaling readers with stories of penitent Dakota men awaiting execution, commanding their children to become Christians and to bear no malice toward white people.[25] "Most of them spoke confidently," we're told, "of their hopes of salvation." They lamented making the choice to go to war. Others, we learn, seemed woefully unaware of their impending deaths "and laughed and joked apparently as unconcerned as if they were sitting around a camp-fire in perfect freedom." A reporter from the *New York Times* also noted behavior that he read as passivity and wrote, "It was a sad, a sickening sight to see that group of miserable dirty savages, chained to the floor, and awaiting with apparent unconcern the terrible fate toward which they were approaching."[26] Some writers wanted drama and repentance, not solemn contemplation or perhaps resignation and preparation for another kind of journey. The correspondent for the *St. Paul Press* was enraged by these men:

> They all appeared cheerful and contented, and scarcely to reflect on the certain doom which awaited them. To the gazers, the recollection of how short a time since they had been engaged in the diabolical work of murdering indiscriminately both old and young sparing neither sex nor condition, sent a thrill of horror through the veins. Now they were perfectly harmless, and looked as innocent as children. They smiled at your entrance, and held out their hands to be shaken, which yet appeared to be gory with the blood of babes. Oh treachery, thy name is Dakota.[27]

What was this correspondent really witnessing? And who was he talking to? It's hard to read such a report as objective, though it's equally problematic to expect objectivity in those circumstances. But were all these men guilty? And if so, of what?

On the day after Christmas thousands poured into Mankato to witness what would be the largest simultaneous execution in US history. The sky was crystal blue, and the early snows had melted. Beneath sunny skies three to five thousand gawkers (along with about fifteen hundred soldiers) gathered wherever they could, seeking out the best vantage points—rooftops, street level, some even gathered on the other side of the river for a clear view. But the crowd was relatively subdued, in part because two days beforehand martial law had been declared and bars closed.[28]

The condemned men painted themselves with "streaks of vermilion and ultramarine" and began singing their death song as preparations began for the executions.[29] One man, Tatemin (Round Wind), had been pardoned overnight, and he was placed with the other prisoners. At about seven o'clock their iron shackles were removed and arms pinioned. When this work was finished they stood as one and sang. Father Augustin Ravoux prayed with them or over them in the Dakota language. Caps of white muslin were placed on top of their heads, not pulled down yet, so they could still see to walk. This gave some of them pause—the hoods were considered shameful because they prevented them from facing death "without flinching" and, thus, dying a noble death.[30] But some of them kept singing.

At ten o'clock the Dakota men were led to the gallows through a tunnel of infantrymen. As they walked up the steps to the scaffold, some began chanting again. The subdued crowd looked on as nooses were placed around the necks of the condemned and then adjusted. Some of them clasped hands. About fifteen minutes later Major J. R. Brown beat a drum three times, and Captain John Duly, who lost his family in the war, took a swing at the rope that would release the scaffold. The first blow was unsuccessful. He swung again, and the scaffold fell. One rope broke, and Hdainyanka (Rattling Runner)

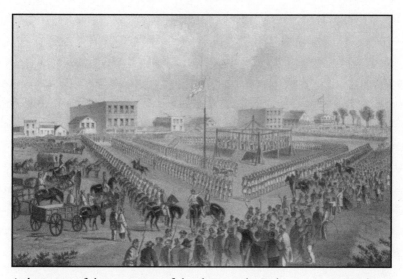

A depiction of the execution of the thirty-eight Dakota men at Mankato, Minnesota, December, 26, 1862. *Library of Congress*

had to be hanged again. Many died instantly, while others struggled as they strangled to death in a scene like no other I've encountered in my research—awesome in size, finality, and purpose.[31] There's no indication that an effort was made to measure the height and weight of each condemned man. Rope lengths would have been mostly uniform and, therefore, it's likely that some men died from strangulation while others from the initial drop.[32] The reporter for the *New York Times* captures some of this in an arresting sentence: "Thirty-eight human beings suspended in the air, on the bank of the beautiful Minnesota; above the smiling, clear blue sky."[33]

The bodies were then cut down and tossed into waiting wagons "like pigs."[34] Onlookers pushed forward, scrambling for what relics they could grab—locks of hair, pieces of clothing, crucifixes—the ornaments of lives lived.[35] The bodies were carted to a sandbar alongside the Minnesota River and unceremoniously dumped into a four-foot-deep common grave. That night the shallow grave was opened. Local doctors, including Dr. William Worrall Mayo (after whom the

Mayo Clinic is named), collected corpses, ostensibly for dissection. Some soldiers tried using one body for target practice until the body was confiscated and reburied.[36]

Lincoln's "Indian bodies" had been sufficiently hidden just a few days before Lincoln's slave-freeing Emancipation Proclamation went into effect.[37] Those Dakota men, though, didn't die anonymous deaths. They did not go quietly. As they stood on the scaffold before the axe fell, the men had called out their names to let the others know they were not alone, to speak their names into being, to bear witness.[38] I am One Who Jealously Guards His Home. I am One Who Walks Clothed in Owl Feathers. I am His People. I am Red Leaf. I am Rattling Runner. I am One Who Stands on a Cloud. I am Wind Comes Home. I am Returning Clear Voice. I am Little Good Stars.

MATERIAL OBJECT, SPIRITUAL SIGNIFICANCE

In reading about this story of the largest simultaneous execution in US history, I discovered that the Minnesota Historical Society has, among its collections, one of the nooses used as part of that massive execution. I e-mailed one of the archivists and asked whether I could come to St. Paul and take a look at the noose. About a week later I got an e-mail from the Historical Society's senior curator telling me I couldn't see it; it's considered culturally sensitive material. They consider requests on a case-by-case basis, and so far only Dakota elders have had access to it. This came as a surprise. What was the problem? Are the Dakota the only ones who can see it? Why don't they want it to be displayed as a symbol of oppression, of their struggle? What makes it culturally sensitive?

This is where I started when I met with Ben Gessner, Collections Associate-American Indian and Fine Arts Collections at the Minnesota Historical Society (MHS), who looks to be in his early thirties. When we met I felt like I was looking at myself—a younger, more intelligent and put-together, hipper version of myself. We both wear beards and the same uniform: shirt, tie, khakis, and hoodie. His shirt is flannel with a gray tie. But Gessner conveyed a composed confidence and took his time approaching the complexities of the Caske noose story.

Gessner told me he learned very little about the US-Dakota war growing up in Minnesota, in part because he grew up in southeastern Minnesota, so it wasn't a part of the community history in the way it was elsewhere but also because what little he was taught about it in his middle school history class didn't register. Then he went to college in Mankato. He noticed the monuments, heard some of the history. But still, like most Minnesotans, he didn't see this narrative as an intrinsic part of his own history, didn't see his place in the narrative. Then he came to work for the MHS, and all that began to change. He was asked to work on an exhibit about the war for its 150th anniversary. They began, he said, by searching the historical society's databases, looking for items related to 1862. That's when they came across the noose.

For MHS to bring this topic up and to make it a public exhibit is doubly difficult given that the founder of MHS was Governor Ramsey, the man who called for the extermination of the Dakota. But Gessner is no Polyanna—he realizes that MHS is a problematic organization for many Dakota people because of that connection.

"And then we ask them," Gessner says in a sort of self-mocking tone, "'So tell me about this noose—should we put it on display?'"

The noose was sent to the MHS seven years after the hanging and was accompanied by a letter from Captain J. K. Arnold, who served as adjutant at the hanging.[39] Arnold claims he cut the noose off Caske with plans to send it to the family of one of his alleged victims. After he cut it off he hid it under his coat and then under his bed. "If Arnold is to be believed," Gessner said, "then the noose in the MHS collection was used to kill Caske." Gessner tells me that it's made of three-strand rope, about ninety-five inches long, with one frayed end and the other tied into a four-turn hangman's knot. He also confirms that I can't see it.

In the summer of 2011 MHS gathered together a number of objects from their collections to show to historians as well as some Dakota representatives to get feedback for a planned exhibit to mark the 150th anniversary of the war. Gessner said that there was a range of perspectives, from those who believed it should be shown as a testament to history, to those who felt like you didn't need to show it in order to tell the story, to those who believed that the noose's very existence is why suicide rates are high among Dakota people. In the end MHS decided not to include the noose in the exhibit and to only allow certain Dakota people access to the object.

What will happen to the noose is unclear. Some Dakota people want to reclaim and, perhaps, destroy it.

Many feel a deep connection to the noose. A Dakota woman I spoke to named Sandee Geshick said she always had a hunch that the noose existed, and when she finally saw it she "felt deep sadness." The noose, she said, like anything used to kill another person, "has a curse attached to it if it isn't disposed of properly." When she saw that it was in the MHS collection, "I felt very bad for the people who took it and kept it. I think many others would say the same."

To Geshick and, perhaps, to other Dakota that noose is not viewed in the way that, say, the John Brown noose is viewed—as a relic connected to an important figure or simply as an artifact from an important event. Caske's noose is a material object imbued with a spiritual significance—like relics of Christ, for example—but unlike Christian relics, holding onto it is disruptive to Caske and, perhaps, to the Dakota community. That's a significant difference. For the Dakota that noose is not just a symbol of those who died—it is those people who died.

Geshick didn't say it should be destroyed, necessarily; she said that it must be disposed of properly and mentioned a ceremony called the Wiping of the Tears. It is a ceremony that comes usually after the loss of a loved one. A year is spent concentrated on living a good life and praying and grieving. Then there is the ceremony. "The person mourning has to move on because the deceased has to move on. The ceremony says it's time to move on with your life." The process is a kind of reconciliation with both life and death and is meant to take the person grieving to a place beyond anger and sorrow.[40]

Ultimately the US-Dakota War artifacts in the MHS collection are vestiges of a problematic colonial ideology to many Dakota people. Gessner hears that criticism and claims to be working to transform not only the image of MHS but also how and what the museum preserves. The noose controversy has taught him a lot because he's been forced to view this artifact from a perspective beyond the merely intellectual.

"The noose is an object that I've had to handle that I don't particularly enjoy handling." Gessner paused, caught himself, and chose his words carefully. "I'm trying hard not to speak for the Dakota people—it's not my place. But I've had this range of people who've said, 'I feel really bad for you.' Because I've had to handle the noose, and people who've actually taken me through a ceremony because I've had to handle it. Then I've had people say they feel bad or forgive the *rope* because that wasn't the reason the rope was created in the first place—somebody turned it into this weapon. There's a lot of very real compassion surrounding it."

Gessner says that typically museums are supposed to preserve objects in their collection. That's different from a traditional Dakota perspective, he says. For the Dakota stewardship could mean allowing something to degrade or, perhaps, feeding the object with sage and tobacco. It requires a completely different understanding, a different set of cultural lenses.

"Listen," he says, "you can be interested in something and read every book about it and even have academic discussions about it, but living it is something different. Sometimes history is lived. I've been exposed to a lot. Before I thought I had empathy, but now I think I'm starting to truly understand where people are coming from when they make certain statements—or I'm working on it."

A Minnesota historian named Carrie Zeman told me that she thinks there is a way for the museum to show the Mankato noose without sensationalizing it. She said she "tried to argue to them not that it wasn't an object of execution, but that there are other stories that the noose told besides 'I am an object that was used to kill people.' For example, there are stories about the rope used in the noose. We have the stories of the military people not having enough rope. And there was the story of Arnold taking the noose."

In a paper she wrote about the noose and other war-related curatorial controversies Zeman suggests a test of the authenticity of Arnold's story: get a coat like an adjutant general would have worn at the time and put the noose inside the coat.[41] Would it work? "If in fact this part of the claim seems improbable," she claims, "then it calls into question the other claims, like that the noose is Caske's. The big idea is to get exhibit-goers thinking about attributions: that claims about history can and should be tested." Ultimately, Zeman writes, "The story is the rope and spectacle, not the noose."[42] She wonders why the executions had to be such a spectacle, noting that authorities went out of their way to get enough rope and to engineer an enormous gallows. Indeed, in the narrative of changes in execution technology, the Mankato gallows is decidedly an anomaly.

So does displaying the noose revivify that spectacle? Does displaying it cause further harm to a community that's already had far more than its share? Is the noose necessary for the museum to tell this story? The noose isn't the only execution artifact of questionable authenticity and taste floating around. There's a cane with a dagger hidden inside, supposedly carved from the wood of the gallows.[43] And somewhere there's the axe that was used to cut the rope that held the gallows together and released the drops. Some have argued that it was at MHS and burned up in a fire in March 1881.[44] Others believe it ended up in a museum in the Northeast, perhaps at Barnum's.[45] But the strangest execution relic is a watch. In the wake of the execution someone cut off Caske's hair and turned it into watchband; it brings to mind the lamps supposedly made from the skin of Jews.

And then there's the beam. Apparently the Blue Earth Historical Society in Mankato has what, for a long time, some believed was a beam from the gallows.[46] It is nineteen feet long and seems to fit the description of the timbers used in constructing the gallows. The museum itself issued a statement in 2012 saying the only real proof they have that the timber is from the gallows is a letter from the guy

Standard Brewing Company beer tray. n.d. Photo by Bob Fogt; *used with permission of the University of Minnesota Press, from the collection of James and Ruth Beaton*

who donated it.[47] These are important questions in terms of historical accuracy, for those with the time and resources to answer them, but are they the *right* questions? Such research does not, ultimately, answer the difficult questions like, "What does it mean to kill another human being in such a mechanized fashion?" And it does not change the legacies of that history. It is wood. It is detritus. It is a rope. It is a knot. It is so much more.

"AS THE WHITE MAN COMES IN . . . "

The desire for revenge against the Dakota people was not sated by the deaths of thirty-eight Dakota men or by their removal to Crow Creek. In April 1863 a federal law called the Dakota Expulsion Act terminated all treaties with the Dakota people, thereby releasing annuity money and banning the Dakota from the state. (The law is still on the books.) The Ho-Chunk, or Winnebago, were also removed. For good measure, Governor Ramsey ordered punitive expeditions into

Dakota Territory, where many involved in the war had escaped, and announced bounties of between $25 and $200 for Dakota scalps. In July a farmer and his son shot and killed Taoyateduta (Little Crow) on his farm near Hutchinson and received $500 from the state of Minnesota. Taoyateduta was scalped and his body brought into town on a cart, where some kids tried to put fire crackers in his ears and nose.[48]

But most Dakota people stayed far away from the state, seeking refuge with Dakota communities in Canada. Among them were Dakota Chiefs Sakpe (Little Six) and Wakanozhanzhan (Medicine Bottle). They had been hiding out in Canada for several years when, in 1864, they were lured out of their hiding by two Canadians (eager to collect a reward), drugged with laudanum-spiked wine, chloroformed, tied to sleds, and then brought back over the border. It was, in a sense, a kind of extraordinary rendition. The Canadians handed over Sakpe and Wakanozhanzhan to Major Edwin Hatch at Pembina, Dakota Territory, and they were taken back to Fort Snelling. Like the other Dakota men before them, they had cursory trials, were found guilty based on hearsay testimony, and sentenced to hang.[49] Almost a year later President Andrew Johnson signed the death warrant.

The two chiefs were executed at Fort Snelling, a stone's throw from Bdote, where the Dakota originated, on November 11, 1865, in front of soldiers and citizens eager to view the execution of two more Dakota men. A newspaper report claimed that "they struggled but little and seemed to die easily. Medicine Bottle apparently retained vitality the longest, but both had their necks instantaneously broken by the fall, and could have felt no pain."[50] Apparently there was a relic frenzy: "The ropes with which they were hung were seized by the bystanders and cut in little pieces as relics. Those who could not secure one of these, cut chips off the gallows. Two fortunate individuals got the hats of the defunct chieftains, and their shoes, even, would have been taken, had a chance been allowed, so great was the demand for relics."[51] Two area doctors came and got the bodies.

There's an apocryphal story that on the way to the scaffold the two chiefs heard a train whistle blow and Sakpe was overheard saying to Wakanozhanzhan, "As the white man comes in, we go out." I asked Sheldon Wolfchild, a descendant of Wakanozhanzhan, about the meaning of that story. He answered me in one breath.

"Well, what they're saying is, 'We have been honest in our dealings from the beginning with the United States government. We kept our end of the bargain, our truth as a recognized government of the Dakota people. We have the integrity and understanding and the dignity and the respect to live up to agreements we sign. Now we're going to die after we hear the train coming, and all these people coming to where we originally started from. And we're going to die today because they, and their representatives, lied, cheated, and distorted the truth because they wanted the land. Now here we are, and we're going to be hung very shortly now. And so we'll go to the spirit world with our head held high, with respect because we kept our bargain, our truth in the eyes of the creator, the great spirit. We lived to the truth of what we said in that treaty. And the way we live and respect this earth is our truth. Now these people and the next generations coming on these trains have to live their lives with the knowledge that what they did was wrong. So I can go to the spirit world with respect because I lived up to my bargain, and they are going to have to live, generations to come and their offspring, with what their government did to the indigenous people of this country.' That's what they were thinking."

The lines on Wolfchild's wide, weathered face creased. This is something close to him, close to the surface, a part of his life. As he talked, he slipped from third person to first person. His great-great-great-grandfather became his grandfather, his father, his self.

The events of 1862 have a fostered a grave sense of loss, a perpetual trauma among many Dakota people, especially those living outside Minnesota. They are the exiles, the children of the diaspora. It became clear to me what this really meant as I drove through the Minnesota River Valley and on west into South Dakota—there are palpable, visible, obvious reasons. An insightful scholar I met in Mankato named Rick Lybeck told me again and again that "the material legacy" of that war reverberates still.[52] And I could see what he meant as I drove across a landscape that stretches and flattens, an occasional hill, but mostly farm as far as the eye can see. Enormous, otherworldly grain elevators that cough up their goods into waiting graffitied train cars, a seemingly limitless line of them, trundling forward and onward, awaiting the grain that will feed a nation, a world. These farms of America's Heartland, where buffalo once roamed, are sustaining the centers of capital.

One area historian named Ben Leonard gave me some stark numbers. "From 1850 to 1880 the population of the Minnesota Territory went from 6,000 to 776,000 white people," he told me. "In 1850 in the Minnesota Territory there were 150 farms, which means 150 barns with wheat fields, etcetera, but of course the Dakota were farming too. In 1880 there were 92,886 farms in Minnesota." This was a sea change not only in terms of the movements of human beings but also for the environment—acres of prairie and woods transformed into wheat fields. For the environment, for Dakota people, it was, Leonard said, "apocalyptic."

The scene of this apocalypse played out on my family's television as I grew up in South Carolina. Reruns of *Little House on the Prairie* played on a constant loop in my house, and as the baby boy with two older sisters, I was forced to watch it. As I drove across Western Minnesota I passed through Sleepy Eye and texted my sister Ellen, "I'm in Sleepy Eye." She replied, "Pa, will you take me on the run to Sleepy Eye." I texted back, "No Half-Pint, the run's too dangerous." Later, as I drove through Walnut Grove, pausing to take a photo of a huge mural depicting the pioneer days, Charles Ingalls seemed less innocuous, less quaint. For their efforts, the Charles Ingallses of the Great Plains gained, in many cases, land purchased for a song and, ultimately, an unparalleled generational wealth. In a Minnesota River Valley tourism brochure I picked up in the vestibule of my hotel, one page depicts carrots and tomatoes, peppers and potatoes, migrant workers tossing bowling ball–size heads of lettuce onto a truck. I turn the page and learn in a brief history of the conflict that if not for the "actions of a few," all of this would not have been lost to the Dakota.

The Dakota lost their buffalo, their seasonal migrations for rice and maple sugaring. The white settlers and their descendants gained a vast gastronomical conduit for a monoculture. The Dakota lost the place they call home, their spiritual center. The white settlers and their descendants gained a food culture centered on the worship of corn. The Dakota lost Mni Sota Makoce. The Dakota lost their ties. The Dakota lost much.

Today there are Dakota communities in Minnesota, South and North Dakota, Nebraska, and Canada. And people like J. B. Weston are trying to hold them together and hold on to what they can. Weston is a tribal historic preservation officer for the Flandreau Santee Sioux Tribe. He addresses tribal protocols and government regulations and works to address misrepresentations.

"When you drove in today before you came to the casino," he asks me, "did you see that wind farm?"

I did, in fact: enormous wind turbines along the South Dakota-Minnesota border. When the windmills were built, he says, workers uncovered many Dakota artifacts, artifacts that are culturally significant but that are now housed in museums elsewhere. Weston works to get artifacts like those back to the community, filing Native American Graves Protection and Repatriation Act (NAGPRA, passed in 1990 to help restore some of the lost cultures of Native Americans) claims and educating the public. He is working to bring the community, the culture back together. This is serious work—life and death work.[53] As we're talking he keeps looking over at two young women and one young man sitting in a booth near us. They look like they're up to something they're not supposed to be. Weston seems distracted by them or by something else. We move out of the bar and over to a little grill restaurant about ten yards away.

Weston is wearing a green hat, navy blue shirt, Lee jeans, and sneakers. He smokes a lot. Smoke. Pause. Smoke.

"You know, suicide rates are very high among the Dakota." And then it's quiet between us. This happens a lot. The conversation moves in fits and starts—well, not a conversation really. I'm quiet, listening.

He speaks in dribs and drabs, saying either what comes to him or maybe what he thinks I need to hear next. In the moment it seems alarmingly random, but when I look at my notes afterward, when I look for patterns, it makes sense.

"So you know," he interrupts the silence, "for you this is a story. For me this is every day. If you write this, I hope that it has a truth for my granddaughter." He gets up and goes to the grill and comes back with some scrap paper and a pen, starts drawing a picture illustrating all the reservation lands in the United States and then a sketch of North and South America. Pointing to the tiny swatch of land on those two continents, he says, "This is all we have left." He draws another picture illustrating how many Dakota people actually follow the ways of their culture, saying it is about 10 percent, that it wasn't until 1978 that Dakota people could legally practice their religion. Things are changing, but theirs is a long road. It's that disconnect—the people and their culture, the land and their culture.

"Do you know your tribe?" he asks.

I think about how to answer this and tell him that my family, the Shulers, came from a little speck on the map called Bibern in what's now called Switzerland. The family, led by a man named Hans Joerg Schuler, immigrated to South Carolina in 1735 with a group of Lutherans.

"I'm surprised you know that much. But do you know your *tribe*? Do you know your people before Christianity? Do you know them? Who they were? They had sacred spaces. Mountains. Rivers."

Tribe is original community. Foundation and bedrock. Something elemental and fundamental that I know nothing about. Tollund Man had a tribe. I glance around the casino, with its mesmerizing clichéd native-patterned carpet and that note played by the slots, somewhere in the key of C, sustained and ringing. A melodic anticipation of an imminent possibility. A buildup to nowhere and no place. In some ways this is a no place, a nowhere. There's a smattering of Native artwork in the hallways, a painting of a powwow on the wall in a hallway. A display case with images of various chiefs and pieces of arrowheads and pottery. There are more cowboy hats here than I've ever seen back East, but still there's nothing special about this building. Nothing real or sacred. I think about my tribe, whatever it was, whoever they were, resting on snowcapped mountains, summer-green meadows with lakes below. They are hunting the land, working through the landscape, in and of it. Silence. Kyle Rudolph has a fourth-quarter highlight reel–worthy catch and trots into the end zone. Viktor the Viking, the blonde-haired conqueror, parades around the field to the adulation of cheering fans. The Vikings win.

Weston has a warranted suspicion of people like me who come looking for a story. In one moment he is a schoolteacher critiquing my ignorance of Dakota culture, chastising me and telling me that this is more about me than it is about the Dakota. And then the next he's a motivational speaker or writing coach, coercing me to remember Caske's family, to remember the victims but also to write something that matters. "You have to put it in the context of putting it on yourself," he reiterates. "Have an impact. What you write should come from your gut."

And then, finally, he talks about the noose. It became a NAGPRA item, a burial item, when the knot was tightened, digging into Caske's flesh. Weston thinks the family should be able to make a claim for it. But how absurd, he says, that they have to use laws to get it back. Why was it there in the first place? Why did Arnold cut it and keep it? Who does that? The noose is another theft of land and lifeways. In this light and in this place I'm thinking about Tollund Man, displaying his body. It's not the same thing and it is.

Weston's telling me to get closer to the story I'm writing and to be honest with myself about what I'm doing. But he's also saying that this particular noose represents Dakota history and getting rid of it goes a long way to helping the Dakota move forward. That noose holds onto something that must be released.

"Where are those men?" he asks me. "You talk about that one noose, but it's much bigger than that. Thirty-eight nooses, but that was a man. That was a man. That was a man."

He says this pointing into the air with his cigarette at imaginary figures, at ghosts.

RELIC HUNTING

I wake up early the next morning. Columbus Day. A frost covers my rental car, and looking east, a red-ribbed sky nudges the day along. Oglala Lakota medicine man Black Elk spoke of "a good red day" and the "the red road . . . the road of good."[54] Today the red road is a pan-Indian concept meaning to be on the right path, to be going in the right direction.

I drive from Royal River Casino through downtown Flandreau and up Highway 13, crossing the ample bends of the Big Sioux River, beginning a four-hour dash back to Minneapolis-St. Paul Airport. I pass the cemetery where Weston told me Little Crow is buried. Dry corn in the fields, prairie grass hugging ditches. Ahead of me is a flat-bed with an enormous white blade, looking like some NASA project in rural South Dakota. I'm thinking about something Weston said: "What's the point of all of this? What are you doing? You'll finish this book and then write another." What's the endgame? What's the motivation? Political? Personal? Can I trace every strand of the knot from beginning to end? Is this about the knot or is this about me? I am becoming, I suppose, a relic hunter. A relic: a sacred object, human remains, a souvenir, the ghostly outlines of a practice, custom, idea. The word has Latin roots, meaning "to leave behind." It's related to the word "relinquish," which means abandon, surrender: a relic contains a part of a past that has been abandoned. Pilgrims embark on grand journeys to contact that which has been surrendered from that past, left behind.

But the noose hasn't been left behind at all—it's very much present, especially in South Dakota and at MHS. And yet I can't see the noose at MHS. I'm not supposed to see the noose. The story is my *not* seeing the noose. It remains offstage and off camera, a spiritual presence manufacturing plotlines and narratives that I can't readily access. There's something in that rope, in that noose, that's hanging on—a spirit, a force, a life. And maybe it's not for me to come close to, what's inside the rope, like the part of the rope covered by wrapping turns, the inner workings of the hangman's knot, what makes it function, what pulls it taut around the human neck. What's inside the rope makes it work. What's inside that rope holds on. What's inside the rope that is life and human wants freedom and air and light. In some ways for the Dakota that noose is not just a symbol of those who died—it is those people who died. Maybe I'm after what's inside the hands that hold the rope, that manufactures the noose, that makes the knot, that makes the death. Those two things—the noose and the noose maker.

A giant John Deere tractor barrels down the hill in front of me. After it passes I make a U-turn and gun it, passing the tractor on another decline. I want to go back to Little Crow's resting place to pay my respects. I turn off the highway and into a weed-choked field next to a dignified little white clapboard Presbyterian Church perched on a rise, cornfield beyond and the calm shine of the rising sun. I pull up the driveway leading to the church and get out. Surveying the small cemetery, I have no idea which one is Taoyateduta's. I don't have time for this. If I miss my flight, my wife will kill me.

The wind blows the lonely churchyard trees, and the dried corn stalks rattle gently. That's when I notice I'm not alone. An old yellow Bonneville with four passengers maneuvers the grassy road between the helter-skelter headstones and then quickly parks, engine idling while the driver, a squat Dakota woman, gets out and leaves a bouquet at one site, returns to the car, and drives away. The Bonneville barrels back down the road, turning left and looping out of the cemetery. Good idea. I hop back in my car and start driving around the cemetery, searching for the path that the Bonneville was on. Somehow this feels sacrilegious, like if my grandmother saw me doing this, she'd proclaim in her low-country drawl, "How tacky!" And I think of my wife at home with our two kids and keep circling.

And then I see a tall prayer flag fluttering in the breeze. Of course. I drive over, park, and walk up to the gravesite. It's reserved, reticent, reluctant. Like Taoyateduta, I suppose. The headstone underscores this. "Therefore I'll die with you." He knew what would happen. The war would be violent and it would only lead to more whites moving into Minnesota. Taoyateduta never really had a proper burial place until 1971, when the Minnesota Historical Society returned some of his bones (which they had among their artifacts) to his family. They buried his remains, over a hundred years after his death, in this innocuous cemetery outside Flandreau.

I get back in the car, turn around, and head back onto Highway 13. On the radio two commentators are talking about the markets—not Wall Street, of course, but soybean and corn markets. And then there's a recap of the news. Again the story of the Somali man, sending young Minnesota-born Somalis to Mogadishu to fight for al-Shabaab and twenty-one-year-old Bangladeshi Quazi Nafis trying to blow up the Federal Reserve in lower Manhattan, a violent echo chamber, questions open for answer and discussion. The day is becoming gray and windy. I can feel it in my gut.

LYNCHING

CHAPTER 8

Alone from a Tree: Lynching in the Post-Reconstruction South

SHERIFF WALDROP UNLOCKED DICK WOFFORD'S CELL in the middle of the night.[1] Outside the jailhouse, enveloped by the roar of cicadas, he and Wofford mounted horses to flee Columbus, North Carolina. Columbus is in Polk County, just over the state line from South Carolina. To the north and west of Columbus the Blue Ridge Mountains, covered in white oak and short-leaf pine, rise serenely from dense thickets of rhododendron and mountain laurel. In the cool of the night Waldrop and Wofford headed toward Asheville, a good forty-five miles away. They followed the Howard's Gap Road, although calling an old rutted wagon trail lined with poison ivy and Queen Anne's Lace a "road" is a bit of a stretch. What's more, it had rained a lot over the past few weeks, and in places Howard's Gap looked more like a bog than a road.[2] The over-mountain trek, skirting the Pacolet River, would be arduous, but it was the best option, the only option, if Waldrop wanted to keep Dick Wofford alive until his court date in November.

Dick Wofford was in double trouble. It was 1894, and he was a young black man accused of raping a white woman in the South. Sheriff Waldrop had kept lookout for several nights as impatient locals demanded that he relinquish his prisoner to them. Waldrop could sense where this was heading—those men gathering outside the jailhouse

159

every night wanted Wofford something fierce. So they fled to Asheville, where Wofford waited until his day in court came.

His trial began just as the last leaves were making their way to the earth. On Tuesday, November 20, the charges were read before the court—Dick Wofford was accused of raping Elizabeth Henderson on July 17, 1894. Jurors were selected, and the state brought forward three witnesses, including James Frank Henderson (Elizabeth's father), and the defense had five witnesses, including Wofford.[3] The day after witnesses appeared, the court reconvened, and a jury of white men found him not guilty of all charges. Many in the courtroom could hardly believe their ears.

The sheriff quickly released Wofford, pointed toward some woods behind the courthouse, and told the likely terrified young man to "cut dirt."[4] If not, he said, "He would be hanged by the people." Based on attempts made on Wofford's life the summer before, Sheriff Waldrop would have known by then that Wofford's best chance of

keeping himself alive was to quickly leave Polk County and not come back. For that reason Waldrop might have suggested he run toward Landrum, just over the border in South Carolina. The quickest route south would have begun along what's now called Peniel Road. But at some point Wofford, who was not too proud to heed Sheriff Waldrop's dreadful but necessary advice, cut through the woods and came out at a place locals call the Rock Cut, where the Southern Railroad slices

Railroad tracks looking south toward Landrum, South Carolina. *Photo by author*

through rock slightly north and west of Landrum and then keeps on chugging.

There he made his way onto the train tracks and no longer had to bushwhack. He must have felt some relief then as he walked along the tracks, as they ran straight and flat into the apparent safety of the town of Landrum.

At around three in the afternoon Wofford spoke to a white man in Landrum named Noah Carpenter and told him he felt safe now. Carpenter told him he best keep moving on or else that girl's friends and family would catch up with him. Wofford then went to a friend's house, a black man named Dan Odem, another mile or so down the railroad from town. About five hours later a posse was spotted passing through Landrum in hot pursuit—eager to get their hands on him. They found Wofford at Odem's house, tied him up, and carried him off into the night.

Early the next morning a black boy walking into town found Dick Wofford's body hanging from a wild cherry tree about a half-mile from the Landrum train station. Wofford had a noose around his neck, and his hands were tied behind his back. There were knife wounds beneath his left armpit and several slashes on his shoulders, and a pool of blood in the road near the tree suggested a struggle—that he didn't go quietly. But as Dick Wofford hanged from that tree, blood dripping from below his left arm, there was little left to hear but the occasional cricket and the creaking of the taut rope, the gentle movement of Wofford's body turning beneath the dark sky.

LYNCHING AFTER RECONSTRUCTION

As we saw in Chapter 6, before John Brown was sent to the gallows he warned the people of the South and of the nation that the "negro question" had yet to be settled but that it would be in due time. And yet even the Civil War did not answer that question. Slaves were freed, but the ideology that had fostered their bondage did not end after Gettysburg or Appomattox. It mouldered, like the bodies of Union and Confederate soldiers left in battlefields or like John Brown's own body, as the song goes.

During the Reconstruction period, generally considered to run from 1865 to 1877, the federal government sought to reform the southern states, even deploying the military when deemed necessary. During this period violence against black people in the former Confederacy increased dramatically. Freed slaves no longer fell under the protection, such as it had been, of their masters, and many white people believed federal law illegitimate because "outsiders" were imposing it on them.[5] What's more, many white southerners saw nearly four million black people suddenly transformed from personal property into potential economic and social competitors.[6] Institutions like the Freedman's Bureau, set up to provide services for and negotiate work contracts for former slaves, often proved incapable of standing in the gap between white and black southerners in any effective way when southern whites took the law into their own hands. So from roughly late 1865 to the early 1870s various groups like the Ku Klux Klan meted out summary justice across the South.[7] This insurgency, this Invisible Empire, as Albion Tourgée called them, intimidated, whipped, and murdered northerners, Republicans, and black people—indeed, anyone who might support or benefit from federal Reconstruction policies—into submission. The Klan and their supporters laid the foundation for Democratic control of the South and the eventual imposition of a white supremacist agenda popularly known as Jim Crow.

Although the Klan exhibited how vigilante thugs could terrorize those they wished to expel from "their" South, the Klan's actions and agenda don't completely explain the massive wave of violence that swept across the southern United States in the late nineteenth and early twentieth centuries, the first extensive period of lynching. There really is no good way to describe all the extrajudicial murder—to describe all the men, women, and children killed and those who permitted the killing. Many writers who tackle the subject admit the problem. Philip Dray writes that when he was working his way through the Tuskegee Institute's clippings file, an unbelievable and terrifying collection of newspaper clippings about lynchings, he was so overwhelmed and that he muttered the words "a holocaust" aloud.[8] Vann R. Newkirk ponders the lives cut short by mob violence, noting that these victims "were real people and that the incidents in which they lost their lives actually happened. Most had families, and since most were young one can only wonder what impact they or their offspring might have made on society."[9]

Some writers rely on the starkness of numbers to give the reader pause. Through their extensive and universally respected research, in 1995 sociologists Stewart E. Tolnay and E. M. Beck confirmed 2,805 lynching victims between 1882 and 1930 in the South, roughly 2,500 of whom were African American.[10] For greater perspective they note that "on the average, a black man, woman, or child was murdered nearly once a week, every week, between 1882 and 1930 by a hate-driven white mob."[11] Researchers at the Tuskegee Institute claimed in 1968 that there were 4,743 lynchings in the United States (3,446 blacks and 1,297 whites) between 1882 and 1968.[12] And in 1919 the NAACP, in their report *Thirty Years of Lynching in the United States*, cite a total of 3,224 lynchings in the United States (702 "White" and 2,522 "Colored") from 1889 to 1918.[13] Although the majority, about 75 percent, of those lynched from about the 1880s to the beginning of World War II were African American, other ethnic, racial, and religious minorities fell victim to Judge Lynch's court—Mexicans, Native Americans, Asians, Italians, and Jews.[14] Women and men, children and adults, white and black were lynched throughout the United States— in Alabama and Arkansas, Minnesota and Mississippi, Wisconsin and Wyoming. And there's no good way, no one way to describe a massacre such as this.

What we do know is that beginning in the 1880s many Americans lynched with impunity. This lynching epidemic peaked sometime in the 1890s and slowed down by the time of World War I. Mob violence came back in earnest in the 1920s and eventually declined in the 1930s. Some might argue that lynching never really went away—that it's a deep-rooted cultural technology and will always return occasionally. Like when members of the Ku Klux Klan murdered James Cheney, Andrew Goodman, and Michael Schwerner outside Philadelphia, Mississippi, in 1960. Or when, in 1998, James Byrd Jr., was dragged to death behind a pickup truck in Jasper, Texas. Or when, that very same year, Matthew Shepard was tortured and left to die on a fence outside of Laramie, Wyoming. But what lynching is depends on who you ask and when you ask them.

The term "to lynch" likely developed during the American Revolution.[15] The word has been connected to stories about either Charles Lynch or William Lynch, Virginians accused of using extralegal means to suppress British sympathizers. At first "to lynch" did not connote "to hang"—that would come later. For these men the whip, not the noose, was the preferred method of discipline, though one story of William Lynch's "lynch men" explains that they would often set a victim on a horse, bind his hands, tighten a noose around his neck, and attach the rope to a tree.[16] The horse might wander off and would, in a sense, become the executioner. But its earliest usages simply imply whipping or roughing someone up, perhaps with tar and feathers, and then sending her out of town."[17]

Almost half a century after the American Revolution "to lynch" someone still meant to rough someone up. For example, an 1827 article in the *Baltimore Gazette and Daily Advertiser* explained that "Lynch Law" is upheld when the "young and respectable members of the community, associate for the purpose of preserving morals" when "common law" does not.[18] The article noted that "the culprit is dealt with in manner and form as the Lynch law directs; which is to go in disguise, seize and blindfold the culprit, and take him to the neighboring woods, and whip him severely—then dismiss him with a promise to double the dose if he does not clear out." Thus, Washington Irving describes the practice as he saw it happen to an Osage man, a suspected horse thief, in his *A Tour on the Prairies* as "'Lynch's Law,' as it is technically termed, in which the plaintiff is apt to be witness, jury, judge, and executioner."[19] He writes that he suspects such actions to foster resentment and exacerbate tensions between native peoples and European settlers. Here, of course, the implication is that roughing up can lead to death. (It's important to remember here that concurrent with the development of the terminology for these extralegal executions was the movement to make legal executions private.)

Lynching, meaning extrajudicial executions, became fairly common in the South in the decades before the Civil War. Historian W. J. Cash believes that the antebellum South was "the home of lynching" in the United States.[20] The victims of southern antebellum lynching parties were often white people. Black slaves were considered valuable property and so, therefore, were (mostly) protected.

Most researchers in the twentieth century define a lynching specifically as an extrajudicial killing by three or more persons who kill someone illegally and claim to do so in service of justice or tradition.[21] Whatever lynching was (or is), lynchings were supported and endorsed by the communities in which they took place either through hands-on participation, public viewing, or the soft complicity of inaction. On many occasions the murderers were well known—they were not the hooded night riders of the Reconstruction era. Lynchers were anything but secretive about their work; many of them looked directly into the camera lens with the earnest belief that their actions were justified. Despite the common report by officers of the law that a lynched person died at the hands of "persons unknown," they *were* known; they were the butcher, the baker, the candlestick maker. Some have blamed lower-class dirt farmers for lynchings, but the evidence doesn't support that accusation—lynchers were from all walks of life.[22]

Though most often associated with the noose, lynching also involved victims being tortured to death (including genital mutilation), burned alive, or riddled with bullet holes. Those who were only hanged and not burned alive still suffered immensely. An account of the Memphis lynching of Lee Walker, who was hanged from a telegraph pole, asserts that "the Negro died hard. . . . The neck was not broken . . . and death came by strangulation. For fully ten minutes after he was strung up the chest heaved occasionally and there were convulsive movements of the limbs."[23]

Lynching victims were generally young, often the sons or daughters of the last enslaved Americans. Sometimes they were well known to the folks who killed them, but more often than not they were outsiders. Lynchings happened throughout the United States but were most likely to occur in the South. The Gulf Plain (from Florida to Texas) and cotton uplands (Mississippi, Louisiana, Arkansas, and Texas) had the highest lynching rates.[24] But the Appalachian Mountain region was a close third due in part to the rural nature of the area, with its poor communication networks and weak law enforcement.[25] In these places lynching was viewed as a method of enforcing law in order to protect whites. But even in places where the law was strong and resources plenty, a lynching was still rarely investigated, and when one was, the accused were rarely convicted. After the trial of thirty-one men in Greenville, South Carolina, accused of the brutal lynching of Willie Earle in 1947, an all-white jury came back to the courtroom with a verdict of not guilty. Judge J. Robert Martin then unceremoniously dismissed them without the customary "thank you" for their service to the state and to the justice system.[26] Such a protest was both brave and rare.

If one were looking to sketch a generic lynching story—though no such thing exists—the story of Dick Wofford might be a good model. It is a "generic lynching story" because Wofford was accused of the "usual crime," which in lynching parlance meant assault or rape of a white woman.[27] It is also a "generic lynching story" because there is little known and recorded about the victim or the crime for which he had been accused. And in the written record of the history of lynching Dick Wofford's has received little attention. When it was first documented recorders often got the date, cause of death, and, sometimes, his name wrong.[28] The details of Dick Wofford's death, like those of many "Unknown Negroes" murdered at the "hands of persons unknown," remain, for the most part, a mystery. Some of this mystery is due to a lack of primary sources and to the poor quality of those that do exist. Court records of Dick Wofford's trial reveal very little, and newspaper accounts of the lynching reveal biases. However, with close reading it is possible to uncover enough details to begin to construct what Dick Wofford's life must have been like in Polk County, North Carolina, in 1894 and the reasons for his murder.

ACCUSER AND ACCUSED

Much of what is now called Polk County was originally Cherokee hunting territory. The first white settlers were traders, swapping gun powder and alcohol for pelts with the Cherokee. Next came Scots-Irish immigrants, with a few English and Welsh for good measure.[29] Many colonists came to the area via Pennsylvania and Virginia, settling in the valleys (or coves, in local-speak) far from main roads and living isolated lives as yeoman farmers. Polk County was formalized as such in 1855, and the county seat was geographically central, a place to be named Columbus after Dr. Columbus Mills, the man who pushed for the county's formation. At the time of its formation there were only about six thousand people countywide.[30] The eastern and southern parts of the county were better suited to agriculture, but even those farms were on the smaller side; the area was never home to enormous plantations like you might see in the eastern part of the state or in the South Carolina Low Country. In Polk County there were just too many mountains and too few stretches of flat land. When the Civil War came, some of Polk's yeoman farmers signed up to fight for the Confederacy out of a sense of loyalty but later deserted when they decided it wasn't their fight.

That doesn't mean that slavery wasn't a part of life in Polk County. As early as 1782 tax records reveal at least 36 slaves in the area that eventually became Polk County.[31] By 1790 there were about 119 slaves with a total of nineteen owners.[32] From 1790 to 1850, because of changing boundary lines, it's difficult to pinpoint individual slave owners within what are now the county's borders, but by the 1850 Federal Census 572 slaves were living within the county.[33] The numbers indicate that most slave owners owned only a few people; "203 were owned by 49 different owners"—an average of about 4 each. Some farms had far more. The largest were home to 53 and 42 slaves, respectively. By 1860 the number of enslaved people in the county had increased, though not by much. In the year before Ruffin and the Cadets fired shots at Fort Sumter, there were 615 enslaved people, with 87 different owners; 399 of them were owned by 19 people.

Life was hard in Polk County after the Civil War. The county was a crossroads of sorts between mountains and the Piedmont, but there was little economic growth. Most people managed to live off of subsistence farms, with a little bit of cotton and corn raised as cash crops. Then there was talk of the railroad, of laying track from Spartanburg to Asheville, opening up the mountains, bringing economic progress. Initially the train was slated to run through Columbus, but that never happened. The train ended up running five miles southwest of Columbus through Tryon and up into the mountains on the Saluda Grade, the steepest railroad grade east of the Rockies. Much of this work was done by hand by convict workers, many of them African Americans. By 1877 the railroad linked South Carolina's ports to the mountains of North Carolina, Tennessee, and beyond.

The railroad offered new opportunities for employment—on the trains themselves and in the hotels and inns that started to spring up around Tryon. Those opportunities attracted many African Americans from the dead-end sharecropping of South Carolina. Some of those workers may have made their way to Columbus, but in 1894 the African American population there was relatively small, and thus, Dick Wofford's presence in the community is somewhat surprising. My initial thought was that he must have been the descendant of slaves from the county, and yet there are few African American "Woffords" in the county in postslavery census records. In 1880 there was only one African American Wofford family in Polk County, a Peter Wofford married to a Mary Wofford.[34] They had two children, neither of whom is named either Richard or Dick. (A fire destroyed much of the 1890 Federal Census, and there are no extant records for Polk County.) Perhaps, then, Dick Wofford was not originally from Polk County. Most likely his story begins in Spartanburg County, South Carolina. The report of his lynching from the *Spartanburg Herald* indicates that he had been working "a number of years over the line in Polk County at Tom Davis' saw mill," meaning on the other side of the border between North and South Carolina. Factories, railroads, and sawmills offered better pay and steady employment for a young black man like Dick Wofford. Thus, he may have gotten wind of a job in Columbus and made his way north from his home.

The location of that home or of his birthplace is hard to authenticate.[35] The 1880 Federal Census records offer two possibilities—two

Richard Woffords in Spartanburg County. The first is a Richard Wofford, a black male about eight years old from Glenn Springs. His father was a thirty-six-year-old farmer named either Milton or Mills; his mother was deceased, and he had four siblings. But then a Richard Wofford shows up again in 1900 near Pacolet, not far from Glenn Springs, in Spartanburg County. This could be the same Richard Wofford from the 1880 Census. If so, it's not the Dick Wofford who was lynched in 1894. The second possibility—and perhaps more likely—is a Richard Wofford living in the city of Spartanburg in 1880. This Dick Wofford was a five-year-old black male, the adopted son of Andy and Betsy Wofford, an older couple. And at some point in either his late teens or early twenties Dick Wofford hit the road and traveled to Columbus, looking for work.

Wofford had been there for at least two years before the 1894 trial. The spring 1892, fall 1892, fall 1893, and spring 1894 Polk County court records reveal he was brought before the court on a warrant.[36] Wofford could have been a career criminal, though there is no record of conviction to support this assertion. Or maybe Wofford was in debt or had been considered a vagrant, but there's no record to support this assertion either. It seems more likely that he was brought into court because the sheriff was rounding up suspects, and in 1894 any African American male would likely have been considered suspicious in Columbus.

For Dick Wofford life would have been complicated, dangerous even. He would have been cautious about his interactions with whites—careful about what he said, the tone of his voice, the direction of his glance. The social customs of Jim Crow existed in this border region of North and South Carolina in 1894, even if the legal frameworks did not. But those laws did come. In 1899 the state adopted voter restrictions—a literacy test, poll tax, and grandfather clause. By the turn of the century the Democratic Party dominated and foisted a white supremacist agenda onto the state that disenfranchised African Americans for decades.[37] But even before they lost the right vote, African Americans in Columbus, North Carolina, would likely have had very little power or influence.

In this climate Dick Wofford was accused of rape by a white woman. The *Spartanburg Herald* writes that his accuser was "an innocent and virtuous girl about eighteen years old named Lizzie Boad." That singular clause brought forth a host of images to the white southern reader's mind. Indeed, it would have led many to instantly assume Wofford's guilt. That's not too surprising. Like the gallows literature of the eighteenth and early nineteenth centuries, stories about lynchings were popular with readers—apparent revenge narratives, salacious details, and blood-stained bodies hanging from the limbs of oak trees added to the popularity of these accounts. Newspapers like the *Spartanburg Herald* were giving their readers what they wanted and, in doing so, were perpetuating the idea that the primary cause for lynching in the South was that black men were raping virtuous white women. This "folk pornography"—to borrow Jaqueline Dowd Hall's term—measured the "ideal" white woman against the "villainous" black man and played on popular notions about black sexuality.[38] This was part of a marked shift in racial stereotypes after the Civil War. Before the war the standard literary and theatrical stereotype of the southern black male was of the contented slave, the "happy darky" or Sambo. After the war and Reconstruction black men were more often than not portrayed as subliterate savages on the prowl for white women.[39] The message was clear—enslaved black men were pliant; free black men are dangerous sexual predators.

These stereotypes held sway in the North as much as they did in the South and were popularized by writers like Thomas Nelson Page and Thomas Dixon as well as by filmmaker D. W. Griffith of *The Birth of a Nation* fame. And they didn't go unchallenged. The pioneer critic of the widely held belief that black men were brutal rapists was Ida B. Wells-Barnett. Her muckraking exposed the horror of lynching as well as the fallacies of the standard arguments for why it was happening. Wells-Barnett mined newspaper reports and pointed to many cases in which white women were in consensual relationships with black men. In Elyria, Ohio, in 1892 a white woman accused a black man of entering her home, drugging her, and then raping her.[40] Later the man was put on trial, found guilty, and sent to jail for fifteen years. The woman later confessed she was lying—her neighbors had seen her invite the man into her home. In other cases the conclusions were more violent. In Tuscumbia, Alabama, before an African American man was lynched "for assaulting a white girl he told his accusers that he had met her there in the woods often before."[41] And in Larned, Kansas, a white woman "held at bay until daylight, without alarming anyone in the house, 'a burly Negro' who entered her room and bed. The 'burly Negro' was promptly lynched without investigation or examination of inconsistent stories."[42] Wells-Barnett also furnished evidence that rape wasn't the primary allegation against black men who were lynched. In her *Red Record* she lists a number of other reasons for lynchings in 1894, including suspected arson, stealing, murder and attempted murder, rape and attempted rape, train wrecking, enticing a servant away, barn burning, writing letters to a white woman, conspiracy, horse stealing, giving information, and conjuring.[43] In that year, she points out, more black men were accused of murder than of rape.[44]

But the real reasons didn't seem to matter. People believed what they did for entrenched historical, social, and psychological reasons, and the white press aided and abetted such rationalizations. In Shelby, North Carolina—just forty miles from Columbus—a newspaper called the *Shelby Aurora* was quite clear on the issue: black people must be controlled, and lynching is one way to do it. In an issue from September 20, 1894, a few months before Wofford's lynching, the newspaper published an article on its front page that gives one a glimpse into the popular sentiments of the day. The article, a reprint of an article from the *Richmond Dispatch*, chastises the English, who introduced slavery to the colonies ("while Virginians 'kicked' against it") and now criticize those who lynch in the United States. The article reads, "Perhaps with their aid and advice a compromise may be effected on the following basis—to wit: That if they will persuade the freedman to give up his besetting sin, the whites will pledge themselves to see that lynch law is abandoned at once and forever."

Edward Ayers writes that "the fear of black rape obviously triggered something deep within the psyche of the white South. Whites had long associated blacks with sexuality, however: why did that association suddenly erupt in a wave of lynchings in the late 1880s and early 1890s? In part, that crisis developed because a new generation of blacks and whites faced each across an ever-widening chasm."[45] There was an intense distrust and ignorance of each other, and thus, fear emerged. In this fashion white women were taught to fear black men and black men taught not to put themselves in a situation that could lead to such an accusation. This fear of black men, fostered by an eager press, could have led a young white woman to accuse Dick Wofford of raping her, even if it never happened.

The *Spartanburg Herald* calls Wofford's accuser Lizzie Boad. But there are no Boads in the 1870, 1880, or 1900 Federal Census of Polk County. We can assume, then, that the name in the newspaper was made up—either to protect her or the newspaper or both—and that the name in the court minutes, "Elizabeth Henderson," is the correct one. There are several Elizabeth Hendersons in census records to choose from, but the most obvious choice is the daughter of James Frank Henderson, who also happened to be a witness for the state during the trial. Henderson was a farmer, miller, and once served as justice of the peace.[46] During the Civil War he joined the Confederate army as a private and served under Stonewall Jackson; he was apparently with the soldiers who mistakenly shot Jackson at Chancelorsville leading to the subsequent loss of his arm. When the war ended he came back to Polk County, married Cynthia Mariah Hannon, and they had eight children—one of whom was named Nora (Bettie) Elizabeth Henderson.

Elizabeth Henderson was born on November 10, 1877, on a farm about four miles south of Columbus proper.[47] Interestingly, Henderson was married to a man named Taylor Alfred Sims on September 1, 1894, just weeks after Wofford was accused of assaulting her. There's no record of witness testimony, so we can only imagine why jurors came to the decision they did. One hypothesis is that he was innocent and the jurors believed him. Dick Wofford and Elizabeth Henderson could have been in a consensual relationship and maybe things ended badly. Maybe she cried wolf out of anger or to protect herself, given that she was about to be married. That the two were in a relationship isn't a stretch—nor was it uncommon, as Wells-Barnett pointed out. But it was supremely problematic for white women to be discovered in such a relationship: it was okay for white men to sleep with black women, but for white women to do the same was unimaginable.[48] For a white woman caught in the act, crying rape was one way out.[49]

After ten years of marriage and five children, Elizabeth and Taylor separated. She lived with her children outside of Columbus for a short while and then worked in mills throughout upstate South Carolina. She moved back home eventually and married again, this time to Frank Giles. When her mother died from cancer in 1913, she assumed responsibility for her father, whose health was beginning to fail.[50] On March 16, 1921, she wrote to the National Soldiers Home in Hampton, Virginia, that her father "has lost his mind and is almost deaf and has no one to attend to him."[51] A letter was sent to her on March 18 that he should come as soon as possible, to bring his army discharge and pension certificate. He died on April 25 and never made it to the home. Elizabeth died on March 25, 1922, of cancer, almost a year after her father. She's buried in a beautiful cemetery next to Green Creek First Baptist Church, about ten miles east of Columbus, with a view of the grassy foothills and a hint of the mountains beyond.

PROBABLE CAUSE

Like many lynchings, there's no evidence that Dick Wofford's was ever investigated. Authorities from Spartanburg County likely didn't see it as their problem, and because it happened over the line, it was out of Polk's jurisdiction. The vivid description of Dick Wofford's body, written by the *Spartanburg Herald* writer, is all we have to work with. One of that writer's assertions is that the lynchers wanted to bring him back to Polk County. But why? Did they wish to torture him? Did they wish to take care of him in their own neck of the woods in order to avoid being charged in South Carolina? And who were the lynchers? Elizabeth Henderson's family? Her new husband's family? Without a doubt those who killed Wofford were angry about some perceived injustice. But according to court records, Wofford was cleared of charges for the supposed rape. Could he have been lynched for another reason?

Economic stress might also lead to resentment among poor whites of a black man in their midst willing to work for low wages.[52] Polk County was likely affected tangentially by the downturn in cotton prices that was hurting parts of North and South Carolina in the 1890s, and economic downturns often led to crime waves, including lynchings.[53] Perhaps local whites resented Dick Wofford's employment at Tom Davis's sawmill, coupled with his outsider status. Or perhaps Wofford was discontented with his pay and demanded more from his boss. Especially in the cotton belt, violent suppression was a useful tool for coercing disgruntled African American workers—and lynching was the extreme use of violence.[54]

But there's no evidence that Dick Wofford was an angry employee. Somehow, some way, Dick Wofford crossed a line that white folks in Columbus didn't want black men to cross. Like white people across much of the South, they desired at any cost—even human life—a social if not legal framework that replicated the racial control inherent in a slave regime. Just because Polk County was never the center of slavery that Charleston County, South Carolina, was doesn't mean that people in that community didn't share a similar ideology. Eric Foner notes that "slavery affected society everywhere in the South and even mountaineers shared many attitudes with planters, beginning with a commitment to white supremacy."[55] This commitment was underscored when the Ku Klux Klan emerged in North Carolina around 1867 and was especially popular in mountainous counties like Yancey and Rutherford (Polk's neighbor to the east).[56] Membership reached about 40,000 in the state during Reconstruction and included all classes and regions. And North Carolina was never immune to lynching; in fact, between 1865 and 1941 168 North Carolinians were lynched.[57] In

1893 the state made lynching a felony, demanded sheriffs secure their jails, and made counties liable.[58] But those laws didn't change things a whole lot; indeed, many sheriffs loathed the prospect of shooting at friends and neighbors.

And yet Dick Wofford was lynched on the southern side of the North and South Carolina border and, thus, was also bound up in the contentious politics and race relations of that state. The fact that his death was, at best, underinvestigated points to the legal system's tacit acceptance of vigilante justice. Things weren't any better for black people in South Carolina in 1894. In fact, they may have been worse. The upstate of South Carolina, the foothills of Appalachia, had a long history of Klan activity, especially in Spartanburg County where Wofford had been lynched. Spartanburg was one of nine counties in South Carolina that President Grant had placed under martial law in October 1871. Though its power had waned greatly, the Klan's model of freelance justice lingered in the upstate; there were twenty-four lynchings in the state of South Carolina from 1890 to 1894, and a third of those took place in the northern corner of the state.[59] Across upstate South Carolina there was a spike in violence in the 1890s, a prob-

Reenactment of Ku Klux Klan in North Carolina. *Engraving made from 1870 photograph by US Marshal J. G. Hester*

lem exacerbated by a culture of feuding in the foothills. An especially hostile and law-breaking area was nicknamed the "Dark Corner" and sat just over the line from Polk County, North Carolina, and Spartanburg County, South Carolina, in Northeast Greenville County.

At the time, "Pitchfork" Ben Tillman was governor of South Carolina. A populist and "friend of the working man," Tillman also had a complicated relationship with lynching and violence in general, walking the line between a business elite who wished to bring business to South Carolina and the poor working classes. In 1892 Tillman famously declared, "Governor as I am, I would lead a mob to lynch the negro who ravishes a white woman."[60] Though, earlier, in his inaugural address, he claimed he wouldn't tolerate lynching and would forever uphold "the majesty of the law."[61] This is the message moneyed classes wished to hear, many of whom feared that the spectacle of lynching would scare away northern investors and black workers.[62] Stephen A. West points out that for many in the large towns and cities in South Carolina, lynching was an affront to their sensibilities, a violation of law, and definitely something with roots in the lower classes.[63] For these reasons it should be controlled. They were "anti-lynching but hardly anti-racist."[64] With equal parts New South and white supremacist, it's uncertain which message his audiences digested.

But Dick Wofford was lynched by a party from North Carolina, and in the year he was killed there were three other lynchings in the Tarheel State.[65] Lynching had become the ultimate cultural technology whites had at their disposal for controlling black people. Before the war slave codes governed black people's movements, access to information, and, in general, the ways in which black people could act in the public sphere. After the war a new world emerged, and whites felt the need to assert their authority anew. By 1896 the US Supreme Court made "separate but equal" common parlance and the law of the land.[66] But it is important to note how closely blacks and whites were connected in the South before and after that decision. The lives of white and black people in the South were connected and disconnected in complicated ways. In rural areas there tended to be closer contacts—"Rural roads, country stores, and cotton gins were not segregated; hunters and fishermen respected rules of fair play, regardless of race."[67] Black people and white people came together at corn shuckings, to help each other when sick, when babies were born, and, sometimes, as Wells-Barnett points out, in the bedroom. Despite all of this seeming goodwill, the reality on the ground for African Americans in the South was more complicated, that in an instant they could become the victims of unspeakable violence and that in big and small ways they were second-class citizens. The terror of the noose and the daily indignities African Americans suffered in the South imposed a quiet and horrible discipline.

The fact that we know exactly where Elizabeth Henderson was buried says a lot about history, about what and who gets remembered. There's no headstone with Dick Wofford's name on it that I could find, but scattered about the Columbus, Landrum, Tryon, area are places—or hints of places—that would have been around in Wofford's day. When he was last seen in Landrum, Wofford spoke to a white man and told him he'd just come across the woods from Columbus, that he'd walked along the train tracks into town beginning at the Rock Cut—that place still exists. About a mile south of Landrum, where Greenwood Road connects with Highway 176, is a new bridge, built in 2001, that crosses what locals call the Rock Cut. If you walk out on the bridge in the winter, you can see clearly the work that must have gone into building this place. But on the summer afternoon I visited, trees draped in kudzu covered much of my view of the tracks below. A storm was rolling over the mountains to the west of me, the Blue Ridge amplifying the thunder in the distance. I walked about twenty feet into the woods, closer to the rock's edge. I stopped and listened and looked. Around me it was quiet except for the occasional whoosh of a car back on the highway. It was cooler in the woods, and soon the rain would come.

FINDING THE STORY

Today Columbus is the first stop in North Carolina for drivers heading northeast on I-26 from South Carolina. From the interstate Columbus doesn't seem like much—the usual conglomeration of chain stores and eateries that typically greet drivers as they enter and exit most American interstate highways. A Waffle House, a menagerie of gas stations, a couple of grocery stores, a McDonalds, and a former Hardees repurposed as a Mexican restaurant. A half-mile from the interstate exit is "downtown" Columbus, a short strip of stores, many of which have seen better days. A pizza joint, a bar, a hardware store, and—one sign of the changing demographics of North Carolina and the southeastern United States—a Mexican *tienda*. Columbus is like a lot of little towns in the mountains of North Carolina—for many years relatively poor and lily white. That's changing as more and more migrant workers stay put. Slowly but surely they are transforming the demographics and culture of these communities. The tension between these immigrants and whites who've long resided here isn't obvious, but a crude poster I saw in the yard of one house spoke the possibilities. "Wake up America! Impeach Obama," the poster read, with the word "Osama" scratched in above the surname. Despite the tepid welcome, Columbus's newest citizens are very visible—working in stores, walking down streets, or smoking cigarettes in front of the Polk County courthouse. The courthouse itself rests amidst a green square peppered by an assortment of memorials to Columbus's soldiers who died in various wars. The building itself is a modest but stately Greek Revival building topped by a white cupola, its bricks baked by slaves as it was being built in 1857.[68]

I went to Columbus because I was looking for the story, looking to see whether someone had ever heard of Dick Wofford. I talked with a secretary in the Clerk of Court's office who let me comb through some old records. She had never heard of Dick Wofford or the lynching and said there were no records of trials from that long ago in the building. She asked around the office, and someone suggested I try the county museum a block away.

When I walked into the Polk County Historical Society's museum, it was empty save for me and a helpful docent named Anna Conner. I explained my research and what I'd discovered thus far. She seemed a little surprised at first, but curious. Conner told me she didn't think too much about race when she was growing up. "There were black communities, but they were totally isolated. Even when I was growing up in the forties and fifties, I never really had a conversation with a black person until I went to college in Greensboro." She grew up in Columbus, and her family, on her father's side, has been here since the 1760s. She remembers an isolated, insular community when she was growing up. She laughs, "My family called anybody who wasn't from Polk County a Yankee!"

About fifteen years ago Anna Conner started writing a book on the history of the nearby town of Tryon, and during that process she began to understand her community. Now she's obsessed with its history. Her research has taught her a lot. For one, she says, "You can't trust most sources. You have to find as many as you can and go with your best guess. People always see events differently." I showed her my sources—the newspaper articles, court records, and a list of Woffords I'd found who lived in Columbus at that time. Looking at the list, she quickly told me all of these Woffords were white because they were buried in white cemeteries. Her best guess is that Dick Wofford wasn't from Polk County, that he was here for work.

"Now, who was the accuser?" she asks.

I told her that according to newspaper accounts she was an eighteen-year-old woman and the *Spartanburg Herald* calls her Lizzie Boad but the court transcript refers to her as Elizabeth Henderson. Based on records and local names, we both agree that "Lizzie Boad" was likely made up. "But Henderson, I'm related to some Hendersons." I mention that her father was James Frank Henderson. "Well, then," she says, "we're related."

Elizabeth Henderson and her ancestors, Anna Conner told me, were well connected to one of Polk County's seminal events, the Battle of Round Mountain.[69] When Europeans began settling in the area, they slowly but surely encroached upon Cherokee territory. In 1767 Sir William Tryon met with Cherokee leaders and brokered a treaty. But for the most part settlers either ignored such treaties or didn't know about them in the first place. When the war with Great Britain began, things got complicated, especially for colonists siding with the Revolutionaries. They were stuck between the English in occupied South Carolina and the Cherokee in the mountains to the west.[70]

As war broke out in 1776, the Cherokee attacked a number of families in western North Carolina. One of those families, that of William Hannon, lived near the Pacolet River, just down the road from what became Columbus. Family members were working in the fields when the Cherokee attacked, and all were killed except for young Edwin Hannon (five generations back for Conner), baby William Jr., and Winnie Hannon. They raced into the woods and followed the river to the safety of another settler's home. After the Hannon Massacre, as it is often referred to, the local militia went after the Cherokee. They were led by a young man named Thomas Howard and a Cherokee guide named Skyuka, who led the militia straight to where the Cherokee were camping on nearby Round Mountain. Under the cover of darkness they slaughtered most if not all of the Cherokee. Because it links Polk County to the American Revolution, it is the source of much consternation and hearsay and many, many local legends. One such legend is that Skyuka was later found hanging from a sycamore tree at the base of Tryon Peak, killed by either British Loyalists or the Cherokee.

In her autobiography, Polk County native and jazz legend Nina Simone tells a different, if not totally historically accurate, version of the Battle of Round Mountain. Nina Simone's version takes place in 1855 when, she writes, "some white settlers and the last band of hostile Indians left hiding out in the mountains. The settlers won, captured the Indian chief and hung him from the nearest tree."[71] The hanged "Indian chief" was called Skyuka. Later, when the railroad was built and a town for workers sprang up just north of Landrum, South Carolina, people debated what to call the new settlement. "Someone suggested that they call it Skyuka after the lynched Indian chief, but the older folks didn't take to the idea of naming the town after a man they had once set swinging from a tree."[72] Even if the dates and details of her story are off, there's a lot of truth in it. Most people don't want to address their own violent past, try to understand it, or make amends for it. What's more, Nina Simone seems to side with Skyuka, and thus, she captures the way many African Americans in the Jim Crow South (like the boy who first discovered Dick Wofford's hanging body) understood their own precarious place in the world and the haunting presence of the noose in their lives.

THE DESCENDANT

Before I left the museum Anna Conner suggested one more possible lead. Elizabeth Henderson's granddaughter, Bernice (Bee) Tompkins, lives just down the road in Tryon, she told me. After a few e-mails and phone calls I was at the doorstep of her brick condo, with an "Obama for President" sign displayed in front. With a smile and a handshake she welcomed me inside her home. At the time I interviewed her she was ninety-three years old and suffering from glandular cancer, but you wouldn't know it because she's so vivacious, so smart and incisive. Bee grew up in Polk County but moved away as a child. Later she married her teenage sweetheart, and the couple ended up in New York City, where she taught in the public schools and sang in the Riverside Church choir for thirty-one years.

I asked Bee about the story of Dick Wofford, and she soon spread out photos and family history books on a coffee table for me to look through. She picked up one photo of a woman surrounded by five children. "Now this is the woman we're talking about—Betty. And this is my mother," she said pointing. "Now Betty had twins, Heddie and Haddie—my aunts—and they were born July 3, 1901. And Heddie died on January 11, 1902, of shaken baby syndrome. I didn't learn this until about six months ago. I'm a genealogist, and you take the bad with the good, but I think this Taylor Sims, he's my grandfather, he might have been involved with this lynching, and he might have been involved with this baby's death."

Bee said that stories about Taylor Sims and his nasty reputation and likely alcoholism were passed down in her family. She assumed that this is what contributed to Betty divorcing him in 1903. "I still hold her in high regard," she said emphatically, "because she had the guts to divorce this man." Not only that but she struck out on her own, working in the appalling conditions of South Carolina mills and then, later, selling moonshine on the sly in order to keep her family afloat.

Bee was only three years old when Elizabeth Henderson died, but she still has some memories of her. "Betty gave me a necklace with a locket on it that she wanted me to have. And when I started the first grade down here in the Green Creek Elementary School I wanted to wear it. And my mom said, 'No, you'll lose it!' Well, I insisted and insisted and wore it to school. And sure enough, I lost it, and lost one of my connections with my grandmother."

We chatted some more. I learned a lot about Bee and her family, her passion for genealogy, for knowing where she comes from. I also got the sense that she's an infinitely humane and kind person. And she is the offspring of someone wrapped up in such violence.

"I think the fact this black man was found not guilty inflamed relatives, and that's how he ended up dead," she speculated. "I regret the death of anybody, and I regret very much the death of black people at the hands of very biased white people." The story, she said, makes her very sad but also curious and desirous of some sort of reconciliation with it: Why did it happen? Why did it happen the way that it did? "I'm just glad," she lamented, "that Dick Wofford had time, if even a little, to live with that 'not guilty' verdict. At least he had that."

Before I left, Bee told me she'd show my research to the one person from the Sims side who might know something about what happened. I was eager to hear the results. But, then, months later Bee told me that the woman had died before she could talk with her about it. So, perhaps, the truth has been buried too. I think about that photo Bee showed me. Despite its poor quality, it's quite telling. Elizabeth Henderson and her children all dressed in their Sunday best. Three children in the front row look directly into the camera. And the children on the second row, two girls, don't look into the camera at all; they stare off to the right. Elizabeth is also on the second row. Maybe it's the poor quality of the image, but it's hard to tell where she's looking. She could be looking to the right like her daughters or directly at the camera. Or maybe she's looking upward, above the camera, into the heavens or beyond.

CHAPTER 9

A Story of Hands:
An Early Twentieth-Century Lynching
in the American Midwest

IN THE FIRST FEW DECADES OF THE TWENTIETH CENTURY more Americans were visibly fighting for an end to the lynching epidemic: activists like Mary McLeod Bethune and Walter White continued the work that Ida B. Wells-Barnett had begun, actively pursuing national legislation to protect Americans from vigilante justice. They were armed with a growing body of scholarship aimed at trying to understand and offer solutions for this horrific phenomenon.[1] One of their greatest weapons was to record and tell lynching stories. In 1937 one such story was read into the record of the US House of Representatives amidst a floor debate about an antilynching bill.[2] The story was horrific: two African American men who had pleaded not guilty to a murder were taken from local law enforcement by a mob of some two hundred people, tied to a tree, tortured with a blow torch, and then shot in Duck Hill, Mississippi. And yet that bill did not pass.

By the beginning of World War II, though, there were fewer and fewer lynchings. Some have suggested lynching died out because of a combination of opposition in the press, the rise of advocacy organizations (like the white-led Association of Southern Women for the Prevention of Lynching), the New Deal, radio-dispatched law enforcement, African American resistance, and migration.[3] But by no means did the practice disappear completely. And curiously, lynching in the first half of the twentieth century was in some ways more visible, as technologies developed that shaped how and where people were killed. Railroad tracks were used to batter down jail doors. People were dragged behind automobiles. People were hanged from telephone and telegraph poles.

Most importantly, though, technology made it easier to document a lynching. This was the heyday of the lynching photograph and the lynching postcard. Indeed, the brazenness of the lynchers and their supporters, who often look directly into the camera lens, is captured for posterity in photo after photo from this era, some of which became postcards and were mailed around the United States.

The knots, the nooses, tied by the hands of murderers stand out in these images in a telling variety of forms. In some cases it seems like the victim was killed and then hanged; lynch victims were often shot, burned, or beaten before being strung up for public display. In those cases, it seems, the knots are quick, haphazard, inelegant, and utilitarian. But this is the first time I begin to see an abundance of hangman's knots, though not always. For example, in the ninety-eight lynching images in *Without Sanctuary*, a book based on the lynching photograph collection of James Allen and John Littlefield, I count about thirty hangman's knots (Knot #1119) or attempts at forming them. I'm reminded of Don Burrhus's assertion that the knot is a tuxedo, an elegant knot to tie for killing someone. It's clear in many of these lynching photographs that the kind of noose used doesn't really matter.

One of the hangman's knots is in an image of Leo Frank, a Jewish man lynched by a Georgia mob in 1915. Frank had been convicted of murdering a thirteen-year-old factory worker named Mary Phagan in a trial that was considered a miscarriage of justice. When Georgia Governor John Slaton commuted Frank's sentence, a mob kidnapped him from prison and hanged him. The photo reveals a noose formed from a sturdy piece of manila rope, laced through the fork of a tree.[4] Before he was hanged he was made defenseless: his legs were bound by

The lynching of Leo Frank.

a square knot and his hands cuffed. Then a noose was placed around his neck. The knot only has five wrapping turns, which could explain why his head arches back rather than being forced to the side. Among the men who lynched him there must have been someone with at least rudimentary knowledge of rope work, someone who knew how to form a knot akin to the hangman's noose. Close examination also reveals that the rope was a bit frayed and that someone had tied a crown knot to stop the fraying.

The knot and rope say something about the lynching itself, a combination of slap-dash and professional, of planned and spur of the moment, of emotion and intellect. But in the moment of the photograph the quality of the knot and rope don't seem to matter anymore. The mob has done its work. Leo Frank hangs in suspended animation, and the lynchers stand near the tree. The hands of the men on the far left and far right of the frame are hidden behind their backs. Most of them wear white shirts and hats (newsboys and boaters), but one man on the right side of the photo stands out. In overalls and rumpled hat, his arms are crossed. His face is stiff and stolid. All of my prejudices boil up—"redneck," "ignorant hillbilly," "cracker." But others in the photo wear ties and fine hats—the classes, the "good" people of the community of Marietta, Georgia, united by race and religion.

A LYNCHING IN THE HEART OF IT ALL

It's important to remember, though, that not all lynching victims were black and not all lynchings took place in the American South. There were willing hands elsewhere. Sherwood Anderson's classic short-story cycle *Winesburg, Ohio* begins with a story called "Hands." The story recounts a visit between Anderson's protagonist, an earnest young journalist named George Willard, and one of George's acquaintances, a man named Wing Biddlebaum. "The story of Wing Biddlebaum," Anderson writes, "is a story of hands. Their restless activity, like unto the beating of the wings of an imprisoned bird, had given him his name."[5] Wing is obsessed with his hands. As he chats with George he alternates between exposing them and hiding them—they are a source of both pride and shame. Although his hands have made him the most prodigious strawberry picker in town and this is how he earns his keep, his hands also caused his fall from grace. Wing was once a beloved schoolteacher in a rural Pennsylvania town, defamed when he is wrongfully accused of sexually abusing a young boy. When the boy's father heard his son's charges he raced over to the school and pulled the teacher outside and assaulted him. As the students watched, the father yelled, "I'll teach you to put your hands on my boy, you beast."[6] That night the schoolteacher heard a knock at his door. He opened it, and standing there was a posse of men. One of them carried a rope. "They had intended to hang the schoolmaster," Anderson writes, "but something in his figure, so small, white, and pitiful, touched their hearts and they let him escape."[7] The schoolteacher ran away, changed his name from Adolph Meyers to Wing Biddlebaum, and moved to Winesburg, Ohio, to live with an aunt. Wing was, from thence forward, fearful of human touch and connection; he lived a mostly solitary existence. Wing also developed the unusual tic of constantly revealing and then hiding his hands.

Hands come up a lot when people talk about lynching, that crime that most often resulted in the death of someone "at the hands of persons unknown." Hands grab. Hands push and pull. They turn and tussle. They whip and maim and cut and bruise. Hands light fires and fire guns. Hands tie knots. Like knots, though, hands also have life-affirming qualities. Handshakes or pats on the back reinforce human bonds. Hands come together, work together, build together. Wing's own escape from the hands of his accusers and tormentors took him into the safe hands of his kin, an escape, a movement west that was repeated again and again in the nineteenth and early twentieth century by people wishing to start life anew. Like Wing, they flew to new and apparently idyllic Midwestern cities and towns like Anderson's imaginary Winesburg.

There are many such towns. Today they are spread around the Midwest like forgotten children. People are moving away from these towns. The most recent Federal Census indicates that growth rates in Midwestern states like Ohio, Michigan, Iowa, and, to a lesser degree, Indiana have dropped compared to states in the southeastern United States.[8] And yet the names of these towns still resonate with hope—Utopia, Felicity, Liberty Center, Goodland, Loveland, Arcadia, Rising Sun, Mount Zion. This is a geography of hope. The names mark places where people went with ideas and dreams, with hatchets and saws. People from the coasts, from Europe, from the South traveled to the great Middle West of the United States and were called "pioneers," "settlers," "homesteaders," "immigrants"—idealistic men and women imbued with a sense of purpose to make the world anew or, more simply, to make a dollar.

But at times it seems these impossible towns lost their bearings. Lynching was, of course, not only a southern disease; it was a national one, and the Midwest was not immune. In 1919 when the NAACP reported that of 3,224 known lynchings that took place from 1889 to1919, approximately 373 occurred in non-southern states. There were at least 12 in Ohio, 19 in Indiana, and 24 in Illinois.[9] Public spectacle lynchings took place in Cairo, Illinois; Duluth, Minnesota; and Springfield, Ohio—events that brought thousands to the street to watch and witness. Even in this geography of hope, people did such things.

They did them in places like Newark, Ohio, just a ten-minute drive from where I teach. Newark is the seat of Licking County, about forty miles from Columbus and just east of the center of the state. In 1910 the central conflict between the city and the county was alcohol. Two years prior the Ohio General Assembly passed the Rose County Local Option Law that allowed each county to choose to go dry or not. (This legislation was pushed by the Westerville, Ohio–based Anti-Saloon League and the Woman's Christian Temperance Union, also based in Ohio.) But Newark's economy was closely linked to alcohol. At one time Newark was supposedly the largest producer of beer bottles in the world.[10] One glass bottle factory in Newark alone, the American Bottle Company, employed about twenty-five hundred workers. And many of Newark's immigrants came from countries with drinking cultures, where going to a saloon after work was routine. In the end Licking County voted dry while Newark voted to stay wet. But the sentiments of the city dwellers didn't matter; the county-wide law went into effect, and shortly thereafter the booze trade shifted gears and unlicensed speakeasies popped up where the saloons had been. There were about eighty saloons in Newark, most of them in the downtown area. Everyone in Licking County knew what was going on; even the chief of police and the mayor were in on it. Indeed, as Sloane Gordon writes, "Vice and crime became arrogant."[11]

Prohibitionists formed a "Law and Order League" to crack down on the saloons, and according to local appearance dockets, people were brought up on charges of violating the law. But saloon keepers and their lackeys harassed those who went after them, and some judges feared for their lives. The Law and Order League contacted the Anti-Saloon League, and lawyer Wayne B. Wheeler got involved. He hired some detectives from Cleveland who mingled with the saloon crowd and collected evidence of corruption and law breaking. On July 3, 1910, a brief story showed up on the front page of the *Newark Advocate*: "Affidavits May Be Filed in Granville." The story claimed that plans were being made to issue warrants and that raids on saloons would likely happen the coming Saturday. And yet life chugged along. As Ray Stannard Baker put it in the *American Magazine*, "Nothing extraordinary had ever happened to disturb the even life of Newark; it was an ordinary, typical, prosperous, American town, like yours or mine. . . . And yet in this very town, on the afternoon of the eighth of July, through the smooth crust of civilization, burst quite suddenly a sort of molten savagery."[12]

There are many versions of what happened the morning of July 8, but all of them begin with a group of detectives filtering into downtown Newark. One of these detectives was a young white man from Willisburg, Kentucky, named Carl Etherington. Some said he was a former Marine, that he had once worked as a strikebreaker, and that he was twenty-two years old.[13] Etherington was actually only seventeen years old and had been discharged from the Marines with "good character" but poor physical condition about a year earlier, and he was quite new to the detective business.[14] Etherington and the other detectives gathered on the steps of the Licking County Courthouse, where Mayor E. J. Barnes of nearby Granville deputized the men and handed out warrants and instructions to raid a number of saloons. Barnes's Granville was a prohibitionist stronghold, and around 1910 Granville was only about fourteen minutes away on the Interurban railroad.[15] Before getting involved in the prohibitionist struggle, Granville played a significant role in the fight to end slavery. Fiery abolitionist Theodore Weld lectured there more than once, and a branch of the Underground Railroad passed through the village. One ardent abolitionist was Ashley Bancroft, whose son, Hubert Howe Bancroft, became one of the most important nineteenth-century American historians and authored many books, including the 1887 *Popular Tribunals*, a two-volume defense of the lynch-law justice of the San Francisco Vigilance Committees of the 1850s. Bancroft wrote, "The vigilance committee is not a mob; it is to a mob as revolution is to rebellion, the name being somewhat according to its strength."[16] In other words, when there's a critical mass, a rebellion becomes a revolution; a mob, a committee; and lynch law, justifiable.

The detectives split up into three groups with about eight men each and moved on three different saloons—Henry's Bar, the Bismark Cafe, and the Old Stock Exchange—none of which was too far from the courthouse steps.[17] But when the detectives began arresting owners and barkeeps and taking them to jail, the police released them immediately, claiming these out-of-town detectives lacked jurisdiction. By the time detectives entered Henry's Saloon word had spread about what was going on. An angry crowd gathered outside, so Carl Etherington and the detectives he was with ran out the back. Etherington hopped on a passing trolley that ran to the train station on the outskirts of Newark. But the mob followed the trolley, running just behind it. Etherington thought he was in the clear when the trolley pulled up to the station and he raced to get on the train, but the mob caught up to him and began to pummel him. The proprietor of another saloon, a former police captain named William Howard, was among the mob. In the scuffle that ensued, Howard nailed Etherington with a blackjack. Etherington pulled out a revolver and shot him. Some say that at this point Etherington's back was up against a tree and that Howard was holding him down when he managed to pull out his gun and shoot. Whatever happened, Howard was mortally wounded.

Shortly thereafter the police grabbed Etherington, threw him in a horse-drawn paddy-wagon, and took him to jail; along the way Howard was dropped off at the local hospital. Maybe the police assumed that Etherington would be safer in the jail—some claimed it was the strongest jail in Ohio and had been built to withstand mobs.[18] But just outside that mob-resistant bastion a crowd began to grow and kept growing throughout the afternoon. The evening edition of the *Newark Advocate* reported what had happened—that Howard had been shot and Etherington beaten—and this brought more folks to the streets. The sheriff let a news reporter inside the jailhouse to interview Etherington. The reporter claimed he "presented a pitiful appearance. His face was mashed to a jelly and was clotted with blood while his clothes were soaked in gore." Another writer reported hearing shouts of "Hang him!" and "Get him!" just outside the newspaper's downtown office. At about 8:00 P.M. Howard died from his gunshot wound—a .44 caliber bullet through his abdomen, exiting below the left shoulder.[19] Upon hearing this, the crowd inched its way toward mobdom. They cut the telephone lines to the jail and then looked for a way in. The crowd grew by the thousands. Newark Mayor Herbert Atherton addressed them, but he was ignored or booed. People threw rocks at the jailhouse and broke out most of the building's windows.[20] All the while neither Newark city police nor sheriff's deputies made any attempts to stop the mob from rushing forward and pounding the front door of the jailhouse, first with a telegraph pole and then with a large piece of train rail. Swaying the rail back and forth, they battered the door like a medieval siege.

At about 10:00 P.M. the door was down, and members of the mob rushed in and up the stairs to the second floor and Etherington's cell. Outside the jailhouse and to the delight of the gathered multitude a man named Robert Cleveland climbed a ladder to the second floor and began a running play-by-play of the action.[21] Down below, the crowd listened attentively. "Okay," he shouted, "now they're outside his cell." Cheers. "They're trying to break in." Shouts of encouragement. Meanwhile Etherington was trying to commit suicide before the mob could enter his cell. He beat his head against the brick wall and then wrapped his head in a blanket and tried to light it. "They got in," Robert shouted. Cheers from the crowd. And then it was nothing but hands: hands pushing, punching, shoving, and carrying him out of his cell. Someone tried to put a noose over his head. He cried out for a moment to speak but was denied.[22] One report claims

Old city of Newark Jail. *Photo by Ron Liniger*

he was overheard repeating again and again, "What will mother say when she hears of this?"[23] The mob forced him out of the jail and out onto the streets with the noose around his neck. As he was carried through the streets he was beaten with hammers and cut with knives.[24] Robert climbed down the ladder to follow the mob. From that day forward some folks in Newark called him "Bloody Murder" or, simply, "Bloody."

When Etherington reached the courthouse square, a place with abundant arboreal options, none of the trees satisfied the mob—most of the limbs were deemed too high. They decided on a telegraph pole at the corner of Second Street and South Park—a symbol of the modern age, of communication, of human connection across the western wilderness. That night, though, it served as an ancient technology. The pole had steps running up it for workmen, and so a few men or boys climbed the pole and attached the rope to a peg, "while those below held the victim clear of the ground. When all was ready Etherington was dropped, and he hung just above the heads of his executioners."[25]

There's a bit of confusion—or perhaps imagination—in the written re-cord regarding his final words. In one story, just before he was hanged, Etherington addressed the crowd saying, "Tell my mother that I died trying to do my duty."[26] Another version of this story that ran in an Oregan newspaper has Etherington channeling the gallows literature of an earlier century. The writer claims that "as [he] mounted the block ready to swing, he was asked to make a speech."[27] To an attentive au-dience he said, "I want to warn all young fellows not to try to make a living the way I have done—by strike-breaking and taking jobs like this. . . . I had better not have worked or I would not be here now."[28] Anti-Saloon League lawyer Wayne B. Wheeler claimed there was no way Etherington could have spoken before he was hanged, that he had been beaten senseless.[29]

At 10:35 P.M. Carl Etherington was hanging from the telephone pole, most likely struggling to breathe, lost in the long fade of stran-gulation while thousands watched. After the fact some speculated that, due to the beatings he endured in the street on the way to the pole, Etherington was likely unconscious when he was hanged.[30] But the coroner reported that his death was the result of strangulation.[31] If that was the case, then those looking on would have witnessed the pain on young Etherington's face—there's no indication a hood had been placed over his head. They would have noticed his body's struggle to survive, twitching and turning and then, perhaps, the gentle sway. And they may have heard the stretching rope in the hot July air or smelled the excrement from his evacuated bowels. The *Newark Advocate* re-ported that some men in the crowd would not allow "their ladies" to gaze upon Etherington's swaying corpse.[32] "Those who did look upon it turned with horror from the scene." Others tried to get their hands on relics of the night's work—pieces of the rope, wood from the telegraph pole.[33] After an hour or so the overstretched rope broke, and Etherington's body crumpled in a heap on the ground.[34] The mob slowly dispersed, and as it did some overheard Mayor Atherton invite a few friends to have a drink with him.[35] An ambulance arrived and took Etherington's body to McGonagle's Funeral Home and Mortuary. The streets grew quiet, and from the west the good citizens of Newark who were still awake could just hear the first rumbles of a thunderstorm headed their way.

The next morning tourists and relic hunters gathered in downtown Newark. Some visited the jail to see the broken windows and discarded battering rams just outside the front door.[36] But train rails were not easily transportable, so the prized possession was wood from the pole on which Etherington was hanged. One relic hunter said he was going to frame his piece of wood from the pole "as a memento of the occasion." Police were brought to the corner of South Park and Second to guard the pole from further destruction, and then city officials had the bottom half of the pole encased in sheet-iron to prevent further relic-hunting expeditions.[37] The pole stayed there, with its sheet-iron skirt, well into the 1950s, when it was finally taken down.

A few days later, after having a moment to breathe and reflect, the *Newark Advocate* published a scathing editorial claiming that "Newark

did not only lynch a man, but Newark lynched the law last Friday night."[38] To repair the damages wrought by the fury of its citizens, the newspaper's editors demanded that Newark arrest those responsible and try to figure out why this had happened. But who was responsible? The Wets (as the pro-alcohol crowd was called) blamed the Drys for meddling in Newark affairs by bringing in outside law enforcement and sending the Granville mayor to deputize them. The Drys blamed the Wets for fostering a culture of lawlessness in Newark and painted the town as some latter-day Sodom and Gomorrah.[39] For years a central tenet

Pole used to hang Carl Etherington. *Used with permission of Licking County Historical Society*

of temperance discourse had been that alcohol fueled violence—this lynching was perhaps proof of that assertion.[40] Furthermore, many Drys thought that Newark's government officials had turned a blind eye to law breaking in general.[41] A lot of attention was focused on Mayor Atherton, and Ohio Governor Judson Harmon exercised executive authority to suspend him; Atherton resigned shortly thereafter. Sloane Gordon offered a more measured approach, pointing out that the struggle over alcohol was beneficial to both Wets and Drys. Both sides blamed each other, he wrote, and both made a living doing so.[42]

But other issues are underdiscussed in the newspapers and magazines of the day: How could a community of people all of a sudden rise up en masse and decide that a man should be put to death by their own hands? Why did people, who would normally shy away from such brutality, commit it with such ease and precision? Who in the crowd knew how to hang a man? And why was Etherington not protected? In fact, Newark is very close to Columbus and, therefore, to more law enforcement officers, and yet no one, most notably the sheriff, had called in the National Guard.[43] Ultimately, twenty-one people were charged with first-degree murder, and a handful received sentences of up to twenty years.[44] Through parole and reduced sentences, though, no one served more than four years of actual jail time for Etherington's murder. Some of the people convicted may have been guilty of taking part in what happened that night, but all were working class, one was from the West Indies, at least two were of German descent, one was described as a deaf mute, and some had priors.[45] These were the scapegoats of a sort. The people in seats of power didn't go to jail. Etherington's father allegedly vowed revenge and wanted to lead a "band of mountaineers from Kentucky" to the streets of Newark.[46] But he would never get his revenge—two years after his son's murder he committed suicide.[47]

CULTURAL KNOWLEDGE

Today the Licking County courthouse sits regally amidst a lawn of green grass and shady hardwoods. Its limestone edifice with statues of Lady Justice perched over each building entrance was completed in 1878. Park benches and memorials populate the square, as they do in every small town in America. Here we're told to abide by the Ten Commandments, to remember the victims of the September 11, 2001, attacks, and to pay homage to Newark native Johnny Clem, the little drummer boy of the Union Army. These are all somber reminders of the past and present. The 1910 lynching of Carl Etherington, though, isn't mentioned anywhere next to that hall of justice. For years the pole from which he was hanged, across the street from the courthouse, was the only reminder of what happened, but even that's gone. The spot on the sidewalk where that pole once stood is distinguished from the rest of the sidewalk because the concrete covering the hole that remained is newer than that around it. From the cracks of that newer patch of sidewalk green weeds push toward the sunlight. And from this spot you have a good view of a statue of Lady Justice on the courthouse roof.

If you walk along the streets that encircle Newark's courthouse square, there's a patina of sadness, a longing for the grand days of yore. Yes, some of the old buildings are beautiful, but the decay is just below the surface. There's nothing particularly unusual about Newark; it's like a lot of small cities in the Midwest that have been hit hard by the loss of manufacturing jobs. The core hangs on by its teeth, while the strip malls, chain stores, and used car lots stretch on—an ugly appendage of a once-graceful body. Towns like Newark have struggled hard to hold on to hope, to find a renewed sense of purpose. A few years ago a song mocking Newark briefly made an appearance on a Columbus radio station. And in the summer of 2010 an article marking the hundredth anniversary of the Etherington lynching appeared in the *Newark Advocate*. Readers responded with shock—that such a thing had happened here. One reader left a rather pithy response: "And thus began the decline of Newark, Ohio . . ."[48]

Local historian Chris Evans doesn't believe that's true. "It's not based in fact. I'd venture to say that one month later everything was going on as before. It didn't change Newark at all. It didn't change the people of Newark at all. There were some that were sorry it happened, but the vast majority probably didn't care one way or the other." That's the kind of comment, he tells me, "that will catch a writer's eye and get printed. No reflection on present company." I laugh.

Evans is a descendant of some of those hopeful immigrants, though his ancestors were Macedonian, not German. It's easy to tell that his roots are in Newark, Ohio, because when he says it, it comes out like "N'erk, Ah-high-ah," in keeping with the local pronunciation. He remembers a time when the downtown was hopping, when all the action was there, but that changed, he says, as it did in many places, with the birth of the suburban strip mall. The lynching didn't kill this downtown—the fifties did.

"Over the years people stopped talking about it," he says. "I don't know why, probably shame. It isn't one of those things you brag about. When somebody would mention that there'd been a lynching in Newark you'd get all kinds of stories. 'Yeah, I think some black guy raped a white girl' and so on." The memory of the event has manifested in some unusual ways. In 1972 some community members proposed a reenactment of the lynching to take place during a local festival, and a great hue and cry ensued. Ultimately organizers decided against it.[49] One organizer noted, though, "The lynching is definitely a part of history no matter how hard it is to accept that." For his part, Evans doesn't think the event should be memorialized at all. When a local businessman approached him about putting up a state historical marker after the hundredth-anniversary article in the newspaper, Evans wasn't interested in helping. "He said it was important that the story be told, but not in my mind. You don't glorify it by putting up a monument." His ambivalence is due to the circumstances of the lynching itself. Both sides, he believes, were in the wrong. It happened because Etherington shot Howard. "With self-defense you're not supposed to use any greater force than is being imposed on you."

"I'm not sure I agree," I protest. "From the accounts I've read, biased and otherwise, Etherington had reason to believe his life was in danger. He'd just been hit on the head by a blackjack. A few more blows and he'd be dead."

Evans says that the mob was a *threat*, not an *act*. "You're not supposed to use more force than is facing you. He was under their control. You're not legally justified in taking the law in your hands."

"Maybe," I say, "but isn't that the irony?"

Locals like Evans will tell you this is a story of prohibition, of Wets versus Drys. And it is, but like all stories of the noose, it's also a story about the things—the awful things—that human beings will do to each other. In the aftermath Ray Stannard Baker opined that "towns are much like individual men; some you will find struggling, resolving, organizing, training themselves for better things. These towns, you say, have a civic spirit. Other towns you will find drifting carelessly, leading a free, selfish, easy-going life, each man absorbed in making money for himself—no cooperation, no town consciousness, no civic spirit."[50] He believed that Newark typified the so-called decline of Western civilization. Newark was founded by the best and the brightest. It had many churches. It had rich natural resources. But somehow, he said, it lost its way. Sloane Gordon was less sympathetic and wrote, "The people in Newark went crazy. That's the only charitable way to describe it. An entire municipality lost sense and reason and human attributes and ran amuck. It lusted for blood, and the blood-lust was sated. It babbled and prayed and shouted and pleaded; it cursed and raged; it dug with claw and fang into quivering flesh . . . Newark, Ohio, 'saw red.'"[51]

Is it that simple? Did the people of Newark just go crazy or lose their way? A man was pulled out of a jail cell, a noose thrown around his neck. He was paraded through the streets, abused along the way, and then strung up from a makeshift gallows for all the townsfolk to see. What happened to Carl Etherington was different from what happened to Dick Wofford. Because there were so many participants in his death—as engineers, spectators, and documentarians—his lynching had more in common with the ritual of the public executions from centuries before. Indeed, it's decidedly part of that tradition.

But does tradition explain how the noose ended up in the hands of Newark's citizens? Does it explain how this Midwestern community permitted such violence to occur, even though the lynching took place in the North and wasn't motivated by racial strife? How does a community come together and get to work tearing down a jailhouse door, stoking a fire, running a rope over a tree limb? How do they know how to do such things, and how do they come to be involved? These were not mere spectators, quietly watching events unfold; those attending a lynching were often very much involved. Certainly some in Newark may have felt a desire for retribution—and it's important to remember that *some* lynching victims were likely guilty of the crime for which they were accused. And yet that doesn't excuse the lynchers.

In the preface to a guide to an antilynching art exhibit, Sherwood Anderson once wrote that lynching is "an assertion, ugly and perverted, of man's hunger for self-respect."[52] He says it's a very elemental, fundamental action, that lynching is a process for individuals and communities to reassert some sort of dominance—be it social, economic, or political—over others. The noose becomes part of this lynching ritual meant to protect community values or reinforce community control over a situation or over a group of "others." Bertram Wyatt-Brown writes that lynching was a kind of "offering to the primal, sacred values of the folk."[53] But this offering, this ritual, did not always follow a particular pattern—every lynching was different, and spectator-participants seemed to choose their killing methods based on their material circumstances. But where did these choices come from, and where did they get the idea to do this or that? Why did so many lynchers revert to the noose? And—this is a question that haunts this book—how did they learn to tie the knot?

CHAPTER 10

Strange Fruit:
The Legacy of Marion

ON THE NIGHT OF AUGUST 7, 1930, in Marion, Indiana, a photo was taken of the hanged bodies of Thomas Shipp and Abram Smith. The photo is iconic because it contains all the elements that one's mind conjures when considering the history of lynching—the tree, the rope, and the noose. Of the two, the noose around Thomas Shipp's neck is a more precise hangman's knot, which makes sense, given that Shipp was the first man killed—perhaps indicative of premeditation and planning. The knots around Abe Smith, the second man killed, are hasty; as we learned in Chapter 1, when people are stressed they tend to use more half-hitches or granny knots because those knots are easier to make. The photo gathers meaning too from the crowd of spectators in the bottom half who look as if they're attending a county fair: the woman who, oddly, wears her fur-trimmed coat as if headed to the opera despite the fact that it was August. The smiling pregnant woman and jovial rube behind her. And the focal point of the bottom half of the photo, the man who looks an awful lot like Adolf Hitler pointing at the community's work. It's not just the noose that makes this image stand out; it's the people who may have tied it or who may have known who tied it—we can't assume the lynchers are in the photo—going through the effort of forming this particular knot with its wrapping turns and taut loop at the end.

This photo didn't appear in the local daily newspapers—the *Marion Chronicle* or the *Marion Leader-Tribune*—the next day or in the Indianapolis papers, for that matter.[1] But somehow the image was disseminated quickly around the nation, in part because a copy showed up at the Acme News Service in New York City a few days after the lynching.[2] It was logged as image number 132856, "Lynching of Two Negroes in Marion, Indiana."[3] The image appeared in many newspapers, including significant African American periodicals like the *Crisis* and the *Chicago Defender*, the latter of which printed it on August 16 along with the caption "American Christianity." Six years after the photo was taken, a New York City high school teacher named Abel Meeropol ran across the image and was so affected that he wrote one of the twentieth century's most important protest songs, "Strange Fruit." Historian James H. Madison writes that "years later Magnum Photo Agency also secured a print. From these two major agencies and the Library of Congress, editors, authors, museum exhibit planners, and others readily obtained copies. By the late twentieth century it had become one of America's most well-known lynching photographs."[4] The image of Shipp and Smith continues to be reproduced. *Life* magazine included it in a 1988 issue devoted to race in America. Rap group Public Enemy included it on the cover of a 1992 release titled "Hazy Shade of Criminal." *Newsweek* ran it twice in 1994. In 2011 *Life* magazine published the photo again in a collection titled "100 Photographs That Changed the World," with the comment that such an image "reminds us that we have not come as far from barbarity as we'd like to think."[5] The photo appeared in *Alistair Cooke's America* (1973) along with the statement, "No one now knows who took this picture, or exactly when. But lynch law ruled the South in the years after World War I. In 1919 alone, 70 Negroes were lynched."[6] But, of course, many people in Marion, Indiana, *did* know who took the photo, when he took it, and where he took it. But no one really knows why he took it.

The photographer was a man named Lawrence Beitler, and he usually took photos of wedding couples and babies, of school and church groups, of parades and public events. His daughter Betty would

Lynching of Abraham Smith and Thomas Shipp, by Lawrence Beitler. *Corbis Images*

later claim he didn't want to take the photo in the first place.[7] But he
did, and he sold it for 50 cents a pop. Beitler apparently stayed up for
ten days and nights making copies of the photo to meet his customers'
demands. Everybody wanted a copy, a modern relic from the event.
James H. Madison wonders whether people saw the photo "as a reas-
surance of white supremacy and of race solidarity in the face of any
perceived black threat, a talisman against murder or rape or inappropriate crossing of the color line."[8]

Beitler's photo isn't unusual as lynching photos go. There are many
photos of lynched men and women, black and white, and there are
many lynching photos with crowds. Yet this particular lynching photograph is memorable. Maybe it's because of its relationship to Meeropol's song or because it came into the possession of a major photo
distributor or because of the clear and visible faces of the spectators
and victims. Or maybe it's because the photo reproduces, at the tail end
of the lynching era, one of the most salient symbols of that era—the
noose. It's the noose that we see in this photo and others like it, and

perhaps this helps the noose become not just a method for execution but also a symbol of white supremacy. The age of mechanical reproduction (to borrow from Walter Benjamin) marks a significant shift because now one no longer needs to get his or her hands dirty to assert racial authority or to provoke fear—the image of the lynching and the image of the noose can do that work.

A former reporter from the *Marion Chronicle* told me he'd heard many stories about the picture still existing "in many Marion households, white and black . . . buried deep in people's drawers." Nobody, he said, wants to talk about it, but the event is not dead. It may be hidden, literally and figuratively, but it's not dead. Those who still have this photographic talisman or relic hidden in their dresser drawers know the power and horror it represents.

ROOTS AND CROP

Indiana is one of the first "square states." Its counties are squares, and its local roads run straight on maps. Marion, Indiana, sits amidst a square called Grant County, about seventy miles northeast of Indianapolis. This is corn country. A friend who grew up nearby told me once that the thing she remembers most about her Indiana childhood is that you could plant anything in the ground and it would grow. And that's the case in Marion—it's all corn and soybeans as far as you can see. Impossible towns rest like islands amidst this green sea. Towns like Fairmount, Gas City, Swayzee, Sweetser, and Upland. Grant County was originally home to the Miami, who were slowly and sometimes violently pushed out of the area.[9] By the 1820s a government land sale opened the area for settlement, and in 1831 Grant County was born. Shortly thereafter Marion was named the county seat. The town developed on the left bank of the Mississinewa River. But there were remnants of previous occupants besides the names they left behind. In Grant and surrounding counties Native American earthworks punctuated the flat landscape. One earthwork was discovered on a spot that later became the courthouse square. It was about ten feet high and sixty feet in diameter, and during one construction project on the courthouse grounds human remains were uncovered.[10]

Before the Civil War over half of the people in Grant County were Quakers from North Carolina. Many of them left North Carolina because they wished to free their slaves but found it virtually impossible to do so in North Carolina. In Grant County many of these freed slaves as well as some who had been freed in the eighteenth century began to settle in an area called Weaver that today is on the outskirts of Marion. Weaver was a haven and a refuge, a place that in many and important ways expressed the hope of the Midwest.

Marion grew considerably in the late nineteenth century, in part due to natural gas reserves and its convenient spot along the railroads that crisscrossed the Midwest. It was a center of manufacturing in glass and iron works, two industries that particularly relied on natural gas to power furnaces. Immigrants flooded the town—Irish, Germans, Belgians, and Czechs, though there were also many from Kentucky and Tennessee.[11] They came to Marion, much like the Quakers and freed slaves did, for safety, security, and a better economic situation. And when immigrants didn't find that security at their places of work, they organized unions and elected Socialist candidates for city council.

In the 1920s, though, Indiana was no longer a place of refuge. Longtime white residents embraced a reactionary politics that sought to blame contemporary social ills and developing economic ones on African Americans and immigrants. This reaction came in part because many whites believed they were losing their nation to a wave of southern and eastern European immigrants. In Marion alcohol sales and union organizing were particular sources of contention in the community. In this social and cultural milieu the Ku Klux Klan came roaring back. This second iteration of the Klan was the brainchild of a defrocked Methodist minister and salesman named William Joseph Simmons. While apparently drunk one night he found himself gazing up at the moon and had a vision of ghosts on horseback. Simmons thought it was a sign directing him to start a new Klan like the one he'd just seen in D. W. Griffith's 1915 film *The Birth of a Nation*, a tale of

Ku Klux Klan parade in Washington, DC, September 13, 1926. *Library of Congress*

white vigilantes saving the Reconstruction-era South from the dangers of savage "Negros"—and even lynching some of them.[12] On the day before Thanksgiving of 1915 Simmons and fifteen other men went to the top of Stone Mountain in Georgia and set a cross on fire—and the Klan was reborn.

Simmons's Klan was akin to a fraternal organization except that this one wished to protect a deeply Anglo-Saxon Protestant vision of the United States—they were no fans of Catholics, Jews, African Americans, unions, or immigrants. By the early 1920s their numbers had grown, especially in the Midwest, and some in the Klan began taking their rhetoric seriously—a spate of whippings, brandings, and tar-and-featherings led to congressional hearings—and an increase in the Klan's popularity. Though decidedly violent on occasion, the second Klan was more prone to theatrics. This was the Klan of the burning cross and parades down Main Streets, USA. Perhaps its most infamous parade happened in 1925 when some forty thousand Klansmen, in all their white-robed glory, marched down Pennsylvania Avenue to the Washington Monument. The march was significant for many reasons: it underscored not only how deeply racist and xenophobic the nation was in that moment but also this particular Klan's close ties to government. This Klan, unlike its predecessor described in the last chapter, was powerful not because of the violence it produced but because of its lobbying efforts.

Nowhere was this truer than in Indiana, where, because of its size and popularity in both city and country, the Klan's tentacles reached deep into both state and local governments.[13] At one point in the 1920s every one of the ninety-two counties in Indiana had a Klavern, and in 1925 there were about 165,000 Klan members in the Hoosier state—more than any other.[14] They rallied or marched in towns large and small, from Indianapolis to Hobart. The Indiana Klan was spearheaded by a former coal salesman named D. C. Stephenson who now sold the Klan to Hoosiers as a bastion of nationalism in a country whose Protestantness and whiteness were being diluted by the immigrant masses. This rang true to a people obsessed with their pioneer heritage, like those in Grant County who had seen an influx of immigrants in recent years. Many longtime residents felt these new residents didn't share their "traditional" white Protestant values. Moreover, these long-timers claimed the immigrants were causing a spike in union rabble-rousing. In fact, union membership was high and Mother Jones and Eugene Debs had each spoken to large crowds in Marion.

But for others alcohol was the catalyst for joining the Klan. The town had gone dry in 1915, a move that essentially deregulated alcohol and opened the door for speakeasies, unlicensed taverns, and, not surprisingly, a crime wave. The Klan blamed these cultural and economic shifts on immigration and responded by staging rallies and parades throughout the county. By 1925 there were 2,329 Klansmen in Grant, or "just over 15 percent of native-born white men in the county."[15] In Marion the Klan led their moral crusade right to the front door, paying visits to Wednesday night church services at congregations with pastors who had yet to join.[16] Dressed in their costumes and carrying an American flag, they'd walk down the aisle, toss some money on the pulpit, and hand a membership form to the pastor. If he didn't sign, he'd be out the door by the end of the week. The Klan was strong in Grant County; a Fairmount woman, Daisy Douglass Barr, was president of the US Women of the Klan. She's buried in a cemetery in Fairmount, just a few rows away from her great-nephew, Grant County native son James Dean. But the Indiana Klan disintegrated rapidly in 1925 when D. C. Stephenson was convicted for kidnapping and raping a woman named Madge Oberholtzer, who died a month after the incident. After Stephenson's conviction, Indiana Governor Ed Jackson wouldn't pardon Stephenson, so Stephenson provided evidence that led to the governor being tried for bribery. The trial was dismissed on a technicality, but the reputations of both the governor and the Indiana Klan were forever tarnished.

By 1930, well after the D. C. Stephenson debacle, the Klan held little power in the state and in Marion. But as one local told me, at the time you couldn't throw a rock without hitting someone who'd once belonged to the Klan. Racist and xenophobic ideologies were not the only things at work on the social dynamics of Marion, Indiana, in 1930. Marion was also on edge because in the past year or so a wave of bombings in the town, most likely connected to labor struggles, had killed five men. The murders remain unsolved. On top of this, the community was also beginning to feel the effects of the Depression: people were being laid off, wages were dropping, and some factories were shortening the work week. Just a year later the American Red Cross distributed three hundred thousand pounds of bread in the county.

On August 7, 1930, these unemployed and possibly hungry people gathered outside the jailhouse in Marion in the midst of a heat wave. Inside, three young black men, Tom Shipp, age nineteen, Abe Smith, eighteen, and James Cameron, sixteen, were behind bars. They had been accused of robbing a young couple, Claude Deeter, twenty-four, and Mary Ball, eighteen, the night before at a place called the Dark Secret, a spot along the Mississinewa River outside of town where folks went to make out. Apparently it was a robbery gone bad: Deeter had been shot and was dying of his wounds in the local hospital. Ball was supposedly recovering from the attack, during which time, newspapers claimed, she had been raped. The young men confessed to the shooting, though who was responsible for what has never really been determined. And some speculate that the young men were coerced into confessing.

When Deeter died in the early afternoon on August 7, who did what didn't seem to matter to the people in Marion and the surrounding communities, especially in Deeter's hometown of Fairmount. Nor did it seem to matter that Deeter, who grew up in a deeply religious family, forgave his assailants shortly before dying.[17] What mattered was that three black men had killed a white man and—"so they said"—raped a white woman. Rumors circulated around town that something was going to happen that night. When a police officer hanged Claude Deeter's blood-soaked shirt from a City Hall window, in clear sight of passersby, the pot began to boil.

At about 8:30 P.M. a mob arrived at the jailhouse. Many people had warned Sheriff Jake Campbell that something was going to happen. The head of the local NAACP chapter, a dynamic woman named Flossie Bailey, had even alerted him. Campbell was either unprepared or didn't much care—he didn't transfer the prisoners to another location, claiming that the air had been let out of his squad car tires and the gas tanks drained.[18] At about 9 P.M. Mary Ball's father entered the jailhouse and demanded the keys but was turned away. The mob then decided that if the keys weren't forthcoming, they'd enter by force. It didn't take them long to figure out how to do the work—they got sledgehammers from a local foundry and beat the doors down. The sheriff and his deputies put up some resistance, tossing canisters of tear gas to a crowd that included former World War I vets who just tossed the canisters back into the jailhouse.

The first man they pulled out of the jailhouse was Thomas Shipp. They took him outside and assaulted him with their hands and feet and weapons. At 10:30 P.M. a rope—three-eighths inch thick, bought from a local hardware store—went around his neck, and he was hanged from the bars of a jail window.[19] Next they went for Abram Smith. Members of the crowd also beat him, but this time they carried him across the street to the northeast corner of the courthouse square and hanged him from a sturdy maple; perhaps they felt the bodies would be more visible from this location. A few went back to Shipp's body, still hanging from the jailhouse window, and put him next to Smith on the tree. Finally they went for James Cameron, who was also beaten and around whose neck they threw a rope. But something happened—a swing in the emotions of the crowd? A twist of fate? A miracle? No one knows for sure. Bystanders claim that a voice was heard above the din saying that Cameron was innocent, that he wasn't involved. As quickly as he was pulled from the jailhouse, the mob mellowed, the rope was lifted, and Cameron was allowed to walk back to the relative safety of the jailhouse.

Cameron claims he was saved by an angel. His story of that night is fascinating, and it focuses, in part, on his personal relationships with the folks doing the lynching. Cameron talks a lot about the hands of these persons unknown, the hands that pulled him from his cell, beat him, and placed a noose around his neck—the hands of a fanatical mob but also the "hands of people I had grown to love and respect as friends and neighbors."[20] When those good neighbors "got their hands" on him they beat him, pushed him, pulled him out of the jail: "Their grips were like bands of steel."[21] As he made his way to the street, "so many clubs and hands were aimed and swung at me that they got in each other's way." And then "rough hands grabbed my head and stuffed it into a noose. . . . I stopped thinking then. In my mind I was already dead. I was glad to be leaving a world filled with so many deceitful people." Cameron, a well-known downtown Marion shoe shiner, says he remembered those hands, recognized those faces, and even knew those shoes because he had shined many of them.[22] The tightening noose began to burn his neck and then, Cameron says, he heard a voice, "Take this boy back. He had nothing to do with any raping or killing!"[23] This angelic voice, it "was sharp and crisp, like bells ringing out on a clear, cold, winter day."

By about 11:00 P.M. law enforcement from surrounding communities showed up to assist. The mob settled down and like vultures gliding the currents, relic hunters began their scavenging, taking pieces of clothing, tree, and rope. They gathered around the courthouse square, swapping stories and offering details to late arrivals. It was a community gathering of women and men, young and old. Someone went to fetch Lawrence Beitler, who set up his camera and snapped the now-famous photo that later inspired Abel Meeropol's words:

> *Southern trees bear a strange fruit,*
> *Blood on the leaves and blood at the root,*
> *Black body swinging in the Southern breeze,*
> *Strange fruit hanging from the poplar trees.*
>
> . . .
>
> *Here is a fruit for the crows to pluck,*
> *For the rain to gather, for the wind to suck,*
> *For the sun to rot, for a tree to drop,*
> *Here is a strange and bitter crop.*

Of course, the image that inspired Meeropol was not of a Southern lynching but a midwestern one. Its imagery is arresting and conjures the singular and iconic image of tree and hanging body, of tree and victim, of burning or rotting corpse. It is an ugly scene: depositing the stunningly brutal into the bucolic pastoral.

"Strange fruit" is a powerful, iconic phrase, evocative of the wrongness of the crimes it describes. And yet in a sad way that fruit, the hanged man, was not strange at all: it was cultivated and harvested in communities across the United States—it came from within. There was "blood at the root" of lynching, of hanging. The fruit is strange, but the people surrounding the tree are not strangers; they are the good people of Marion, Indiana, and they were in good company. Their behaviors were unusual but not unique—those "bod[ies] swinging" were visual reminders of the outcomes of an age-old practice of hanging someone by the neck until dead.

It wasn't until 5:45 A.M. on August 8 that the "strange fruit" was cut down from that maple tree in Marion. At that point most of the previous night's spectators had gone home to rest, easily or not. Some cut pieces of the rope on their way homeward.[24] Things quieted down in Marion, but as a precaution two companies of the Indiana National Guard were sent in to patrol the streets. Meanwhile Flossie Bailey was contacting NAACP headquarters in New York, who were in turn contacting the governor. They demanded swift justice and immediate protection for the black community in Marion. A few weeks later the NAACP sent acting Secretary Walter White to Marion to begin its own investigation. Newspapers across the state and nation followed the story. The *Marion Chronicle* ran an editorial entitled "Mob Psychology." Echoing the sentiments of those commenting on the Newark lynching, it claims that "Marion is about the last place on earth where we should have expected to witness a lynching. Yet, this very thing happened here." It was committed by men "stung to the quick by an atrocious crime and spurred on to their violent act by a want of confidence in the processes of the courts." Ultimately the editorial concludes that "it is sad to reflect that, human nature being what it is, and social conditions being what they are, what has taken place here in Marion is not unlikely to befall any community. Mob psychology may break out anywhere."

Not everyone in the state of Indiana—or in the United States, for that matter—was willing to write this off as an aberration, a momentary outbreak of "mob psychology." Individual human beings were involved—they tied the noose and bruised the bodies. A Court of Inquiry began a week after the lynching, and the depositions of the thirty people interviewed in that court are telling. In one exchange between Prosecutor Harley Hardin and Assistant Chief of Police Roy Collins, Hardin asks Collins whether he could identify anyone in the crowd. He says he could not, that "it looked like a whirling mass of humanity."[25] This is repeated again and again in the pages of these depositions—those two men died at the hands of persons unknown. The depositions also reveal that law enforcement in Marion was not investigating the lynching. When Deputy Attorney General Earl Stroup asked a sheriff's deputy named Orville Wells whether he had been trying to gather information about what happened, he treated the interview with disdain:

> STROUP: Have you talked to anybody about this lynching?
> WELLS: Just casually; not from the standpoint of getting information, anything like that.
> STROUP: I suppose you regard it your duty to learn, if you could?
> WELLS: Yes, yes, sir. I haven't secured anything.

Not surprisingly, the trials that followed in late 1930 and early 1931 were a sham from the start. In the first place, they took place in Marion. Two men from the mob, Robert Beshire and Charles Lennon, were put on trial; both were acquitted, and then the attorney general essentially gave up. One outcome of the trials, though, was that the black community in Marion, despite the lynchings, showed a united and fearless front; this was in large part due to the leadership of Flossie Bailey. And yet that united front didn't matter. Justice was never served. No one was ever convicted. Another gaping wound in Lady Justice's side festered.

SMALL MIDWESTERN CITIES

The similarities between Newark and Marion are uncanny. Both were small industrial Midwestern cities—towns really—built on a landscape dotted with Native American earthworks. Both were towns where glass manufacturing and iron works fueled economies and significant population growth. And both were experiencing growing pains when their respective lynchings occurred, though the issues that prompted each lynching were quite different. Newark was still booming, while Marion was in the midst of hard times. But something prompted hysteria and violence. And in both cases law enforcement turned its gaze or barely offered protection to the prisoners as citizen mobs broke into jails, got their hands on the accused, and slipped nooses around their necks. The victims were hanged and their bodies displayed on or near the county courthouse. In both towns the wounds perhaps never really healed. The two events and cities had a lot in common, but in some ways the only "real" thing that connects them is the noose and the human hands that made it.

There's a story that some locals tell in Marion, that the tree from which Smith and Shipp were hanged died shortly after the lynching. In this story the tree's death is symbolic of the community's decline—that after the lynching nothing was the same in Marion. In Paul Laurence Dunbar's poem, "The Haunted Oak," a personified oak tree speaks to a passerby who wonders aloud why the tree is so bare and haunted looking. The tree explains that it bore witness to a lynching and the experience has forever transformed it:

> *I feel the rope against my bark,*
> > *And the weight of him in my grain,*
> *I feel in the throe of his final woe*
> > *The touch of my own last pain.*

> *And never more shall leaves come forth*
> > *On the bough that bears the ban;*
> *I am burned with dread, I am dried and dead,*
> > *From the curse of a guiltless man.*[26]

The tree could no longer produce life and light in a world of such cruelty. The Marion tree story is reminiscent of the reader's comment about Newark, Ohio, declining in the wake of the Carl Etherington lynching. But as in Newark, history doesn't support that story either. Something may have died in that community that night, but the community itself did not die—economically or socially.

"It wasn't the lynching that killed this town—it was factories closing," a retired Marion high school teacher named Bill Munn told me. But, he says, the lynching is a part of community memory—perhaps locked away, but it's there. Because he was a well-liked history teacher and has close ties to the county museum, folks will often call him when they want to get rid of stuff they think might hold some historical value—for example, copies of Beitler's photo of Thomas Shipp and Abe Smith.

"It's always the same picture, an 8 x 10," he says. "It was their grandmother's or some family member, and they want to get it out of their house. Almost like they want to exorcise this demon from their house." One time a woman called him and said she found a Klan robe and hood in a deceased relative's home and asked whether he could come get it. The local museum had all the robes and hoods they needed, thank you. But the caller was insistent. When he finally went to the house to get the hood, the woman walked him down a hall and opened a door to a room.

"She told me it was in the closet but that she didn't want to go in the room. She was literally scared to be in the same room as that Klan robe."

More than artifacts, though, Bill Munn is a collector of stories about Marion and Grant County. And he has collected a lot of stories about the lynching.

There are countless stories from countless perspectives, Munn says, and he's given up trying to reconcile them all. For example, he asks aloud, Who was Mary Ball really? Some say she was in a relationship with Abe Smith, others that she was friends with all of the men involved, that they were a criminal gang and had often used Mary to lure men to the Dark Secret, where they would then rob them. Others believe the original story, that she was raped. Munn isn't sure what to believe. Her family has been quiet through the years, and Mary Ball left Marion shortly after the lynching. Munn heard a rumor in the 1970s that Mary Ball was living in San Bernadino. He was out there on vacation and looked her up. He called her, but no one answered.

I ask him about the tree story. He chuckles.

"It didn't die. They were always cutting them down. Maybe they get too big, and so they cut them back or down. They've done it at least twice since I've been here. Now, I can see why they'd want it out of there." The lynching had a long-term effect on the community, but he thinks the stuff about the tree is just "too karmic."

"But was there a long-lasting impact? Yes." Munn says the lynching represented a breakdown in law enforcement and that ultimately justice was never pursued. "You had murderers loose on the street who were never punished and people knew who they were. And of course, if you were a black person, and maybe the guy working next to you was one of the people who put the noose around one of the guys. And so what are you to think? Look, white people will kill and get away with it." But there have been some public admissions of past wrongdoing. In 2003 the Grant County government apologized for the lynching; the city of Marion never has.

Bill Munn came to Marion by way of Ball State in Muncie. When he finished grad school he got a job in Marion, married a local girl, and settled down. "When I started out it was not to be talked about. In the seventies there were still people around who had had their hands on the noose. When I was doing some research I found the name of a guy who was accused of being an instigator, and I knew him. He had since died, but I did not know that while he was living. Now, I'm not a cynic, but I'm enough of a student of human nature to know that people can do just about anything." Even in places like Marion, he says, "somebody had to know how to tie that knot. That wouldn't have been easy."

I talked to Bill on August 6, the day before the anniversary. I assumed there would be some recognition of that day. Bill told me not to hold my breath. "There won't be anything. There won't be a peep."

And there wasn't a peep. It was just another quiet Sunday morning. High humidity, a patch of fog here and there. Some people slept in. Others went to church. I drove down to the banks of the Mississen-awa, to the place once called the "Dark Secret," and I could just hear a trickle of water from the river. I drove over to the courthouse, passing the former (seemingly bombed-out) RCA factory along the way. The courthouse square was quiet too. I kept driving and left Marion on State Highway 9. Following Bill Munn's directions to the Weaver community, I turned right down a narrow, barely two-lane road deep into fields of summer corn, higher than my head. I passed a small cemetery, close to the road, where Bill Munn told me Abe Smith and Thomas Shipp are buried. He said that for years he'd heard rumors that this was where they'd been buried, on the edge of Weaver's African American cemetery. And then he spoke to a ninety-year-old man who grew up in Weaver. The man said he knew they were buried there, that a few days after the lynching he watched from his bedroom window as several men dug their graves by car light.

It's a desolate stretch of Midwestern corn-lined road. Nothing but field and sky, and I imagine the place is windswept and frigid come winter. This was the Midwest where former slaves fled and first felt something akin to freedom. I get out of my car to listen to the wind roll in and out. Above me a red-tailed hawk is at work, floating and then diving into the corn. It's a quiet, beautiful place. I'd like to believe that this is, in fact, where Thomas Shipp and Abe Smith are buried, peaceful in the warm morning sun.

A GOOD DEATH

CHAPTER 11

When the
Gallows Come Down

THIRTY-THREE-YEAR-OLD RICHARD HICKOCK and thirty-six-year-old Perry Smith were hanged after midnight on April 14, 1965, at the Kansas State Penitentiary. Hickock and Smith had been convicted on March 29, 1960, for the murders of Holcomb, Kansas, farmer Herb Clutter, his wife, and their two children. Hickock had heard from a former Clutter employee that this farmer and former member of the Federal Farm Credit Board kept a safe in his house with $10,000 in it. No such safe existed. For their efforts, a nighttime robbery and multiple homicides, the pair earned $43, a radio, and a pair of binoculars. After an extensive manhunt authorities apprehended Hickock and Smith in Las Vegas. And after almost five years on death row and four appeals, their time had run out.

In the final twenty-four hours of their lives Kansas Governor William H. Avery denied clemency, "a federal judge denied a writ of habeas corpus, and a US Supreme Court justice denied their final petition for a stay of execution."[1] That was it. Smith and Hickock ate their final meal of jumbo spiced shrimp, French fries, soft drinks, garlic bread and hot rolls, and vanilla ice cream and strawberries with whipped cream in separate interrogation rooms, and they waited there until their executions.[2] Because of all the press the murders garnered, it was no routine execution for the witnesses present. Indeed, for one of them, Truman Capote, it was more than just an execution:

it was the obvious conclusion to a book he was writing called *In Cold Blood: A True Account of a Multiple Murder and Its Consequences*, a book that would examine violence in America through the lens of this case.

Capote begins his narrative of the Hickock and Smith executions with a "breakfasting" Alvin Dewey, the hard-nosed Kansas Bureau of Investigations (KBI) detective who had doggedly pursued Hickock and Smith and had just watched them die. Capote explains that Dewey "had never attended an execution, and when on the midnight past he entered the cold warehouse, the scenery had surprised him: he had anticipated a setting of suitable dignity, not this bleakly lighted cavern cluttered with lumber and other debris."[3] It was a dumpy warehouse with stone walls and a large gallows on which hung two nooses in a corner.[4] The nooses were crafted by an executioner brought in from Missouri, "attired in an aged double-breasted pin striped suit overly commodious for the narrow figure inside it" and a cowboy hat.[5] With a driving rain falling hard on the warehouse roof, the witnesses waited for Hickock and Smith to arrive.[6] They talked among themselves, making "self-consciously casual conversation."[7]

They were killed in alphabetical order. Hickock entered first, at 12:14 A.M., accompanied by six guards and a chaplain. He wore "an ugly harness of leather straps that bound his arms to his torso."[8] Hickock looked around and asked a guard whether any Clutters were present. "When he was told no, the prisoner seemed disappointed, as though he thought the protocol surrounding this ritual of vengeance was not being properly observed."[9]

After the death warrant was read Hickock gave his final words: "'I just want to say I hold no hard feelings. You people are sending me to a better world than this ever was'; then, as if to emphasize the point, he shook hands with the four men mainly responsible for his capture and conviction, all of whom had requested permission to attend the executions: KBI Agents Roy Church, Clarence Duntz, Harold Nye, and Dewey himself."[10] He walked up the steps, and the chaplain spoke as the hood and noose were put in place. The trap

Kansas state gallows. *Used with permission of the Kansas State Historical Society*

opened at 12:19.[11] Seven minutes later a doctor checked—Hickock's heart was still beating. Rain fell harder on the warehouse roof. At 12:41 he was dead.

Capote records a conversation between two reporters as the witnesses waited for Smith. For one it was his first hanging: "Nobody in our office wanted the assignment. Me either. But it wasn't as bad as I thought it would be. Just like jumping off a diving board. Only with a rope around your neck," he says.[12] The other replies, "They don't feel nothing. Drop, snap, and that's it. They don't feel nothing."[13] The first, again, "Are you sure? I was standing right close. I could hear him gasping for breath." The second: "Uh-huh, but he don't feel nothing. Wouldn't be humane if he did." And then Smith walked in, chewing gum, and, writes Capote, appearing "jaunty and mischievous." He made his way to the gallows and gave his final speech. "I think it's a helluva thing to take a life in this manner. I don't believe in capital punishment, morally or legally. Maybe I had something to contribute, something. . . . It would be meaningless to apologize for what I did.

Even inappropriate. But I do. I apologize."[14] Smith dropped at 1:02 A.M. and was pronounced dead at 1:19 A.M.

There is a kinship between *In Cold Blood* and the gallows literature of centuries before—both illustrate that hanging is a dramatic ritual deeply connected to our culture, where we work out social tensions and alleviate our deepest fears. It's a planned and calculated process that we are all, as citizens of this land, deeply connected to. These are our laws protected and enforced by our legal system. But it's also a process from which we seem to wish desperately to distance ourselves. The hanging happened late at night in a dank warehouse with a handful of witnesses, and the hangman was an out-of-state consultant and not a state employee.[15] The hanging execution has become a necessary but shameful bureaucratic process—but it is still violent, it is still about killing a human being. Indeed, the hanging execution is, as Capote's subtitle explains, often the culmination of a process that begins in violence and ends in violence.

Capote's book begins with the randomness of the Clutter murder and concludes with the planned nature of a state-sanctioned execution. This is an important juxtaposition worth parsing. The Clutters lived in farm country and had achieved the American dream; they were killed by two men who certainly had not. Such violence was not supposed to happen in the Sunflower State, the breadbasket of the world. And such violence is not supposed to happen in Newtown or Aurora or Blacksburg or Littleton. It's not supposed to happen in Holcolmb, Kansas, not in Newark, Ohio, not in Marion, Indiana. But it does. And when it does it disturbs a certain privileged sense of separation from the grosser nature of humankind or from certain shameful technologies of death.

Thus, the action in *In Cold Blood* leads to this double hanging. Capote writes his way to this execution regardless of whether he meant to when he began. With any judicial execution comes a desperate desire for catharsis, and this is painfully evident with the Clutter murders. Bill Brown, editor of the *Garden City Telegram*, witnessed both the crime scene and the execution. He said that after Smith made his comment about the death penalty he thought of the day of the murder and the scene he encountered at the Clutter house: "I thought of the shotgunned and mutilated bodies of the Clutter family . . . they were shown no mercy whatsoever. I think the feeling of the people of Garden City is one of relief. They have been waiting, some impatiently waiting. Some doubted they would ever go to the gallows."[16]

The irony was that there would be no relief. Capote's book was soon released and then the film, and to this day the community continues to relive the Clutter murders again and again—most recently in 2012 when the bodies of Smith and Hickock were exhumed in order to help solve a Florida murder mystery.[17] Capital punishment doesn't always bring catharsis. The execution simply becomes one more through-line in a complex narrative about the horrible things that humans are capable of doing to one another—sometimes planned and calculated, sometimes not.

The 1967 film adaptation of Capote's novel, starring Robert Blake as Perry Smith and Scott Wilson as Dick Hickock, makes editorial choices similar to those in the book. The noose is inevitable. We know it is coming from the beginning of the film. We watch Perry Smith tying knots with ease when, in a hardware store, the two prepare for their crime. When investigators puzzle over the scene, Dewey comments on the knots used to tie up members of the Clutter family. "All tied with the same square knot," he declares. "Used by anybody who works with livestock." And later, still trying to figure out who would be motivated to kill the Clutters, he notes, "Unless we can place the killers in this spot. Unless we can tie the killers to that piece of rope, they'll never hang." There is rope in the beginning, middle, and end, when the movie concludes with the hanging: Perry Smith looking scared as the pastor reads Psalm 23 and we hear the heartbeat. Perry asks, "Is God in this place too?" The trap door releases. We hear his heartbeat slow down as his body sways and the rope groans.

Hollywood may well have played a significant role in shaping our contemporary understanding of the hangman's knot. One victim of a noose incident I spoke with told me that when he saw a noose left on a timeclock at his workplace, he immediately pictured himself hanging from a tree like in a movie.[18] In western films, especially, well-wrought hangman's knots and gallows are often employed as plot devices or villainous omens, in a sense romanticizing frontier justice.[19] A great example—and there are plenty—is Nathan Juran's *Good Day for a Hanging* (1959), which centers on a marshal, played by Fred MacMurray, struggling with the duty his position entails versus the reasonable doubt he and the community have about a man condemned to die for murder. In the end the condemned man breaks out of jail and dies on the gallows in a shoot-out with the sheriff—not the ignoble death of the hanged man but the haphazard one of the outlaw. The film's closing shot is of the noose rocking back and forth with the outlaw, shot dead, resting on the gallows.

It is curious how this conquest of the West is wrapped up in the American imagination with popular myths and popular culture, most notably the western film. It's even more curious how this film genre has forever linked the West with the noose. Do-gooder sheriffs and their manly posses ride on horseback to avenge some wrong done to the community, be it by outlaws or Indians. Hollywood has profoundly affected our thinking about the conquering of the West. A recent advertisement promoting rereleases of Columbia/Tri-Star westerns, after listing all the films, ends with the tagline, "It's how the West was won." Hickock and Smith, for their part, disrupted the life of a western farmer and his family and were chased down by a posse and brought to justice at the end of a rope. And their story was refashioned into gallows literature and film—the genre keeps on.[20]

THE LAST HANGING EXECUTIONS

In the late nineteenth and early twentieth centuries the transforming nature of corrections, spurred on by an apparent humanitarian bent, led many to view hanging as an archaic punishment out of step with modern sensibilities. To many, hanging brought to mind barbaric public spectacles and even lynching. Furthermore, it was increasingly viewed as both unnecessary and barbaric. And yet for years some hangmen had tried to make executions more humane. Their efforts centered on perfecting the drop from the gallows, believing that with a longer drop a person would die more quickly, in most cases from a severed spinal cord.

From the perspective of these innovators, the hangings in the early chapters of this book were crude affairs with little attention paid to engineering a swift death. The positioning of the knot of the noose had been studied closely for some time. Originally the noose was placed behind the head, but eventually both hangman and hanged preferred to place the knot behind the ear and pulled tight. There's evidence that the hangman's knot (Knot #1119) was used in nineteenth-century American executions; in Great Britain, however, a rope with a metal eyelet was more common. There were other differences in execution style across the Atlantic.

By the middle of the nineteenth century hangmen in Ireland and England began to pay attention to the distance of the drop as a way to hasten death and avoid prolonged strangulation. Irish doctor Samuel Haughton proposed that a longer and more exact drop would dislocate the neck and produce a quicker death.[21] His formula for determining such a drop was to "divide the weight of the patient in pounds into 2240, and the quotient will give the length of the long drop."

Perhaps prompted by Haughton's essay, English hangman William Marwood, working from 1872 to 1883, devised a table of drops that took into account the height and weight of the condemned person when determining the length the execution rope.[22] British hangmen adjusted these measurements from time to time, but the general science remained the same. In the United States a "standard drop" (between four and six feet), a drop longer than the old-fashioned short drop but not measured based on a prisoners height and weight, was often used.[23] But this drop didn't always break the neck, though the condemned were often made unconscious by it, and if it were too long, the head could decapitate. (The use of a measured drop officially made its way into American executions when the US Military included a table in its 1947 execution field manual.[24])

And yet no matter how precise the drop, no matter how much the process was perfected, hanging still made people squeamish. It was a simple but old method of killing often administered by sheriffs with little experience. It could never be precise: there's no way to anticipate how an individual human body may react to traumatic violence. All manner of dreadful outcomes ensued: necks exotically bent, heads pulled off, and, worst of all, victims who suffered but didn't die. Hanging put the body on display and maybe was shunned, in part, because of a kind of Victorian fear of the body and impropriety. Or perhaps it was shunned because of an earnest belief in the progressive nature of humankind. In 1885 New York Governor David B. Hill noted in his annual address that "the present mode of executing criminals by hanging has come down to us from the dark ages, and it may well be questioned whether the science of the present day cannot provide a means for taking the life of such as are condemned to die in a less barbarous manner."[25]

The new technologies, most notably the electric chair and the gas chamber, supplanted the noose in the United States. In 1889, in Auburn, New York, William Kemmler was the first to be electrocuted. By 1923 even Texas had abandoned hanging, citing "the 'fact' that hanging 'is antiquated and has been supplanted in many states by the modern and humane system of electrocution.'"[26] A year later, in Carson City, Nevada, Gee Jon became the first American to be executed by lethal gas. These new technologies were widely believed to kill more humanely. If we look at the long history of executions in what is now the United States, it's clear that the turn from the noose was quick. From 1608 to 2002 61.3 percent of all executions were hangings (9,324 people), but 29 percent were electrocuted (4,425 people).[27] And then, from 1900 to 1999, 4,361 were electrocuted, 2,722 hanged, 593 gassed, 432 injected, and 33 shot.[28] But hanging was not completely abandoned. Though private affairs in twentieth-century America, hanging executions still excited and disturbed the popular imagination as they had before. Perhaps this was due to the simplicity of the act of hanging compared to the complicated engineering of the electric chair or gas chamber.

The last public hanging execution was of Rainey Bethea on August 14, 1936, in Owensboro, Kentucky. Bethea, an African American farm-hand, had been convicted of raping and murdering seventy-year-old Eliza Edwards. Bethea was never tried for the murder; instead, he was convicted of the rape by a jury that deliberated for about five minutes. At the time Kentucky law stipulated that someone convicted of rape would be executed in the county where the crime had occurred. Bethea's execution was witnessed by a crowd of about twenty thousand. Kentucky prohibited public executions in 1938.

From that day forward hangings, like all executions, were exclusively behind closed doors. Hickock and Smith were hanged on April 14, 1965, and on June of the same year George York and James Latham were also hanged. Those four Kansas hangings were the last hanging executions in the country until the early 1990s. The 1972 Supreme Court decision *Furman vs. Georgia* invalidated existing death penalty laws, prompting a hiatus until the Supreme Court declared the death penalty constitutional in 1976. In 1977 Utah's Gary Gilmore was the first to be executed after that hiatus—by firing squad. Sixteen years later, in 1993, the first of three hanging sentences was carried out. The first, Westley Dodd, murdered three boys, hanging one of them, post-mortem, in a closet. The second, Charles Campbell, slashed and killed two women and an eight-year-old girl. And the third, Billy Bailey, shot and killed an elderly couple in their rural farmhouse. Apart from the heinous nature of their crimes, these three men had a lot in common. They were all white, had problematic childhoods, and were sentenced to death by hanging.

If there were a scale for determining the relative heinousness of crimes, of the trio, Dodd might be at the top. He was a serial pedophile who kept a diary of his crimes and his plans for others.[29] After the three murders—stabbing ten- and eleven-year-old brothers to death and later brutally raping and then killing a four-year-old—he was caught in November 1989 trying to kidnap a six-year-old boy from a movie theater. Shortly thereafter he readily confessed to his crimes. Dodd waived all appeals, and his execution date was set for January 5, 1993, in Walla Walla, Washington. Dodd chose hanging over lethal injection because he had hanged one of the kids he tortured and murdered.[30] In his final statement Dodd claimed there was no way to stop a sex offender but through execution and that he had made peace with that through his new faith in Jesus Christ.[31] The noose was placed around his neck, and he dropped about seven feet through the trap door as witnesses watched through glass windows in the state's two-story execution room. When he dropped there was little struggle. One of the witnesses, Dodd's lawyer, Darrell Lee, claimed he was surprised by how smoothly the execution went. "I came away with the view that, 'Hey, if you are going to be executed, hanging is the way to go.'"[32] A coroner's report revealed that he died two to three minutes after he was dropped.[33] The examiner claimed that he hadn't died of a broken neck or hangman's fracture but instead of a "combination of neck damage and strangulation . . . ligaments in [his] neck were damaged enough for neck bones to separate." The coroner had told the state beforehand that Dodd would likely die of a "hangman's fracture," but that isn't what happened. Anti-death-penalty advocates pointed to this as proof of the unpredictable nature of hanging.

Charles Campbell was another story. He worked every angle he could to not be executed. His lawyers appealed to the 9th Circuit Court of Appeals in part on the premise that hanging was a cruel and unusual punishment. Ultimately his sentence was upheld, but the dissenting opinion, penned by Judge Stephen Reinhardt, argued that hanging is a "medieval" form of execution that isn't "compatible with society's evolving standards of decency."[34] Reinhardt claimed that hanging "inflicts unnecessary pain, both physical and emotional, on those condemned to die."[35] Washington state protocol relied on a 1959 military execution manual that, Reinhardt pointed out, "had never been used in an actual hanging, even though the Washington state officials had no idea how the procedure set forth in the manual had been developed."[36] He argued that the Constitution allows for people to be executed "with as much dignity as possible."[37] The Army's manual is "hardly some set of scientific equations which magically eliminates all possibility of decapitation or strangulation . . . [it] contains no scientific references."[38] To this degree he was right: as we have seen, hanging is violent and always has been, and there's no way around that.[39]

Reinhardt noted that most states and even the US Army have rejected hanging.[40] But it's not just objectively wrong: it's contrary to "human dignity" and "savage and barbaric."[41] He continued, "We are convinced that judicial hanging is an ugly vestige of earlier, less civilized times when science had not yet developed medically-appropriate methods of bringing a life to an end. Hanging is a crude, rough and wanton procedure, the purpose of which is to tear apart the spine. It is needlessly violent and intrusive, deliberately degrading and dehumanizing. It causes grievous fear beyond that of death itself and the attendant consequences are often humiliating and disgusting."[42] But Reinhardt's most salient argument was that in the United States "hanging is associated with lynching, with frontier justice, and with our ugly, nasty, and best-forgotten history of bodies swinging from the trees or exhibited in public places."[43] To emphasize his point he footnoted the words to "Strange Fruit."

On the night of his execution, Charles Campbell refused his last meal and had to be subdued and pepper sprayed because he wouldn't be handcuffed in order to be moved to a holding cell.[44] He had to be strapped to a board because he was too weak to stand up straight for the execution. Witnesses described prison employees fumbling about, trying to fix the hood over his head despite all the straps on the restraining board. Campbell made no final statement, and so witnesses never saw his face; a curtain separating witnesses and Campbell stayed in place so all they could see was shadows moving the machinery of death into place. The noose was cinched up, and at 12:08 A.M. the lever was pulled and the trap opened. After twelve years and about $2 million, thirty-nine-year-old Charles Campbell plunged to his death on the same gallows that had been used for Dodd.[45]

Like Dodd, Billy Bailey, the last man to be hanged in the United States, didn't fight the sentence. When he was asked to choose the needle or the noose he claimed, "Asking a man to choose how to die is more barbaric than hanging. . . . The law sentenced me to hang and I should hang."[46] Bailey grew up poor and abused in South Carolina, the nineteenth of twenty-three children.[47] In 1980 he robbed a liquor store and went to the rural farm of Gilbert and Clara Lambertson in rural Kent County, Delaware, intending to steal a truck. Drunk and high on valium, he shot Gilbert in the face and Clara in the back.

Bailey said later that he wasn't really sure why he did it: "It hurts sometimes when I think about it. When I say hurt, I think about the Lambertsons and how much they hate me and I start to cry and sometimes I cry myself to sleep at night."[48] After being sentenced to death he became a model prisoner, fixing furniture, mending clothes, and earning a good reputation among prison guards who spoke up for him at his last clemency hearing.[49] But Bailey wasn't granted clemency, and his hanging sentence was set in motion. The night before his execution reporter Bob Faw from NBC, noting his size, quipped that "once 220-pound Bailey wondered out loud if prison officials would be able to find a rope strong enough to hold him. Early tomorrow morning, he'll find out."

In the hours before his execution on January 25, 1996, Bailey was moved to a location closer to the gallows.[50] He met with his lawyer and a chaplain, and he visited with his sister for the last time. He also ate his final meal: steak, a baked potato, rolls, peas, and vanilla ice cream. Before midnight Bailey was escorted to the large gallows set up in an outdoor area at the Delaware Correctional Center in Smyrna. He climbed the steps to the top and stood in the freezing night, waiting for witnesses to arrive. When they did they immediately saw Bailey on the gallows above them, with a bald head, white sneakers, and a light denim jacket.[51] Flanked on both sides by guards wearing black hoods topped with black baseball caps, a clench-fisted Bailey gazed down upon the witnesses, including the victim's son, and they looked up at him.[52] The noose swayed in the wind and the yard was quiet, with no one talking or whispering—they had been told if they did, they'd be kicked out.[53] And then, at 12:01 A.M., the warden asked whether Bailey had any final words, and he said no.[54] They put a black hood over his head and moved him closer to the noose, put it over his head, and adjusted it.

The lever was pulled at 12:04 A.M. Bailey fell through and stopped suddenly, "spun around six times in one direction and then twice in the other."[55] Silence. A curtain was closed over his hanging body, and eleven minutes later he was pronounced dead. Gary Tuchman, one of the witnesses for the media, says, "It doesn't matter how you feel about the death penalty, when you see something in this fashion it's quite shocking to the system . . . for many days afterward I had a tough time sleeping. It stays in your mind a long time when you witness something so unusual as death by hanging." Bailey's lawyer, echoing Reinhardt, called the hanging "mediaeval and barbaric."[56] Witnesses from the victim's families told the media that justice had been served.

GALLOWS IN A WAREHOUSE

Today hanging is permissible in New Hampshire, if lethal injection isn't possible, and Washington, where there is a choice between hanging and injection.[57] Despite the technological advances of execution engineers, the hanged human body will expire how it sees fit. A snap of the neck. A tear of muscles. A slow suffocation. The gallows is still made of wood, and the noose is still a knot in a rope.

Kansas hasn't executed anyone since 1965. For years the state gallows, built in 1944, collected dust in that warehouse, still intact but taking up space. In 1986 officials from the State Penitentiary in Lansing contacted the state museum to see whether they wanted it. John Zwierzyna, a former curator at the Kansas Museum of History, went to check it out with some other colleagues and assess whether they could find a place to store it. As Zwierzyna tells it, they were taken to the warehouse where it was still set up, a cavernous but nondescript building on the prison grounds. It was a strange thing, he says: "from the outside you wouldn't expect it to be the place where that gallows was." When they got closer the gallows looked like it was thrown together in the prison carpentry shop—crude, makeshift, ugly. Someone had carved little crosses on one of the support beams. Graffiti, markers of the dead. But the innocuousness of it all, he recalls, made it seem like it had just been used. They took it apart, transported it back to the state museum in Topeka, and put it in storage, where it's been ever since. With the gallows came a few other items: a harness used to restrain the condemned, a hood, a roll of adhesive tape and a tongue depressor (the tape held the depressor in place to prevent the condemned from biting his tongue during execution), and a pair of shoelaces used to tie the condemned prisoner's feet together.

The governor at the time opposed capital punishment and so opposed exhibiting it, and, besides, there was no room for it in the museum. It has never been displayed, in part, Zwierzyna says, because anything associated with the death penalty is complicated to display. "They're an important part of the state's history, but it's hard to display them. How it's displayed, the lighting or whatever, can make an object appear sinister." The curator doesn't want it to appear macabre because that might come off as an attempt to exploit people's emotions. Zwierzyna wonders whether there's any possible way to display the gallows objectively. About a decade ago, while working for Pennsylvania's state history museum, they held a single-day symposium to discuss the feasibility of exhibiting the electric chair. They didn't come up with an answer for that one. In Delaware state officials held a press conference, where they ran a chain from the gallows to a backhoe and yanked the gallows down.[58]

My amiable tour guide at the Kansas State Museum is curator Blair Tarr, who ushers me down a hall and swipes a key card that opens enormous steel doors, and all of a sudden we're in a huge warehouse chock-full of Kansas history—cars, tractors, signs, windmills, an old soda bottle dispenser, and boxes upon boxes upon boxes. It's all neatly organized on three floors of metal storage racks, with a staircase in the middle to allow easy access. Tarr says part of the reason they haven't exhibited it is because of lack of space. They've talked about setting it up in the lobby of the museum, but the museum is often rented out for parties and the like. "It might put a damper on festivities," he chuckles.

But really, Tarr says, it's the Clutter murders. That's what prevents them from displaying the gallows. "Even after—what is it now, fifty-four years? It's still extremely sensitive, particularly out around Holcomb and Garden City. Members of the Clutter family are still around. And a lot of it has to do with Truman Capote. Many feel he glorified Hickock and Smith too much."

"It's interesting," I point out, "that of all the people hanged on this gallows, two people after them . . ."

"There were nineteen altogether—fifteen by the state and four by the military. But it's those two who stand out, and it's mostly because of the book *In Cold Blood*. Otherwise they'd be forgotten for better or worse. It's a problem that doesn't go away because as long as people are using Capote in high school or college classes or writing about it . . ." There is an awkward pause, then, "It's not gonna go away. Someday we may be able to put it up." They have displayed a beam from the gallows used to execute the Lincoln conspirators—there was no controversy about that.

We walk through the warehouse and up to the third floor, our feet clanging across the metal floor. He points to objects along the way—a pinball machine here, some bullets there, a Carrie Nation poster here, the original Hickock and Smith's gravestones there (they were stolen and ended up on a farm in southeastern Kansas). We move on down the narrow aisles between shelves on the third floor and over to a corner.

"There it is," he points.

Several piles of wood. Some stairs. Boxes with screws and nuts and bolts. (I'm tempted to take a relic, but I don't.) There are little notes attached to various pieces explaining what the pieces are and where they should go, but Tarr says that if it ever gets put back together, there's going to be a whole lot of trial and error in the process. I tell him what John Zwierzyna said about there being crosses on some of the wood, and so we poke around a bit but realize that it would be quite a project to locate anything in that mess. Tarr says a few others have come to see the gallows before me but not many—mostly television stations wanting a shot of the trapdoor and stairs whenever they're doing a story about capital punishment. There are some folks in Lansing who'd like to put it in a museum there. But people from the Holcomb area say it sounds like they want to use the gallows for tourism. "That doesn't sit right with them, of course."

We walk back down the stairs to look at the platform, which rests on its side in a rack full of other items. As I walk around to the other side to get a better look at it Tarr says, "And you're about to pass by the trap door."

I pivot and see it, a long, black metal lever attached to the metal trapdoor. It's stunning, in a way. The handle is gray, seemingly worn away from use or just a bad paint job. It's up on a platform to protect it from flooding.

"Wow," I say, surveying the scene around me. "What a strange collection of objects!"

"Yes, it is," he agrees.

"Here's a tractor, here's a trap door, here's an old vending machine . . ."

"And here's a jail," he points to a box-like structure in the corner made of wooden bars. "Well, more like a drunk tank."

It's all disorienting, but I turn back to the worn handle of the trapdoor. I'm mesmerized. I look at it closely and get the courage to touch it. I think of the people who have touched this thing. It's a strange sensation, at once sinister and sad.

"Through that," Tarr says without prompting, "nineteen people met their end."

Even though it's a pile of wood, it still carries meaning. Deconstructed, disassembled, scattered in parts about the warehouse, to reconstruct this machine would require much effort. To build it in the first place certainly did. I think of Sandee Geshick's remark that the rope didn't want to be a noose. The wood didn't want to be a gallows. People made it into a gallows.

Later that day, reading through the files of James Latham and George York, the last two executed on the gallows, I came across a slip of paper with these notes scribbled across:

Latham 11:59 PM W
12:04 AM Sprung
12:20 AM Deceased
York 12:30 W
12:34 Sprung
12:53 Deceased
Called Townsend 1:03 AM

There's nothing more. After that the page ends.

CHAPTER 12

The New Burning Cross

A STUN GRENADE CONTAINS ONLY A FEW GRAMS OF MAGNESIUM, aluminum, and ammonium perchlorate, but it's enough to cause intense disorientation of sight and sound. The blast and flash last about five seconds, they say—brief and effective. So when a Lima Ohio Police Department SWAT team kicked in the front door of Tarika Wilson's modest home and one team member tossed in a stun grenade, this is what Wilson's six children experienced, disrupting their play and the drone of a television.[1] It was an otherworldly juxtaposition of sharp light and dull sound—the black-armored SWAT team and multicolored children's toys—at about 8 P.M. on January 4, 2008, a Friday night. The dozen heavily armed men had entered the home because a petty drug dealer named Anthony Terry was supposedly living there. They used the stun grenade to create a distraction in hopes of catching Terry and finding a stash of cash and drugs. But the SWAT team didn't find Terry; they found his girlfriend, twenty-six-year-old Tarika Wilson, cowering in an upstairs bedroom with her six children, the oldest of whom was eight. One officer, Sergeant Joseph Chavalia, fired his automatic rifle at Wilson, shooting through the left shoulder of her fourteen-month-old boy, Sincere. When the firing stopped, Wilson was dead.

The response from Wilson's neighbors was almost immediate. They gathered outside the house, demanding to know what was going on inside and what was happening with the children. Over the following days, as they learned what happened, they continued to demand justice and the truth. The day after the raid they marched to City Hall and kept up pressure on the police. Throughout the cold Ohio winter Tarika Wilson's community kept the pressure up. Most said the police raid and the killing of Tarika Wilson were a tragedy but not surprising. For years, many said, the police had singled out African Americans for stop-and-frisks, for abusive treatment.

At the time, one of the most vocal critics of the Lima Police Department was Jason Upthegrove, an area businessman and president of the local chapter of the NAACP. Upthegrove's ties to Lima run deep: he was born and raised in Lima, and his family on his mother's side has been here for over a hundred years. He's seen the changes too—the enormous loss of jobs that accompanied the closure of a steel foundry, the loss of jobs in the area. When I meet him in Lima it was the fall of 2011, in the midst of the Great Recession. Upthegrove notes that Lima today looks like a lot of communities across the Midwest, across the United States. "Unless you knew the people in the community," he says, "you wouldn't know what community you're in. The faces are different but the situations are very similar."

But what separates Lima from some of these places is a sizeable African American community, many of whom are descendants of folks who moved north looking for jobs, escaping the Jim Crow South. Upthegrove's grandfather was such a person, moving from Rome, Georgia, in search of work and security. And this, Upthegrove notes, is why tension over crime and policing in these communities is rarely about an actual spike in crime. The real issue is race. "Traditionally law enforcement in this country has felt that the way you deal with black people is by force; that you can't communicate with them in a civil manner." This is what led to Tarika Wilson's death, he says. It was a battle between two law enforcement agencies, the county sheriff's department and the city police, to see who could get the most drug dealers off the street, and that's why they went after Anthony Terry, a petty drug dealer, with a SWAT team and semi-automatic weapons. If it wasn't a SWAT team kicking a door in, it was racial profiling or "pin-point policing," the current euphemism. Because of his position of leadership in the NAACP, Upthegrove was pushed into the spotlight by Wilson's death, and he has had to try to make sense of what happened for the African American community. What he saw was another example of the reckless behavior of policemen when encountering poor black people. "You know, how can you go past Big Wheels and Barbie dolls on the porch at eight o'clock on a Friday night, knowing that there were children in there, and then do what they did?"

At rallies and press conferences Upthegrove pointed to a pattern of racial profiling. He was not off the mark. In 2007 61 percent of the 323 drug arrests made in Lima were black people, whereas 39 percent were white.[2] And in 2008 a reporter from the *Toledo Blade* found that more than half of the 5,000 arrested each year in Lima were black.[3] That same year just 2 of 77 police officers were black. None of these numbers are proportionate to the actual demographics of the community: in 2005 73 percent of Lima residents were white and 26 percent were black. According to the 2010 Census, Lima's population was 38,771, with a 3.3 percent decline between 2000 and 2010.[4] In the same year 67.1 percent of the population was white and 26.4 percent black. In this predominantly German-Catholic city African Americans arrived in the 1940s and 1950s to work in the oil refinery; they stayed, and resentment simmers just below the surface. Lima's inequities and tensions are perhaps connected to a poor economy. Unemployment is staggeringly high, and Lima has lost about eight thousand jobs over the past fifteen years.[5] Per capita income for Lima hovers around $16,000, versus about $25,000 for the state as a whole.[6]

For some time, African Americans had complained of harassment and poor police work in general. When the police finally explained the raid, the complaints of the African American community seemed, if not vindicated, underscored. According to Lima Chief of Police Greg Garlock, the "flash-bang" grenade was for Terry, whom they assumed would be armed and dangerous.[7] But Terry wasn't in the home, and the police never located a gun. They did find about eight grams of marijuana and less than a gram of crack cocaine. This came after several weeks of investigation and obtaining a "no-knock" search warrant. The police claimed they raided the house because they had tracked Terry leaving it to make a drug sale and then returning to it later. They said they didn't know Wilson and her children were there, even though they claim to have surveilled the house for some time. These admissions of sloppy police work came well after the raid—in the weeks immediately afterward they weren't as forthcoming, and Jason Upthegrove, among others, applied pressure whenever and however possible, marching in the frigid winter to City Hall and speaking to the media at every opportunity.

The media, both local and national, picked up the story. That's when the pushback started. First it was phone calls. Then racist flyers on cars and lampposts. Not just targeting Upthegrove but also other leaders in the community—basically any black person they could find in Lima, including Tarika Wilson's mother. The flyers mocked Wilson's death and told African Americans to keep quiet. And then on Valentine's Day, about a month after the killing of Tarika Wilson, Jason Upthegrove's wife handed him the mail as he was sitting in his car in the driveway. He noticed a large envelope. "I opened it," he remembers, "and it had some racist literature with Tarika Wilson's face on it and the word 'nigger' and some other stuff written on it. And then I opened up a package, and inside the envelope was a little nylon rope tied into a noose." It was a small hangman's knot, complete with wrapping turns. He went straight to the Sheriff's Department, and they passed it on to the FBI. The case got traction because the noose came via the US Postal Service. Upthegrove was not the only African American resident in Lima to receive the literature, but he was the only one to receive the noose.

Upthegrove felt like his life might be in danger. He changed his patterns and habits: drove down different streets, went to work at different times, became hypersensitive to what was going on around him. One day he noticed a Dodge Ram pickup truck parked near his house, and then he saw it later in the day heading down the street toward him. He slowed down. As the cars passed each other, he stared at the man in the truck—then the truck raced off. After that, Upthegrove was worried about the safety of his family. He wouldn't let his children leave the house—no parties, no basketball games, no nothing. He slept when he could during the day and sat on the floor with a gun in his lap at night. That this was standard procedure for many African American civil rights activists in the fifties and sixties wasn't lost on him at the time; he says he was accustomed to people being angry with him for some reason or other, but these people had "invaded" his home and, in doing that, threatened his family.

But the machinations of justice were working all the while. The FBI jumped on the case and traced the noose to an Oregon man named Daniel Lee Jones, apparently a member of a white supremacist group called the National Socialist Workers Party. He wasn't hard to find—Jones had left his fingerprints all over the literature and skin cells from his hands all over the noose. On May 17, 2010, Jones entered a guilty plea and, on November 8, 2010, for using the US Postal Service to mail threatening communications, he was sentenced to eighteen months in a federal prison and three years of supervised release.[8] At the sentencing Jason Upthegrove tried to explain the significance of what happened, to put words to feelings complicated by history and emotions. He claimed, "Sending a noose isn't just like saying, 'I don't like you.' It is not like saying, 'I disagree with you.' It's not just an objection to my position. Sending a noose is tantamount to sending a picture of a gas chamber to a Holocaust victim, tantamount of sending a bullet to a shotgun victim, tantamount of sending a knife to a stabbing victim, or a stocking cap to a victim of rape. . . . The noose is the most egregious thing that can be threatened against an African American because of its long history. We've come a long way since the Jim Crow South, but this is a constant reminder in the African American community that there are people out there that feel as though the African American has not evolved, that we are not deserving of citizenship."[9] Upthegrove explained that the noose disrupted his family and work life. He was scared, he said, anytime somebody walked through his business door. He wondered, "Is that the guy, is that someone who wants to harm me?"[10]

Nothing violent ever ended up happening to him, and that, Upthegrove seemed to say, gave the court a unique opportunity to rehabilitate and perhaps educate the perpetrator of this crime; it was an opportunity because the intent of the hate behind the literature and the noose he was sent was clear—"clear indicators of his intent, clear indicators of how he feels, what the essence of this man are."[11] He made a choice, Upthegrove said, and now he has to pay the consequences, but perhaps he would learn something. He concluded, "His hands were on the rope. He's the one that sent it to my house where my wife, where my children stay. He could have called me like any other coward . . . but he chose to [send a noose]."[12]

Jones's defense attorney, Andy P. Hart, noted that the FBI's investigation revealed that most of Jones's friends and associates were surprised he would do such a thing, and those not affiliated with the hate group were surprised he held such beliefs: "They found him affable, and just an average everyday person."[13] Jones, he said, had no history of violence; he seemed only to wish to create attention. But that's the problem, Judge David A. Katz said. This was not a community that needed any more attention in this moment. The real danger in this case was "its impact on an already-supercharged community," that this could have opened the door for more people with Mr. Jones's leanings to act, and it could have led to violence.[14] It's not just about whether Jones would have done anything; it's that it could have encouraged others to act. Shortly after the sentencing the Department of Justice issued a press release in which Civil Rights Division Assistant Attorney General Thomas E. Perez noted that "a noose, an unmistakable symbol of hatred in this nation, was used by this defendant as a threat of violence aimed at silencing a civil rights advocate. . . . The Department of Justice will vigorously prosecute those who use threats of violence to silence proponents of racial equality."[15]

Upthegrove came face to face with Jones at the trial—the man who had threatened his life. "I found myself getting really angry the first time I saw him." But Upthegrove says his anger wasn't just about what

Jones had done to him and his family; rather, it was that he seemed like such a normal, simple man. There was nothing that screamed *Aryan Brotherhood!* about him. "He just looked like a normal guy you'd see working anywhere, in a factory or as a mechanic. Always talking to the judge, 'Yes sir, your honor. No sir, your honor. Yes sir, I understand.' Just on his best behavior, and that was just sad because it showed and demonstrated that he had the capacity to be respectful. He wasn't one of them minutemen types who were just like, 'F the justice system.' He certainly wasn't that guy. And when we went to the first hearing I remember coming out of the courtroom, he had to walk past me to leave, and he nodded at me. In that moment I just felt like busting him in his face."

That look, he said—how could Jones even look at him after what he'd done? It wasn't a game for him, for his family. Upthegrove hasn't encountered or heard from Jones since that sentencing hearing. "I wouldn't be opposed to sitting down with him and talking to him," he says. "I'm not harboring any ill feelings toward him. I think what he did was foolish; I think he's probably a product of his environment like I'm a product of my environment. It would be injurious to me to walk around with a spirit of unforgiveness. He paid a penalty, what I consider a heavy penalty—a year and half in a federal penitentiary is a heavy penalty. He paid a heavy price, and it's not for me to judge him."

At the time Jones did it Upthegrove thinks Jones didn't take what he was doing very seriously. As he tied that knot, as he made those wrapping turns, he didn't care about the repercussions for the recipient and what it would mean to him. That noose, Upthegrove says, felt very real. "Black men were hanged in front of their wives and children for doing nothing more than speaking to a white woman or not kowtowing to white supremacists or preaching the gospel of Jesus Christ or refusing to sell their land. Not for murder or rape, but just trying to be a typical citizen. The remedy for scaring those men and women, to prevent them from being citizens, was to have these public hangings. Daniel Jones kept that cycle flowing. There cannot be a new paradigm when you're re-creating old wounds like that."

FROM TOOL TO SYMBOL

From 1952 to 1954 researchers at the Tuskegee Institute who had been tracking American lynching since the late nineteenth century did not record a single incident.[16] The era of the large-scale public lynching was over. There were no Newarks or Marions after that year. There were, however, Emmitt Tills, Cheneys, Schwerners, and Goodmans. There were Medgar Everses and Martin Luther King Jrs. The end of the spectacle of lynching does not mark the end of the history of the noose: tracing the noose from its wide use as a tool of execution and then lynching to its manifestations in the hands of those who wish to threaten violence without actually committing it—in some cases—an interesting thing begins to happen: the noose becomes a synecdoche, a part that stands in for the whole.

As both lynching and hanging executions became less public, the noose as tool of intimidation began to take on a more public role. Hanging someone in effigy had been practiced for many years, but in the twentieth century a similar message is conveyed by displaying the noose on its own. Mark Potok, a senior researcher for the Southern Poverty Law Center (SPLC), claims that the noose emerged as a symbol of intimidation during the 1950s and 1960s; for example, a noose was mailed to NAACP secretary Roy Wilkins in 1959.[17]

But there are earlier examples of the use of the noose as symbol. On May 3, 1939, in Florida, a Klansman riding shotgun in a car held a hangman's knot outside a window during a "parade" through an African American neighborhood of Miami the night before a municipal election. The motorcade rolled along, stopping at least twenty-five intersections and burning crosses. Along the way they threw out leaflets that read, "Respectable Negro citizens are not voting tomorrow. Niggers stay away from the polls. KKK."[18] But they didn't stay away. In fact, black voters showed up in record numbers; about "twenty times the number recorded" in the previous election turned out to vote.[19] There is some evidence that more recent iterations of the Klan and white supremacist groups have used the noose as a ready symbol of hate and intimidation in the latter half of the twentieth century.[20]

Roy Wilkins with noose, 1959. *Agefotostock*

Klansman with noose, 1939. *Corbis Images*

During the civil rights era the noose migrated from one site of contention to the next, from the offices of the NAACP to the streets of African American communities and even to the schoolhouse. On September 11, 1956, in Texas, the noose appeared again in its role as tool of intimidation, dangling from a tree at Texarkana College amidst a battle over integration.[21] That incident brings to mind the events of Jena High School, of course, and how the public school has been for some time a central site of contention. This is a history that has been suppressed or, at least, underacknowledged—in the United States the noose has a long history of being dangled from sturdy trees in order to keep racial and ethnic minorities "in their place," so to speak.

In American art the noose has served as a stand-in for this history. Aaron Douglas's 1928 painting "Charleston" evokes the jazz clubs of the Harlem Renaissance—the music, dance, the quiet corners where African Americans could feel a modicum of liberation in a country that still provided very little political freedom. Douglas reminds viewers of this via a figure of the noose, centered on the canvas, and eerie hands grasping from the bottom of the painting—perhaps the hands of lynchers who seek to disrupt those who seek freedom. Those hands and the noose are a reminder of the reality for many black Americans who cannot find their way north—those hands reaching up from some dark place, some present, some past.

Most recently Kara Walker examines the link between the past and present in American culture. Her cut-paper silhouettes drip with tar, metamorphose, perform sex acts. Indeed, her work is at once sexually provocative and horrifying. In "Slavery! Slavery!" (1997) trees covered with Spanish moss also sport tangled ropes that appear almost alive. Her work, though, is both reminder and caution—that this history, these nooses can perform their own choke-hold on us, entangling both perpetrator and victim, performing the past in the present. John Sims's "The Proper Way to Hang the Confederate Flag" uses an actual hang-man's knot and Confederate flag and is, in some ways, more explicit than Walker in addressing the history and legacy of the noose, combining as he does two lingering and powerful symbols of America's violent past. The first iteration of the piece was in 2004 at Gettysburg College's Schmucker Gallery. Publicity about the exhibit, which was to include a large gallows outside the gallery, angered local historians and the Sons of Confederate Veterans.[22] Sims even received death threats. Given the controversy, college officials decided to move the exhibit indoors and not construct the gallows. The piece was then simply a Confederate battle flag hanged from a noose of thirteen wrapping turns with a picnic basket on the floor beside it—a symbolic lynching of the Confederate past. In protest of the college's decision, Sims boycotted the exhibit opening. In 2007 Sims installed the work at the Brogan Museum in Tallahassee, this time building a gallows and dangling a Confederate battle flag through a hangman's knot. The first display, perhaps, evoked the extralegal steps to dealing with America's past and, the latter, a more legal, state-sanctioned manner.

Is something lost when the knot is reproduced, as the image of Sims's piece is likely more powerful, more visceral in person? What is lost when a YouTube video or iPhone app can teach anyone how to tie the hangman's knot? There is no Glenn Dickey, no rope or knot expert to admonish and instruct knot tyers about the dangers of the knot, the very real possibility of death that can come quite easily from

John Sims, "Proper Way to Hang a Confederate Flag," 2004. *Used with permission of the artist*

such a knot. Perhaps in this age of one-click copying we feel so distant from the potential harm that the noose can and has inflicted that we do not take it seriously.

But it is serious, and as Jason Upthegrove sensed, it can produce and reproduce harm simply through its symbolic presence. In the twenty-first century there is something uniquely American about the noose. It is at once an expression of racist hatred but also of the possibilities of extralegal punishment—the kind of extralegal punishment any individual can mete out. It is a particularly American symbol because it is at once an expression of the racial categories that developed with the formation of this nation as well as the tension between the individual and the community. Vigilante justice existed and exists in other countries, of course, but the term and iconography have American roots. (Actually, commentators called the mob killing of a man in Brazil in 1982 a *linchamento*.[23]) The United States at once values the rule of law while at the same time glorifies the pioneer spirit of the individual who bucks the system, breaks the law, and seeks retribution for some perceived wrong. America is the orderly narrative of the Constitution and its system of checks and balances, but America is also the nation of Ahab's revenge, of the Lone Ranger, of Rambo, of Dirty Harry—and of George Zimmerman.

Indeed, the noose has become a synecdoche for this history in part because, compared to a burning cross, it is simple and quick to manufacture. Hardware stores sell rope, and online videos can instruct any patient person on how to tie the knot. If the rope isn't too large, it's easily concealed and portable. The noose is instant hate. And what happened in Jena, Louisiana, was not an anomaly. It wasn't the first noose incident, and it wasn't the last. The noose has become the new burning cross, the ready symbol for expressing hate and fostering a climate of fear in workplaces, schools, and neighborhoods throughout the United States.

But should noose incidents really be taken seriously? To address this question we must seek out patterns, causes, and effects. The incidents fall into a number of obvious categories. Quite a few of these incidents, like what happened to Jason Upthegrove, are racially motivated attempts to intimidate African Americans. Such incidents reveal a desire on the part of the perpetrator to control a minority group or individual, to limit their free speech or social mobility—the latter is particularly common. Nooses are often displayed as a way to censor, discipline, or intimidate a perceived outsider or outsider group.

- In Ruston, Louisiana, a Honduran immigrant found a noose hanging from her garage on June 13, 2008.[24] A neighbor, Robert Jackson, placed the noose there to intimidate African American men who had visited her house. Jackson was prosecuted under the Fair Housing Act and sentenced to twelve months in a federal prison.
- On August 30, 2010, in Elwood, Indiana, twenty-five miles down the road from Marion, the only African American employee at a small manufacturer found a noose dangling from a time clock a week after he began work there.[25]
- In October 2010, a few weeks after moving into a predominantly white neighborhood in Noblesville, Indiana, an African American family found a noose in their yard—this in addition to people driving by and shouting racial epithets.[26]
- Specialist Adam Jarrell was the lone African American in his unit of the New Mexico Army National Guard stationed in Afghanistan. After being called various racial slurs, he found a noose hanging outside his barracks.[27] Jarrell may have been harassed also because he reported the physical abuse of two subordinates by another officer.
- A series of complaints of racism lodged against US Capitol architect Stephen Ayers's office exposed racial tension among the blue-collar workforce on the Capitol grounds. In one reported incident a noose was discovered hanging in a break room.[28]
- In May 2012 a noose was found hanging from a tree outside Varina High School in Henrico County, Virginia (where Gabriel Prosser lived). The culprit was a student who claimed that he didn't mean it to be seen as a racist symbol or an attack on any specific person.[29]
- On June 7, 2012, an interracial couple moving into a new home in Brazoria County, Texas, found "No Niggers" spray-painted on their garage and "KKK" along with a picture

of a noose on a sidewalk that led to their front door.[30] The next day the community came out to support them with welcome cards and gifts.

- In April 2013, in Meridian, Mississippi, black mayoral candidate Percy Bland found a noose hanging outside his office.[31] Bland ultimately became Meridian's first black mayor on July 1, 2013.

The noose is also being transmitted via communications technologies. These high-tech lynchings, to borrow Justice Clarence Thomas's now-famous phrase from his Supreme Court nomination hearing, occur via fax machines and cell phones. In March 2010 South Carolina Democrat and then–House Majority Whip Jim Clyburn was faxed a picture of a noose in the wake of the House's vote to approve health care reform.[32] In January 2011 California state Senator Leland Yee also received noose faxes.[33] High-profile politicians are not the only victims of high-tech nooses. In early September 2010 an African American student at a mostly white high school in Johnstown, Pennsylvania, received a text message of an image of a brown beer bottle with a noose and three beer cans dressed as KKK members.[34] His family had recently moved to the community from Philadelphia. Police filed charges against suspects for ethnic intimidation and harassment. Later someone spray-painted "Go back to Philly or else KKK" on the Fletchers home while they were on vacation. And in early February 2011 a school bus driver in Fort Mill, South Carolina, sent a text to several friends and coworkers with an image of a noose hanging from what appears to be a swing set.[35] A message attached read, "I called Fisher Price and asked if they had black swing sets. They sent me this one. Sweet." The bus driver said it was just a joke, but she was fired nonetheless.

Perhaps it is the anonymity of some communications technologies that fosters such incidents. Some noose incidents are not anonymous in part because the perpetrator claims other intentions, like the bus driver did. One particular manifestation of the noose happens every year in late October when some homeowners decorate their houses and yards for Halloween and incorporate nooses—either just the noose itself or a mannequin in a noose hanging from a tree.[36] Some Halloween displays are more public than others, though. In October 2011 a highway billboard in Pittsburgh displayed a hanging person to help advertise the Haunted Hayloft and one of its main attractions, a reenactment of the 1889 hanging of the Nicely Brothers.[37] Other seasonal decorative nooses are both obviously racist and borderline ridiculous. In December 2010 a white separatist in Hayden, Idaho, built a snowman in his yard, complete with Klan hat and noose in hand.[38]

Since Barack Obama became president in 2008, one source reported in October 20, 2010, there have been over 106 noose incident–related lawsuits.[39] And the political rhetoric, directed toward President Obama and his policies, has also brought out the noose. In September 2010, in Miles City, Montana, a Tea Party affiliate displayed a hangman's noose at their booth at the Eastern Montana Fair.[40] The incident created a heated debate in the community—on the streets and in the local media outlet. A member of the group that displayed the noose claimed that "a lot of ads use symbolism to make something stick in your mind. That's all it was." But this noose appeared in a display of a political organization whose rhetoric specifically attacks the policies of the United States' first black president.

In the weeks prior to the 2012 election there were a number of noose incidents directed toward President Obama. Some involved hanging chairs, a reference to Clint Eastwood's GOP convention speech in which he addressed an empty chair, a stand-in for President Obama.[41] Certainly this isn't the first time a political leader has been depicted wearing a noose—this is a global phenomenon. Around the same moment the Obama nooses were appearing in the United States Greek protestors were depicting German Chancellor Angela Merkel wearing one. A year or so earlier Egyptian protestors did the same with Hosni Mubarak. More recently, when the Italian government's first black minister, Cécile Kayenge, visited the town of Pescara, an extremist group hung nooses from lampposts. (Two days beforehand a white senator had compared her to an orangutan.[42]) Certainly there is free speech, but perhaps there are *limits* to what is considered "free speech." The noose is, of course, violent and threatening speech. And there's something all the more problematic and prescient here: the people responsible for the Obama noose incidents were white males targeting the policies of a black male.

Mark Potok thinks the return of the noose is part of a reaction from white people who have become more aware of the Census Bureau's prediction that by 2050 they'll lose their numerical majority in the United States. And now there's a black president in the White House. Some people feel threatened, he says, "and these are just those feelings playing out."

"What does the noose symbolize for you?" I ask.

"Well, the noose symbolizes that if you don't act the way I want you to, you will die. That's essentially what the threat is. The threat is rarely followed by murder. I don't know of a single case, but that's the obvious implication of the threat. The noose has no other purpose other than to hang people until they are dead."

Potok's job is to expose and, sometimes, humanize these crimes. He's very honest, abrupt, and to the point. When I ask him whether hanging a noose is a hate crime, his answer is straightforward. "If the intention is to frighten or somehow warn someone about the way they better act—it absolutely is a hate crime," he says. Without taking a breath, he claims, "It's a form of terrorism. It's not blowing up buildings, but it's a form of instilling fear in your enemies or also in someone you see as your enemy and everyone else who looks like that person. And that's what makes it terrorism."

According to Potok about 56 percent of hate crimes go unreported, so it's hard to tell whether we are witnessing an increase. What he will say with some certainty is that we are witnessing a backlash to inevitable change, something our country has always gone through. "There was a backlash after slaves were freed, after women got the right to vote, against Catholics at the beginning of the twentieth century, certainly with the civil rights movement and the gay rights movement— each of these things produced a major backlash. It takes a while," he says, "to change a society's reactionary ways."

"POSTRACIAL" NOOSE

Should noose incidents be considered hate crimes? A hate crime means, essentially, a crime that targets someone because she belongs to a particular group. Laws protecting victims of such crimes are a relatively recent phenomenon, but certainly they are rooted in the violent histories discussed in this book. This is not surprising: hate crimes are about enforcing a social order. They are, as Barbara Perry writes, "a mechanism of power intended to sustain somewhat precarious hierarchies, through violence and threats of violence."[43] In other words, hate crimes act out already-present conditions on a more intense scale.

Hate crime laws have their roots in the wake of the American Civil War, specifically in the Fourteenth Amendment's guarantee of equal protection under the law, and they were enhanced, in part, by the passage of the federal Civil Rights Act in 1964. Hate crime began being monitored as such in 1990 when George Bush Sr. signed the federal Hate Crimes Statistics Act into law. It requires the US attorney general to compile information on crimes motivated by religion, race, ethnicity, or sexuality. But reporting is mixed. Every state reports differently, and some states report no crimes for certain categories. (And nongovernmental organizations like the SPLC and the Anti-Defamation League do their own monitoring as well.) Laws about who is protected from hate crime differ across the nation as well. For example, although most states have laws protecting victims of crimes based on hatred of specific races, ethnicities, or religious faiths, fewer protect against crimes motivated by someone's hatred of the victim's sexuality. (Though a 2009 bill in the wake of the high-profile Matthew Shepard case may change this at a federal level.) In March 2013 the Department of Justice released a report estimating that over 250,000 hate crimes (with victims over the age of twelve) occur each year.[44]

It is in the very nature of hate crimes that they destabilize already fragile community relations. This may have been what Daniel Lee Jones was thinking when he mailed the noose to Jason Upthegrove—an activist, an agitator, in Jones's mind, most likely. A black man who didn't know his place. But it's not just the violent threat implied by the crime itself; it's also the psychological effects of the crime on the community—the fear and intimidation produced—and these effects are largely incalculable. Communities learn of these crimes. They imagine it could happen to them. And then they change their lives and patterns. This fallout is what the judge addressed during Jones's sentencing. Jones, he said, was not just threatening Jason Upthegrove and his family; he was also threatening a community already on the edge and perhaps giving the green light to other racists. For Daniel Lee Jones, this nexus of race and hate did not pan out. The federal government, backed by the Constitution and legal precedent, protected Upthegrove and, in a sense, reinforced his right to free speech in the public sphere.

Thinking about First Amendment rights—of the victims and of the perpetrators—is important, but legal scholar Jeannine Bell believes it's more important to consider the impact of the noose on victims. She notes that in popular culture it holds a particularly negative connotation for African Americans, and the media often pick up on this; the media "almost uniformly describe the noose in a manner consistent with its historical meaning as a racially offensive symbol used to intimidate."[45] They will offer the commentary of experts, of numbers of lynchings, or they will bring up analogies to the swastika or burning crosses.[46] This coverage can add to the impact of the incident itself and perhaps exacerbate the effects of the hate crime.

In the wake of Jena many state legislators rushed to ban the noose, but noose hangings were already illegal according to employment and criminal law as well as civil rights legislation.[47] And yet legislatures in North Carolina, New York, and Louisiana, among others, made noose hanging illegal.[48] In New York, for example, legislation was a response to a spate of noose incidents in Hempstead, Long Island, and in New York City.[49] On October 22, 2007, the New York State Senate passed legislation (S6499) sponsored by Republican Senator Dean Skelos of Rockville Centre. This legislation makes "it a felony to etch, paint, draw, or otherwise place or display a noose on public or private property with intent to threaten, intimidate, or harass." Skelos claimed that "there is no place for racism and intimidation in America and this rash of incidents clearly demonstrates the need for tough new penalties." State Senate Majority Leader Joseph L. Bruno added, "This legislation recognizes that a noose continues to be a powerful symbol of racism and intimidation towards African Americans." He added that noose incidents are "menacing and disturbing."

Bell says such bills are a good start but don't address situations in which the noose is hung as a joke or prank—"those who, like the students at Jena High, do not appreciate the significance of the hangman's noose. Such perpetrators impart fear and intimidation, but cannot be punished under the legislation specially aimed at the harm they cause with nooses."[50] For noose hangers to be prosecuted there must be a clear intention to intimidate. This, she says, is problematic because it negates the feelings of the victim. Even if the perpetrator meant it as a joke, a burning cross or a noose could cause a great deal of harm for those who see it. Bell says that whenever hate symbols are displayed, courts need to "incorporate the victim's perspective."[51] She advocates a "victim-centered" approach that "focuses only on punishing the 'wordless speech' in readily identifiable extreme symbols of racial hatred like the hangman's noose."[52] When courts reject the victim-centered approach, "the hangman's noose changes from what victims and the rest of society sees—an unmistakable sign of violence wrought by the Ku Klux Klan—into a harmless prank. Validating the perpetrator's perspective in this way is symbolic of the lynch mob all over again."[53]

THE NOOSES IN JENA[54]

When the nooses appeared on that oak tree in Jena, Louisiana, on the morning of September 1, 2006, some of the black students who heard about it didn't understand the significance of them.[55] Or at least that's what former Jena High School student Robert Bailey told Alan Bean, a Baptist minister and activist from Tulia, Texas, and the man who helped publicize the Jena 6 case. But when those students went home that day and told their parents, their parents were livid. They organized a meeting at a local Baptist church and made plans to speak at the next school board meeting. And those black students, perhaps armed with a better understanding of the meaning of the noose, held a sit-in the next day beneath that oak tree. Reactions from white students to the protest were mixed: some agreed, some were indifferent, and others were angered by it. There was some shoving, some pushing, some yelling. Clear divisions were being drawn in the schoolyard.

As Bean tells it, there had always been some animosity between black and white students, and even between black students and white teachers. After the noose incident and student protest, tension in the school was palpable. The campus was put on lockdown—law enforcement officers swarmed the place, and the school administration called an assembly. At that assembly all of the white kids sat on one side of the auditorium and all of the black kids on the other. At one point during the assembly District Attorney Reed Walters addressed the students, saying he was tired of their behavior. And then he said, "I just want you all to realize that I can make your lives disappear with a stroke of my pen."[56]

The noose hangings were discussed at the next school board meeting. The high school principal wanted the noose hangers expelled, but he would not get his way. The noose hangers claimed they meant it as a joke aimed at kids on the school's rodeo team. They claimed to have recently seen an episode of the television show *Lonesome Dove* that inspired them to make the nooses. They said they didn't really understand the history of lynching in America and, according to at least one journalist, "became visibly remorseful" when told about it.[57] The students were given nine days suspension in an off-campus alternative school, two weeks in-school suspension, and a number of Saturday suspensions.[58] They were also required to attend a discipline court and undergo psychological evaluations to determine whether they were a threat to themselves or their classmates.

In an interview with *Jena Times* reporter Craig Franklin, LaSalle School Superintendent Roy Breithaupt and LaSalle District Attorney Reed Walters said there was a "full investigation" in the wake of the noose hangings.[59] The investigation found that the nooses were first seen early in the morning, at about 7:55 A.M. They were made of nylon ski rope and were cut down almost immediately. According to La-Salle School System Child Welfare Supervisor Melinda Edwards, they conducted multiple interviews with the perpetrators and came to the conclusion that the students "did not have a knowledge of black history in relation to the hanging of black citizens in the south."[60] When they learned the history "they really were very remorseful," Edwards said. Besides, she notes, when the student asked the assistant principal whether he could sit under the oak tree in the school yard, "Everyone laughed including the black student who asked the question. That exchange has been misconstrued by certain persons to formulate a reason for the hanging of the nooses."

When a group of African American parents was allowed to speak at one of the meetings, they protested what they saw as the board's leniency toward the noose hangers. They wanted the school board to acknowledge it was a hate crime, that it was motivated by race. They were allowed to speak for five minutes. After they spoke the meeting went on as scheduled; the nooses, along with the history they raised from the dead, were apparently ignored. Life carried on in Jena. By the end of September 2006 the Jena Giants football team was having a winning season, and all seemed well—as it does in small southern towns with successful football programs. Two of the team's star players were black students Mychal Bell and Carwin Jones. But victories on the gridiron couldn't erase the history of race relations in Jena, Louisiana, or in the South, for that matter. Tensions mounted on and off campus. On Thursday night, November 30, 2006, someone set fire to a classroom building at Jena High School. The culprits have never been apprehended. The incident made the situation more difficult. For one, the school administration was thrown for a loop—they had to figure out where to have classes. And secondly, many assumed the fire had something to do with the bubbling animosity between black and white students.

The next evening two black students, Robert Bailey and Theo Shaw, tried to attend a private dance at a local dance hall. A few black students had been invited and were already inside. Bailey had gotten a call from one of these students, telling him to come on in. But when he tried to enter the hall, he was asked to leave. Then Bailey was attacked by a white man named Justin Sloan, who was later charged with simple battery. The next day, at a local convenience store, Bailey and two friends encountered one of the white men who had attacked him the night before. The white man took a shotgun out of his truck, and Bailey and his friends wrestled the gun away.

The following Monday a white student named Justin Barker was assaulted as he was walking out of the gym. Barker was apparently knocked out with one punch. Some say he was kicked while on the ground. The primary assailant, according to teachers, was Mychal Bell. According to Alan Bean, it's virtually impossible to know for sure what happened—and he even wonders about who was involved. Some have said that Barker had been teasing Bailey for getting beaten up on Saturday; others have said that Barker was friends with the noose hangers. Six students were arrested in connection with the fight or attack at school: Carwin Jones, Robert Bailey, Jesse Ray Beard, Mychal Bell, Bryan Purvis, and Theo Shaw. Eventually they were all charged with attempt to commit second-degree murder and conspiracy to commit second-degree murder, charges that could carry a maximum sentence of life in prison. The six were expelled for the year, but the harsh charges brought the media to the story and about twenty thousand activists to Jena on September 20, 2007—so many people that cell phones wouldn't work and roads were clogged with buses of protestors never making it into town to march.

Eventually the charges facing the Jena 6 were reduced. Those young men have moved on, moved away, gone to college. But Alan Bean told me that to focus solely on the fights and the charges against those young men is to miss the point. The point is that there was an underlying issue that wasn't being addressed in the community, and the noose brought it to the surface. And when it got there, it was ignored. On a number of occasions investigators and school officials have said the initial noose incident had no relation whatsoever to the violent confrontations that happened that fall. "That makes no sense to me," Bean said. The noose was what set off the community. The noose is what led to the fights, to the fire, and to the charges of attempted murder filed against six black youths. It was the noose that led to one of the largest civil rights marches in the United States since the 1960s. The noose made it all happen.

And it was the noose that led many to quickly paint the community with a broad stroke, to dip into the narrative of the past.[61] An area newsman claimed that the media got it all wrong and that the experience led to a deep distrust among folks in Jena of anyone from the outside. The community of Jena looked inward and, in some cases, upward. One local pastor claimed the "community saw the church as a rallying point and point of unity and we grew closer than we were before. That's not an admission that there was some problem just that that event brought us closer. Jena is more close-knit than it was."[62] In the wake of the incident the community formed a task force of local clergy and leaders to talk about some of the things that happened, but they remain, not surprisingly, hesitant to talk with outsiders.[63]

Community-rooted efforts like the Human Relations Committee happened after all the violence and tension, Bean noted. "It wasn't phony." They were trying to address what happened, but there was no real effort to address the heart of the matter, which is an ugly and complicated history.[64] And the heart of the matter, he said, was buried deep in the community, buried deep in the history of the South, an ugly history that almost no one wants to address. "Everybody wants to feel good about their heritage," Bean said, "but neither black nor white southerners can do that." The history of black people in the South is a story of slavery and racist violence. And for white people it's being the perpetrators and being on the losing side of the Civil War. Bean notes that "white people in the South had cobbled together this myth of the lost cause." But then the rest of the world, the rest of the country disrupted that myth in the 1950s and 1960s, and "it was a tremendous blow to white southerners." Addressing the underlying issues in Jena would mean actually confronting that messy past, and that would be overwhelming. That, Bean said, explains why the school board so desired a quick resolution.

It also might explain why white students at Jena High School claimed they were ignorant of the history of lynching in the United States and in Louisiana. In fact, Louisiana has seen the fourth-most lynchings in the United States—behind Mississippi, Georgia, and Texas—and second-most in lynching per capita.[65] And by 1923 Louisiana had the top three lynching counties in the nation with number of recorded lynchings—Ouachita (19), Caddo (18), and Bossier (15). So what are young people learning about the history of race and violence in the United States and their surrounding communities? Are they learning anything about lynching? There's no way of knowing what takes place in every classroom across the United States, let alone in a small town like Jena. Some Louisiana textbooks do mention lynching.[66] But Louisiana's State Department of Education has curriculum standards, and they do not mention lynching directly.[67] The only mention comes not in the US history classroom but in standards for teaching African American studies, one of nine options that students can take to fulfill a high school social studies elective requirement. Louisiana standards do address Jim Crow, but the vigilante justice that kept those laws and customs in place, the over 391 people lynched in the state, isn't required knowledge. Of course standards do not define everything that happens in a classroom, but they are about accountability and measurement. Standards are also about what state departments of education think well-rounded citizens of the state should know.[68]

The problem is exacerbated because the offspring of those who lived through 1950s and 1960s don't really know each other. Bean told me that "a lot of the white kids had gone to white schools in towns around Jena. They were country types, into hunting and fishing, and many of them racist—they were having culture shock. Some of these folks were on the rodeo team, and they cooked up this idea to hang nooses from that tree." He thinks of what happened as indicative of a deep resentment. "The white kids should have been punished in some way as a sign that this will not be tolerated, that it's a breach of the social compact. An expulsion for a month or something. But the real thing is that there was no acknowledgment on the part of the leadership and no desire to educate about the past."

Jena isn't alone in ignoring this history. "Look," Bean said, "there are still scars from integration. That's what this is about, fundamentally, whether or not whites and blacks can get along or whether a multicultural society can work." It disappointed Bean then and disappoints him still that this was never a part of the story. Like many places in the South, in the United States, "they couldn't handle it, the nooses, a real racist symbol in your face. They couldn't handle it as a community." It showed the real differences in perceptions in that community, and the white community experienced a bit of "cognitive dissonance." The tree, he knew, would be central to the story because most people can make that connection. But he was shocked that few people connected the dots between the noose, the tree, and the schoolyard and that adults in the community didn't recognize this moment for what it really was—a litmus test for the future.

From the outside looking in, the story seemed clear-cut, at least from the perspective of the national news media. What happened in Jena was evidence, as one BBC News story headline screamed, that "'Stealth Racism' Stalks Deep South."[69] Alan Bean said he was concerned about such stories from the beginning. "I didn't want it to be about an unreconstructed South. I wanted it to be a story about what happens post-civil rights when schools are integrated and people can't unpack their baggage from the past, the trauma. It was a festering wound." So the stories were either "This is Jim Crow racism!" or "This is being blown out of proportion." The South today is a different place from the South of the 1960s, he allowed, but there are still things below the surface that mustn't be ignored. There's evidence, though, that some white folks down the road were learning something. On the day of the march in Jena a teenager from nearby Alexandria named Jeremiah Munsen hung nooses from his truck as he drove past demonstrators. Munsen was sentenced to four months in prison for interfering with the marchers' right to travel.[70]

The noose incident is an easy target. Newscasters with pained faces report on this visible symbol of hatred and note the fear it has provoked in the victim. And yet the noose reveals a more complicated set of truths—the still underdiscussed narrative of violence in American history and the long arc of violence in human history. Interpersonal racism is easier to address than the institutional racism that, perhaps, privately sustains and permits it. In Jena, in an effort to put the past behind them, they cut down the supposed "white tree," but the history was still there, of course.[71]

It is one thing to point to a symbol and say that symbol is bad; it is another thing entirely to engage with the history that symbol represents. Displaying the noose in the United States carries the resonances of our nation's long lynching history, a history we have yet to reconcile. When we see the noose, whole worlds open up in a terrible and tremendous fashion. To trace the noose's wrapping turns is to trace a violent American history perpetrated against social others, in particular against racial minorities. This includes both a kind of legal "justice," the death penalty, meted out by the state—with all the biases that kind of justice entails—as well as another, extralegal "justice," the democracy of the mob.

There are also plenty of examples in which the symbol becomes much more. On June 7, 1998, an African American man named James Byrd Jr. was dragged to death behind a truck in Jasper, Texas. During the trial prosecuting his killers, it was revealed that one of them, John William King, was a member of a white supremacist prison gang and had a tattoo of a man hanging from a tree.[72] Wade Michael Page, the neo-Nazi who walked into a Wisconsin Sikh Temple, killing six and wounding four, was a member of a "white power" band called 13 Loops. But perhaps the most salient example in the last few decades was when, on March 21, 1981, Michael Donald was found hanging from a tree, a noose around his neck, along a street in Mobile, Alabama.[73] The autopsy revealed that Donald was dead before he was hanged from the tree, and yet that isn't the point: the position of the body and public nature of its display signaled the long history of lynching in America. It wasn't enough to simply kill Donald; his killers, both Klansmen, wanted to display his body in such a manner in order to maximize fear in the black community. One of Donald's killers, James Knowles, described in court the deliberate nature of his own contributions to this lynching.[74] He first went to friend and fellow Klansmen Frank Cox's house to get the rope, used a lighter to seal the ends of the rope, and then tied the hangman's knot. The lawyer questioning him asked him whether he could replicate the knot for the court. Knowles did so, explaining the process and care he took in tying the knot almost as if in passing, like it was second nature. He said, "There was a strand left over, about like this [indicating], it was cut off and burned, just similar to this right here . . . both ends were cut and burned prior to the time of the noose, so that they wouldn't, neither of them, unravel." Then the lawyer asked him why he got the rope from Cox in the first place. Knowles's answer was blunt: "I intended to use it to hang a black person. . . . Henry [Hays] and me went to East Mobile, and we drove around for a while. Exactly how long, I don't remember. And eventually, we came on Michael Donald, and we kidnapped him and took him to Baldwin County and killed him, and brought him back to Herndon Avenue and hung him up earlier Saturday morning."

Where the nooses used in the Jena incident were a threat, this noose was shaped, turned, and crafted as a tool for killing. In literature a "turn" is a major transformation in a poem's narrative, rhetoric, or form. Poet and friend David Baker tells me the turn "is both a turn in the language, story, argument, and often—like in a sonnet—a turn of the line and visible re-turn of the poem's shape itself." It's a dramatic change. "It's magic," he explains. When a noose is formed from rope a kind of sorcery occurs, indeed. The structure is transformed—the meaning of the rope is transformed.

The noose signifies an international history of execution, legal or otherwise. The knot itself was crafted as a technology of execution; it was the way of death for young and old, men and women, rich and poor—but mostly poor—across centuries. According to one

CHAPTER 13

The Noose in Our World

THE DEATH PENALTY SEEMS TO BE ON ITS WAY OUT around the world. Ninety-eight countries have abolished it for all crimes.[1] The United Nations has called for a moratorium on the death penalty, most recently in 2010, with 109 votes in favor and 49 votes opposed. In 2013, 173 of the 193 UN member states were execution free.[2] That same year, though, the United States was the only country in the Americas to carry out an execution. And yet in the United States rates of execution have dropped precipitously over the last century. James L. Payne points out that "if the United States were applying the death penalty at the same rate it was applied in the 1640s, there would have been more than 88,000 executions in the decade 1990–1999, instead of the 478 there actually were."[3] The total number of executions has dropped since about the middle of the twentieth century.[4] And in the first years of this century they have as well: in 2000 there were 85, and in 2013 there were 39.[5] The death penalty is applied with less and less frequency, in a fashion that borders arbitrariness, but still disproportionately affects the poor and racially marginalized—as it always has.[6] Numerous studies underscore that the death penalty is not a deterrent, that it costs more to put someone to death than to incarcerate them, and, increasingly, families of murder victims are suggesting that the drawn-out process of capital cases do not bring them closure.[7] And sometimes the wrong person ends up on death row. Since 1976, 144 people have been exonerated from death row.[8] In turn it's becoming less popular. A 2013 Pew Research Survey found that 55 percent of Americans support the death penalty, down from 78 percent, the year Billy Bailey was executed.[9]

And yet this punishment has not gone away entirely. In 2013 at least 778 executions were carried out in twenty-two countries worldwide.[10] This figure is likely much higher, though, because it doesn't include China, which, according to some estimates, executed several thousand people in 2012 and 2013.[11] The methods for these executions included firing squads, lethal injection, and even hanging, which is still used regularly in Bangladesh, Japan, India, Iran, Pakistan, and Singapore, among others. Currently the United States ranks in the top five worldwide for number of annual executions, trailing only Saudi Arabia, Iraq, Iran, and China. In the time it took me to write this book, 101 people were executed in the United States, though none of them by hanging and none of them in public.[12]

If I want to witness a hanging execution—if I really want to see the noose do its work—I don't have to go very far. I don't even have to leave my office. There's plenty to see online. Indeed, *you* don't have to go anywhere special to watch an execution today. Pull out your smartphone. Turn on your laptop. It's right there on the screen: real human beings hanged.

The most famous hanging in recent years is that of Saddam Hussein on December 30, 2006, and it is readily accessible online. Ostensibly Hussein was executed for crimes against humanity related to his orders to kill 148 Shia men and boys in the town of Dujail in 1982. (His government also seized property and bulldozed homes.)

On YouTube and elsewhere you can see for yourself one result of the war in Iraq. The disgraced former dictator of Iraq was executed on December 30, 2006. At 5 A.M. that day he was transported from Camp Cropper near the airport to Camp Justice and, wearing a wool cap, scarf, and long black coat, handed over to the Iraqi National Police.[13] Camp Justice is in Kazimain, a suburb northeast of Baghdad, and it used to be called Camp Banzai. And it was where his own operatives, the Istikhbarat (military intelligence group) had used the same gallows to kill Iraqis.

Saddam execution still from Iraqi State Television.

At Camp Justice he was led into a small, dingy room, cramped with a film crew, guards, and witnesses, including Munkith al-Faourn, deputy prosecutor for the court; Munir Haddad, deputy chief judge for the Iraqi High Tribunal; and Sami al-Askari, member of Iraqi Parliament. The executioners took his hat and scarf and bound his hands in front. They sat him down, and the final verdict, which detailed his crimes against humanity, was read aloud. As it was read, he shouted, "Long live the nation! Long live the people! Long live the Palestinians!"[14] He was asked "if he had any remorse or fear" and replied negatively: "No. I am a militant and I have no fear for myself. I have spent my life in jihad and fighting aggression. Anyone who takes this route should not be afraid."[15] Curses flew. One guard shouted, "You have destroyed us!" To which he replied, "I have saved you." The guard retorted, "God damn you!" Hussein responded, "God damn you."[16]

The videos of the execution show what happened next. To be clear, there are two videos of Hussein's execution. One is official—shot from the platform and aired on television without sound—and doesn't show the drop. The unofficial one—shot from below the scaffold and with sound—is from a cell phone and a bit grainy. You can see and hear the masked executioners, who are apparently Shia.[17] Hussein is led up to the gallows, and his hands are unbound and retied behind his back. He is offered a hood but refuses. Then you see one of the executioners talking to him, explaining what will happen when he's dropped, that the rope might cut through his neck.[18] That executioner then takes Saddam's black scarf and wraps it around his neck. The noose is adjusted with wrapping turns under his left ear. Hussein prays, and then you hear shouts of the name of Shi'ite leader Moktada al Sadr.

"Moktada! Moktada! Moktada!"

Hussein replies, "Moktada. . . . Is this how real men behave?"[19]

Then shouts and noise.

And from somewhere, "Go to hell!"

"Please no! The man is about to die."[20]

His head held high, eyes open. Hussein prays the Shahada, his final prayer before death. He says it once, and then, as he's about to repeat it, in midsentence—the drop. After the execution there are shouts of "The tyrant has fallen! May God curse him!" And in the cell phone video there's a close-up of his eyes—again wide open but now glassy. Later he was placed into a pine box and flown 110 miles in a helicopter to his hometown of Awja, courtesy of the US military.

But the story of the Saddam execution wasn't just that he was hanged; it was that things got out of hand, that the execution was not "civilized" and that images of the execution leaked. If the hanging had happened smoothly in private, few would have cared and it wouldn't have been an embarrassment for the Bush administration. Instead, a supposedly dignified affair was chaotic. Commentators noted that his executioners were clearly his enemies. A *New York Times* editorial called it a "Shiite lynch mob."[21] The editors claimed, "Mr. Hussein has now gone to his grave. But the outrageous manner of his killing, deliberately mimicking his own depraved methods, assures that his cruelty will outlive him." The scene did have an air of revenge rather than the apparently high-minded dispensation of justice. Furthermore, amidst the yelling and name calling, Hussein appears to die a good death. He's calm, almost noble, when juxtaposed against that mocking masked crew. Daoud Kuttab, a Palestinian media critic, notes, "If

Saddam had media planners, he could not have planned it better than this. Nobody could ever have imagined that Saddam would have gone down with such dignity."[22]

In the wake of the Hussein execution and viral videos there were at least a half-dozen copycat hangings around the world, including a ten-year-old in Texas, a nine-year-old Pakistani boy, and a twelve-year-old boy in Turkey, among others.[23] Two weeks later Hussein's former intelligence chief Barzan Ibrahim al-Tikriti, and Awad Hamad al-Bandar, the former chief of Hussein's revolutionary court, were hanged.[24] Al-Bandar's went smoothly, but the calculations for al-Tikriti's drop were apparently off—his head was ripped off from his body after a drop of nearly eight feet.

The war produced other moments of destruction, degradation, and violence, not just for elite former leaders, and much of that was also caught on camera: Saddam's statue is noosed to the ground on April 9, 2003; on March 31, 2004, four armed contractors from Blackwater Security are attacked by a mob, beaten and burned, and their bodies hung from a bridge that crossed the Euphrates River, where civilization began; and then there was Abu Ghraib, with Lynndie England's "thumbs up" next to a pile of naked bodies or with cigarette dangling from her mouth as she yanks a dog collar on another naked body, and, of course, the hooded and robed figure of Abdou Hussain Saad Faleh. His arms are outstretched, Christ-like, the ghostly black sleeves of the robe hanging down, but with the tall black Klan-like hood, he looks almost sinister. He's standing on a box with wires attached to his fingers, toes, and penis; he'd been told that he'd be electrocuted if he fell. The photo was taken on November 4, 2003, and was later published in the *New Yorker* and quickly became the iconic image of the Abu Ghraib scandal. The image is compelling because, as art historian Dora Apel writes, it "resonates with allusions to the crucifixion, robed monks, the Statue of Liberty, the Klan, the executioner, the mask of death."[25] It also reminds one of the suspended figure of a lynched man. Artist Richard Serra made a sketch of the photo and mounted it on a billboard on Tenth Avenue in New York

City, an image that was later displayed in the Whitney Museum of Art's Biennial.[26]

The noose is missing in the Abu Ghraib images, but its work is not. The messy war in Iraq brought forth some of America's basest impulses, including, it seems, that of lynching. Dora Apel suggests that despite different motivations as well as historical moments, we can learn something from putting the Abu Ghraib images and lynching photographs in conversation with one another.[27] Like lynching photographs, the viewer focuses attention on both the victimized body and the seeming shamelessness of the apparent perpetrators—a terrifying juxtaposition. She writes, tellingly, that these scenes are staged by people who assume their actions are community sanctioned, and "the viewer is meant to identify with the proud torturers in the context of the defense of a political and cultural hierarchy."[28] America doesn't have the same history with Arabs and Muslims as it does with the history of slavery, but, she argues, "the old and unresolved Israeli/Palestinian conflict, and the effects of the first Gulf War in 1991 have encouraged many Americans to view many Arabs and Muslims with grown suspicion and distrust, which burst into open and wanton violence in the United States following 9/11."[29] Now "just as black men were stereotyped en masse by white supremacists" as "'black beast rapists'; now they are all 'terrorists,' making them far easier to humiliate, torture, sexually exploit, and kill."[30]

Egyptian-born artist Haitham Eid made these connections in his 2008 painting "Noose," which was first displayed at New Orleans African American Museum at the Tenth Annual MLK Commemorative Art Exhibit and later at the New Orleans Jazz and Heritage Foundation Art Gallery.[31] Eid was taking a graduate course at the New Orleans African American Museum of Art, Culture, and History, in a hall where an African warrior suit and mask were on display. The display mesmerized him—it looked lifelike, like a human being hanging. Somehow, he says, that display merged not only with the image of Abdou Hussain Saad Faleh in his subconscious but also with the history of African Americans in the United States. Out of that merging he

"The Noose," painting by Haitham Eid, 2008. *Used with permission of the artist*

created an enormous mixed media painting of a figure with memories as a film strip coming out of his head.

"He's remembering," he told me in an interview, "what's happened to him or to his people." The suit is that of the African warrior that was the genesis of this painting, the photos are from Abu Ghraib, and the noose, he says, represents the lynching of African Americans in the United States.

"It's three different cultures, three different injustices coming together, three different unnecessary sufferings."

Eid, who is working on a PhD in museum studies, insists that museums should be dynamic public spaces that contribute to the public conversation about controversial issues. His painting obviously fosters such a public conversation. At one of its showings it stirred up controversy. Some museum goers thought it was in bad taste and inappropriate for the eyes of young children. At least, he says, that's how the complaints were framed.

"I used to stand near it and look at people's expressions, and I saw different expressions. Most were shocked, and one person almost cried." Perhaps it was shocking and disconcerting, but can't images also be used to teach us, to provoke us? "With this painting I think I'm trying to ask a very basic question: What kind of memories are we trying to make for ourselves and the generations that come when we create violence? Peace, justice, and human rights can never come through violence."

THE OTHER HANGING VIDEOS

As I wrote this book I kept coming back to the obvious: the violence of modern punishment and its concomitant culture of retribution have old roots, and despite much progress, we still aren't far from them. Me-

Execution in Iran, a still from Iranian State Television.

dievalist Robert Mills gets it right when he notes that although there may have been a shift from regularized public torture, "tell that to the people being tortured now, in the police cells, prisons, detention centres and execution chambers of—yes—the modern West. And tell that to all the people watching violence on television and the silver screen."[32] And also, of course, watching execution videos online. There are dozens if not hundreds readily available. In 1908 the US Postmaster General banned mailing lynching postcards, but the World Wide Web doesn't function in the same way.

There's much to be seen if you wish to look. Iraq's neighbor to the east, Iran, still uses the noose and often in a very public manner. Hangings are often publicized events, some are televised, and many are recorded and available on YouTube. At least 580 people were executed in Iran in 2012, and 625 in 2013.[33] In Iran murder, rape, drug trafficking, sodomy, adultery, and apostasy, among other things, can lead to the death penalty. In 2012 the majority of all executions were for drug-related charges—murder accounts for only 6 percent.[34] In 2013 Ahmed Shaheed, the UN Special Rapporteur on Human Rights in Iran, claims that, again, the majority of people executed were for drug charges.[35] Iran executes more juvenile offenders than any other country and sets the bar at puberty—age fifteen for boys and nine for girls.[36]

Hadi Ghaemi, executive director of the International Campaign for Human Rights in Iran, told me that Iran, like most places, has a long history of hanging executions, but now it has become an important social and political control for the Islamic Republic. After the 1979 Revolution the number of executions in Iran spiked because of the new penal code, the Islamic penal code, and a number of crimes punishable by execution. During the first decade there were tens of thousands, he said. "We don't know exact numbers, but in the summer of 1988, in the aftermath of the Iran-Iraq War, there were about 4,500 prisoners hanged throughout the country." At first executions were mostly by firing squads, but when a penal code was established, hanging became the preferred method, and the Islamic Republic justified it with religious doctrine.

Ghaemi says that capital punishment has become a major method for the Islamic Republic to maintain control. In the 1980s, he points out, most executions were of a political nature, but now public executions are often for "moral" issues—drug crimes, perceived sexual deviance, and so on. "According to their own admission and our accounts too, they have occurred over 70 percent for drug-related crimes. . . . But Iran does have a huge drug problem, being a neighbor to Afghanistan and Pakitsan." Officials will target poor local dealers who can't buy their way out of the judicial system. They think they could use capital punishment to fight the drug problem, but there's been no indication that it has worked—the drug problem continues to grow. In a sense, Ghaemi says, this is "a war on poor people, ethnic minorities like Baluchi or Kurdish people, for example. These people are being targeted and sacrificed."

But the increase in public hangings, Ghaemi says, is most disconcerting. "I'm troubled by the psychological impact of the hangings on the viewer, particularly children. It desensitizes the public through violence, preparing them for further acts of official violence and making violence a formal element of public policy." And they are happening more often, he believes, than they did in the pre-Revolution era. There were at least fifty-eight public executions in 2012, and fifty-six in 2013.[37]

Ghaemi has paid close attention to where the hangings are happening, when they're happening, and who's attending them. It's this last trend that he's most interested in. "There seem to be three types of audiences. One, people who know the person to be executed and are angry. Two, people who are coming from the community where the crime was committed, full of this idea of revenge that they have made people accept. And the third are just curious and were raised after the Revolution to believe that this form of public execution is commonplace among people. Remember the majority of Iranians are under thirty-five. So you get a lot of young men who come out of curiosity, and that lynching atmosphere. Hanging people publicly has become normalized."

"But what do you think about the videos online? Don't they do that too?" I ask.

"Iran is a closed society, but people are very tech savvy, and they resort to any method to get the material on the web. Many of the pictures come from the regime's own news agency."

"Who are they for?"

"They are intended to spread the message that they are capable of extreme violence, a warning to the broader public that any kind of dissent or challenge to our role, we are capable of extreme violence and are not shy about it and international pressure will not deter us." And yet they can have the opposite effect.

"Globally, we're progressive. Things have changed. Change requires a generation of kids to learn something new, different, better." He tells me that he remembers in the 1980s hearing environmentalists talk about the need for widespread recycling. And now, lo and behold,

people recycle. "And that happened because young people were educated in schools and in popular culture."

Maybe we should see these images as a weapon against tyranny.
By documenting atrocities, they can hold a regime accountable in the
public sphere. Responding to questions about violent content from
the Syrian War posted on YouTube, a spokesperson for the website
claimed, "People around the world have used YouTube to document
humanitarian disasters, war zones, and human rights abuses. This material can be quite graphic, yet the Web is a vital source of news and
information, and these are events and perspectives that may otherwise
never be seen."[38] Images can raise awareness, the argument goes: the
Marion lynching photo, the body of Emmett Till shown in an open
rather than a closed casket, or that of Trayvon Martin. The hanging
videos can teach us to respond to the noose in a certain way.

But what does seeing this violence do to us, viscerally, even if we're
being educated? I've watched these videos, and I can't help wondering:
How can this ever be normalized? I'm grasping for words here, trying to
say something critical and articulate about watching these films, but I
can't. I'm reaching, in my mind and in my body, the limits of this history
of the noose. In one film a crane slowly lifts a man off the ground, red
rope tied into noose.[39] In another, the daytime hanging of an alleged rapist, crowds of spectators hold up their cell phones to take pictures.[40] And
then, five men standing on oil drums at a city intersection, the drums
are kicked out, and they kick and lurch.[41] The dark sky and a street light
with rope attached, white pickup truck, red brake lights, truck goes into
gear, moves forward, a man falls, but the film continues; he kicks, swings
his arms, kicks, swings.[42] The last one I watch gives me some hope: a
crowd of onlookers rushes the gallows and pulls the hanged men down.[43]

THE HANGED MAN'S TALE

In 1996 a man named Niazali was hanged in Iran after having been
convicted of manslaughter. After twenty minutes in the noose his face
turned black and his tongue thrust forward.[44] His executioners took

him down from the rope and sent the body to the morgue. There the coroner began his inspection and discovered that Niazali was alive. He was revived in a local hospital and unceremoniously sent back to prison. He said, "That first second lasted like a thousand years. I felt my arms and legs jerking out of control. Up on the gallows in the dark, I was trying to fill my lungs with air, but they were crumpled up like plastic bags."[45] Niazali speaks to us from the ghostly interstices of limbo, somewhere between the living and the dead, from a place few can talk about—from beneath the execution hood.

Surviving the gallows, though, is extraordinary, but if the hanged could speak, what would they say? Would they be able to speak of their experience? Would they offer us a rarified calculus of pain? Would we comprehend it? Elaine Scarry notes that we have no words to describe pain, "unlike any other state of consciousness—[it] has no referential content."[46] Most importantly, Scarry asserts, "physical pain is not only itself resistant to language but also actively destroys language, deconstructing it into the pre-language of cries and groans. To hear those cries is to witness the shattering of language."[47] Indeed, the knot constricts the throat, the vocal cords, and it effectively silences speech. It is, to borrow from John Conroy, an unspeakable act.[48] Unspeakable because the deceased can't describe what they've experienced. Unspeakable because violence, any kind of violence, happens when we abandon speech, when we abandon language. Unspeakable because it is an act that I, the writer, cannot ever adequately describe.

And yet the hangman's noose can tell us a story across time and place. It represents a history of violence, a history that for some signifies the proper execution of justice and, for others, the limits of government (or, better, human compassion). It represents horror, helplessness, and hopelessness. In a very material way the body hanged from the noose is a sign that someone has been accused and convicted, that some form of justice—popular or governmental—has been passed. It is an ignoble way to die, chosen for its victims in part because of the kind of death it imposes—prolonged strangulation, the kicking legs, and the added shame of the body left to twist in the wind.

In the 1920s Danish explorer and anthropologist Knud Rasmussen recorded the songs and stories of Inuit people living throughout the Artic. In a Netsilik Inuit community near Hudson Bay he recorded the song of a shaman named Orpingalik. In translation it reads, "Songs are thoughts, sung out with the breath when people are moved by great forces and ordinary speech no longer suffices."[49] Those are some of the most beautiful words I've ever encountered, words that connect me with Orpingalik because I can empathize. I know what he's talking about; you know what he's talking about—the beautiful things that make us all sing.

Rasmussen recorded these songs because he believed, as I do, that our humanity is found in what we leave behind. Our history is recalled, as any archaeologist or museum curator will tell you, in the objects we use, touch, and carry: a coffee mug, a hammer, a steering wheel. This is the kind of history I have been pursuing while writing this book: the history of an object and the human hands that formed it, the human necks it touched. Despite the morbid nature of this object and the topic, I've learned that despite all the death, there is life here. Much life. Beautiful life. Life in the fearless activism of Jason Upthegrove and J. B. Weston. Life in the stories of Bee Tompkins. Life in the artistry of Glenn Dickey.

When I was in that casino in Flandreau, South Dakota, just after J. B. Weston told me a third time that I needed to think about putting that noose around my own neck, I lost it. Just a bit.

"Listen," I told him, "I've been researching and writing about this thing, the noose, for a few years now. Do you think that I haven't thought about that? About what that might mean? When I was in high school my friend Pierce put a noose made from a belt around his neck and hanged himself. I get it. So you can just stop with the putting the noose around my neck stuff."

"Right there," he said. "That. You need to write from that. That's from the heart."

This is not a book about suicide. I never intended it to be. But in that moment, the most confusing moment of this project, that's all I could think of. Herman Melville writes in "Benito Cereno" at the moment Captain Amasa Delano finally understands the truth of his situation: "All this with what preceded, and what followed, occurred with such involutions of rapidity, that past, present, and future seemed one."

At Flandreau my past, present, and future collided, and all I could see was an image: I'm sitting on the floor of Pierce's bedroom. The place where it'd happened. Other teenagers too, in a circle on the beige-carpeted floor in an innocuous red-brick McMansion on an innocuous suburban street. Beige carpet. Beige walls. It's late in the afternoon, and the lights are off and the blinds drawn, sunshine and shadows on one wall. I didn't know Pierce that well. I'd met him a year before at South Carolina Governor's School for the Arts, a summer-long arts program for aspiring young artists. It was a pivotal moment for me—for once someone besides myself thought of me as an artist, a writer. And I met other people like me and discovered I wasn't alone in this universe, that I could claim common cause with these people. Over the next year, my senior year in high school, a group of us gathered on occasion—two actors, some painters, some musicians, and me, the writer. One August we went to Lollapalooza; Pierce came too. Someone brought a shampoo bottle full of bourbon, and they were drinking from the bottle in the backseat of my air-condition-less Jeep Cherokee as we drove to the concert. The windows were rolled down, and the noise from the Charlotte traffic competed with the sounds of teenage boys and Nirvana on the radio. And then, almost a year later, Pierce killed himself.

I can hear J. B. Weston as I type at my desk, a rope formed into a hangman's knot buried under some scissors and pens and a hidden flask of bourbon in the desk drawer next to me. I hear him say, "That was a man. That was a man. That was a man. That was a man." An incantation. A prayer. That was a man, arms bound behind his back, a walking spectacle, moving slowly down the road or across the prison yard. Up the steps of the gallows or ladder. The noose is placed around his neck. Adjusted. The drop, and that was a man, that was a man, that was a man, that was a man.

Notes

PREFACE

1. Kouross Esmaeli, Rick Rowley, and Jacqueline Soohen, *The Jena 6*, pt. 2, Big Noise Film, 2007. One local journalist claims there was no "whites-only tree," but others contradict that story. There's enough evidence to believe that many black students believed it to be true. See Craig Franklin, "Media Myths About the Jena 6," *Christian Science Monitor*, October 24, 2007, www .csmonitor.com/2007/1024/p09s01-coop.html.

2. Craig Franklin, "DA/School Officials Grant Exclusive Interviews," *Jena Times*, October 3, 2007.

3. Quoted in Ibid.

4. "EEOC Chairwoman Responds to Surge of Workplace Noose Incidents at NAACP Annual Convention," US Equal Employment Opportunity Commission, Press Release, July 13, 2000, www.eeoc.gov/eeoc/newsroom /release/7–13–00-b.cfm.

5. I tracked from September 2010 to September 2013. My method for tracking was pretty simple and unscientific: I created a Google alert with the word "noose" and looked for stories that more than one media outlet covered.

6. See Bill McKelway, "Thomas Dale Students Charged with Assault in Noose Incident," *Richmond Times-Dispatch*, May 17, 2011, www.times dispatch.com/news/thomas-dale-students-charged-with-assault-in-noose -incident/article_5d7e84cb-ab5f-57bd-9da7–09c488b0564e.html? mode=jqm; "Teens Suspended After 'Bullying' Girl with Noose at High School," WBTV (North Carolina), January 11, 2012, www.14news.com /story/16497338/student-makes-noose-out-of-string-at-high-school-deputies -say; Larry McShane, "3 White Chicago Teens Busted for Putting Noose Around Neck of Black Teen for Dating White Woman" (New York) *Daily News*, January 26, 2012, www.nydailynews.com/news/crime/3-white -chicago-teens-busted-putting-noose-neck-black-teen-dating-white -woman-police-article-1.1012379; "School Probes Noose Hazing Accusations," Fox16.com, October 3, 2012, www.fox16.com/news/local/story /School-probes-noose-hazing-accusations/d/story/9c2FtcPFzUC _KArafDaNxg.

7. Sheldon H. Laskin, "Jena: A Missed Opportunity for Healing," *Tikkun* (November–December 2007): 29–73. For more general information

about lynching in Louisiana, see Michael J. Pfeifer's "Lynching in Louisiana," http://academic.evergreen.edu/p/pfeiferm/louisiana.html, and "Apologizing to Lynching Victims and Their Descendants," US Congressional Record 151, no. 77 (June 13, 2005): S6364–S6388.

8. Daniel T. Williams, *Amid the Gathering Multitude: The Story of Lynching in America, A Classified Listing* (Unpublished: Tuskegee University, 1968). This number has been questioned by scholars in recent years because there were frequent inconsistencies in how events were reported. See Chapter 8 for more on these numbers. Useful places to start researching the numbers of lynching include the Tuskegee Institute News Clippings File (Tuskegee Institute, Alabama: Division of Behavioral Science Research, Carver Research Foundation, Tuskegee Institute. Sanford, NC: Microfilming Corporation of America, 1976), NAACP's *Thirty Years of Lynching, 1889–1918* (New York: NAACP, 1919), and Stewart E. Tolnay and E. M. Beck's *A Festival of Violence: An Analysis of Southern Lynchings, 1882–1930* (Urbana: University of Illinois Press, 1995). See also, Lisa D. Cook, "Converging to a National Lynching Database" (May 2011), https://www.msu.edu/~lisacook /hist_meths_lynch_paper_final.pdf.

9. Christopher Waldrep, *The Many Faces of Judge Lynch: Extralegal Violence and Punishment in America* (New York: Palgrave Macmillan, 2002): 149.

10. Susan Sontag, *Regarding the Pain of Others* (New York: Picador, 2003), 92.

11. Natalie Zemon Davis, *Society and Culture in Early Modern France* (Stanford, CA: Stanford University Press, 1975). See also Raymond Williams, *Television: Technology and Cultural Form* (New York: Schocken Books, 1975) for another way to think about cultural technologies.

12. When I began work on this project a friend gifted me a 1953 edition of Charles Duff's *A New Handbook on Hanging* (Chicago: Henry Regnery Company, 1953), a revised version of his original polemic, *A Handbook on Hanging*. Duff's satire is a trove of anecdotes covering the vast history of hanging, and it is an important work in the anti–capital punishment canon. I owe much respect to Duff as well as to August Mencken's 1942 *By the Neck: A Book of Hangings* (with a foreword written by his older brother, journalist and essayist Henry Louis) (New York: Hastings House) and Negley K. Teeters and Jack H. Hedblom's *Hang by the Neck . . . : The Legal Use of Scaffold and Noose, Gibbet, Stake, and Firing Squad from Colonial Times to the Present* (Springfield, IL: C. C. Thomas, 1967)—these books helped shape my own vision.

CHAPTER 1

1. Cyrus L. Day, "Knots and Knot Lore," *Western Folklore* 9, no. 3 (1950): 230.

2. Ibid., 231.

3. Donald P. Ryan and David H. Hansen, *A Study of Ancient Egyptian Cordage* (London: British Museum, 1987), 9. Some knots may be shared across species. In 2005 primatologists Chris Herzfeld and Dominique Lestel published an article claiming there is some verifiable evidence that great apes can in fact tie knots *in captivity*. They surveyed a number of captive apes that had demonstrated some ability to tie knots, and from this, they assert that much of this behavior could be learned from watching their keepers. They note that knot-tying skills would be useful for making nests but add that, with only one exception, no one has seen apes doing this in the wild. See Chris Herzfeld and Dominique Lestel, "Knot Tying in Great Apes: Etho-Ethnology of an Unusual Tool Behavior," *Social Science Information* 44 (2005): 621–653. Naturalist—and latter-day cryptozoologist, a.k.a., Bigfoot hunter—Ivan T. Sanderson claims to have discovered dozens of knots (grannies and reef knots) in a gorilla nest during an early twentieth-century expedition. See Ivan T. Sanderson, *Animal Treasure* (New York: Viking, 1937), 187.

4. "What Does the IGKT Do?" International Guild of Knot Tyers, www.igkt.net.

5. Tim Ingold, *The Perception of the Environment: Essays in Livelihood, Dwelling and Skill* (New York: Routledge, 2000), 347.

6. James George Frazer, *The Golden Bough: A Study in Magic and Religion*, vol. 1, pt. 1 (New York: Macmillan, 1922), 80.

7. Rodger Ide, "Knots Under the Microscope: Part 1," *Knotting Matters: The Magazine of the International Guild of Knot Tyers*, June 2009, 25.

8. Ibid.

9. Middleton A. Harris et al., *The Black Book* (New York: Random House, 2009), 55.

10. Mel Distel, "What Happened Tonight: Hanging a Noose on Someone's Door Is Not a Crime," Facebook, October 28, 2010, 10:36 P.M., http://facebook.com/meldistel.

11. Clifford Ashley, *Ashley Book of Knots* (Garden City, NY: Doubleday and Co., 1944), 203.

12. Richard Godwin, "Power Dressing Now Means a Pair of Plimsolls," *London Evening Standard*, May 23, 2012.

13. "The Burden of Being 'Most Likely to Succeed,'" *Talk of the Nation*, National Public Radio, May 31, 2011.

14. Ashley, *Ashley Book of Knots*, 203.

15. Ibid., 204.

16. Ibid., 118.

17. Ashley mentions a few heaving line knots, including #538 and #540. Author, IGKT member, and respected forensic knot expert Lindsey Philpott suggested to me in an interview that it may have a relationship to a heaving line. That's his "best bet," he said, and added, "the people who took cargo

from one place to another, they were using a monkey fist as a heaving line. But they also used the heaving line knot, which used multiple wraps around the rope and then is tucked through to make weight. And they realized that this is a very stiff object. And then I guess they put two and two together and said, 'well, if I can put multiple wraps on the rope to make it stiff, maybe that will help to make it stiff and can help snap their neck when they drop.' And then you just have to get them to drop far enough."

18. Ashley (*Ashley Book of Knots*, 204) notes that a knot with a similar appearance is mentioned in Diderot's 1762 *Encyclopedia*.

19. "Man Survives Passing Out with Head in Museum Noose," *Associated Press*, September 23, 2010.

20. "Teen Worker at Haunted House 'Creepyworld' Found Caught in Noose," *St. Louis Post-Dispatch*, October 28, 2011.

21. Julian Kesner, "Quick, Painless End, Unless, . . ." *New York Daily News*, December 30, 2006.

22. Richard Clark, "Hanged by the Neck Until Dead! The Processes and Physiology of Judicial Hanging," *Capital Punishment UK*, www.capital punishment.uk.

23. Harold Hillman, "The Possible Pain Experienced During Executions by Different Methods," *Perception* 22 (1993): 746.

24. Quoted in Jacob Weisberg, "This Is Your Death," *New Republic*, July 1, 1991, 24.

25. Hillman, "The Possible Pain Experienced," 746; The *Oxford Handbook of Forensic Medicine* notes that if the rope is behind the head, death might be caused by "compression of the arteries to the brain." If the rope is to the side, there may be other factors involved like "laryngeal disruption and airway disruption" or brainstem/spinal cord injuries, blood flow to the brain, and so forth. See Jonathan Wyatt et al., *Oxford Handbook of Forensic Medicine* (New York: Oxford University Press, 2011), 106.

26. Hillman, "The Possible Pain Experienced," 745.

27. Ibid., 50.

28. Ibid., 749.

29. Elie Boghossian et al., "Respiratory, Circulatory, and Neurological Responses to Hanging: A Review of Animal Models," *Journal of Forensic Sciences* 55, no. 5 (September 2010), 1272.

30. Anny Sauvageau and Stephanie Racette, "Agonal Sequences in a Filmed Suicidal Hanging: Analysis of Respiratory and Movement Responses to Asphyxia by Hanging," *Journal of Forensic Sciences* 52, no. 4 (July 2007), 957.

CHAPTER 2

1. Christian Fischer, *Tollund Man: Gift to the Gods* (Stroud, Gloucestershire: History Press, 2012), 31.

2. As of late there have been many thoughtful discussions about the ethics of displaying a body in a museum. A good place to start is Samuel J. M. M. Alberti, Rose Drew, Piotr Beinkowski, and Malcolm J. Chapman, "Should We Display the Dead?" *Museum and Society* 7, no. 3 (November 2009): 133–149.

3. P. V. Glob, *The Bog People: Iron-Age Man Preserved*, trans. Rupert Bruce-Mitford (Ithaca, NY: Cornell University Press, 1969), 33.

4. Fischer, *Tollund Man*, 49.

5. Glob, *The Bog People*, 32.

6. W. A. B. van der Sanden, *Through Nature to Eternity: The Bog Bodies of Northwest Europe* (Amsterdam: Batavian Lion International, 1996), 155.

7. The exact ethnic origin has long been in dispute among historians.

8. Ahmad Ibn Fadlan, *Ibn Fadlan's Journey to Russia*, trans. Richard N. Frye (Princeton, NJ: Markus Wiener Publishers, 2005), 66.

9. Cornelius Tacitus, *The Germany and the Agricola of Tacitus: The Oxford Translation Revised, with Notes, with an Introduction by Edward Brooks, Jr.* (Philadelphia: David McKay, 1897), 31.

10. Ibid.

11. Morten Ravn, "Burials in Bogs: Bronze and Early Iron Age Bog Bodies from Denmark," *Acta Archaeologica* 81 (2010): 112–123, 115; Richard J. Evans, *Rituals of Retribution: Capital Punishment in Germany, 1600–1987* (Oxford: Oxford University Press, 1996), 3–7.

12. Glob, *The Bog People*, 147.

13. Ibid., 192.

14. Fischer, *Tollund Man*, 180.

15. Ibid., 181.

16. Ibid., 182.

17. Ibid., 184–185.

18. Ibid., 186.

CHAPTER 3

1. Pierpont Morgan Library, Manuscript.M.390, Catholic Church Book of Hours, Bruge Belgium, ca. 1500, 197 Leaves (1 column, 17 lines), bound: 230 x 170mm.

2. Sophocles, *Sophocles I: Oedipus the King, Oedipus at Colonus, and Antigone*, trans. David Greene (Chicago: University of Chicago Press, 1991), 1274.

3. Eva Cantarella, "Dangling Virgins: Myth, Ritual, and the Place of Women in Ancient Greece," *Poetics Today* 6, no. 1/2 (1985): 91–101, 94.

4. Homer, *The Odyssey*, trans. Robert Fitzgerald (New York: Vintage, 1990), 422.

5. An interesting exception when hanging may have been used is discussed in Frederic Wood Jones, "The Examination of the Bodies of 100 Men

Executed in Nubia in Roman Times," *British Medical Journal* 1, no. 2465 (March 28, 1903): 736–737.

6. Richard A. Bauman, *Crime and Punishment in Ancient Rome* (New York: Routledge, 1996), 23

7. Quoted in Cantarella, "Dangling Virgins," 95.

8. Joshua 8:29 and Joshua 10:26. See also II Samuel 4:12.

9. II Samuel 17:23 (NIV).

10. H. H. Halley, *Halley's Bible Handbook* (Grand Rapids, MI: Zondervan, 1965), 258.

11. Marvin Meyer, *Judas: The Definitive Collection of Gospels and Legends about the Infamous Apostle of Jesus* (New York: Harper, 2007), 21.

12. Matthew 27:5 (KJV).

13. Trans. in Otfried Lieberknecht, *Death and Retribution: Medieval Visions of the End of Judas the Traitor* (Collegeville, MN: Saint John's University, May 13, 1997), 2.

14. Acts 1:18 (KJV).

15. See *Gospel of Judas*, trans. Rodolphe Kasser et al., in collaboration with François Gaudard, from *The Gospel of Judas*, eds. Rodolphe Kasser and others (Washington, DC: National Geographic Society, 2006).

16. Lieberknecht, *Death and Retribution*, 6.

17. Kurt Weitzmann, "Age of Spirituality: Late Antique and Early Christian Art, Third to Seventh Century," *Metropolitan Museum of Art Bulletin* 35, no. 2 (Autumn 1979): 70–71.

18. Quoted in Susan Gubar, *Judas: A Biography* (New York: Norton, 2009), 113; see also St. Jerome, *Contra Jovinianus*, Book II, para.25.

19. St. Ambrose's *Three Books on the Holy Spirit*, Book 3, trans. H. de Romestin, E. de Romestin, and H. T. F. Duckworth, from *Nicene and Post-Nicene Fathers*, 2nd Series, vol. 10, eds. Philip Schaff and Henry Wace (Buffalo, NY: Christian Literature Publishing, 1896), 123.

20. Leo the Great, Sermon 55, sec. 3, trans. Charles Lett Feltoe, from *Nicene and Post-Nicene Fathers*, 2nd Series, vol. 12, eds. Philip Schaff and Henry Wace (Buffalo, NY: Christian Literature Publishing, 1895).

21. Thomas Aquinas, *Catena Aurea,* Catecheticsonline, www.catechetics online.com/CatenaAurea-Matthew27.php.

22. Archer Taylor, "The Gallows of Judas Iscariot," *Washington University Studies* 9, no. 2 (1922), 135.

23. Ibid., 140.

24. Ibid., 142, 144.

25. See Richard Axton's "Interpretations of Judas in Middle English Literature," *Religion in the Poetry and Drama of the Late Middle Ages in England*, eds. Piero Botani and Anna Torti (Cambridge: D. S. Brewer, 1990).

26. Recto, Judas: Returning Silver: miniature, full-page, quadripartite, Bologna, Italy, 1325–13351 miniature, 206 x 151mm (Manuscript M.360.8), MLM.

27. Quoted in Lieberknecht, *Death and Retribution*, 5.

28. *The Hanging of Judas*, c. 1520, Stained glass, 57.2 x 44.6cm (22 1/2 x 17 9/16in.), Kate S. Buckingham Endowment, 1949.494, Art Institute of Chicago. Of course, throughout the Middle Ages Judas is also associated with the Jews. For more about the relationship between Judas and myths of Jewish evil, see Hyam Maccoby, *Judas Iscariot and the Myth of Judas Evil* (New York: Free Press, 1992).

29. Lee R. Sullivan, "The Hanging of Judas: Medieval Iconography and the German Peasants' War," *Essays in Medieval Studies* 15 (1998), 101.

30. Curiously, in an article exploring a more "humane" method of hanging, Samuel Haughton writes that hanging executions should be regarded as an Anglo-Saxon method of punishment which seems to have been used in the past for "cases in which especial ignominy was intended to be attached to the criminal." "On Hanging Considered from a Mechanical and Physiological Point of View," *The London, Edinburgh, and Dublin Philosophical Magazine and Journal of Science* 32 (1866), 23.

31. Lynn White Jr., "The Legacy of the Middle Ages in the American Wild West," *Speculum* 40, no. 2 (April 1965), 199.

32. Robert Mills, *Suspended Animation: Pain, Pleasure, and Punishment in Medieval Culture* (London: Reaktion Books, 2005), 23–25.

33. Robert Bartlett, *The Hanged Man: A Story of Miracle, Memory, and Colonialism in the Middle Ages* (Princeton, NJ, Princeton University Press, 2006), 44.

34. Ibid., 43.

35. The hangman's knot is absent from images of hangings in the Middle Ages, but that doesn't mean that the knot, or a version of it, didn't exist, of course. (Although there seems to be one around Mel Gibson's neck in the incredibly historically inaccurate film *Braveheart*.)

36. Bartlett, *The Hanged Man*, 45–46.

37. Peter Linebaugh, "The Tyburn Riot Against the Surgeons," in *Albion's Fatal Tree: Crime and Society in Eighteenth-Century England*, eds. Douglas Hay et al. (New York: Pantheon, 1975), 102–105.

38. Bartlett notes that some were blindfolded but that wasn't a universal practice until the nineteenth century (*The Hanged Man*, 43). Robert Mills notes the problem of archive: few hangings were recorded, really only the most noteworthy ones, and "detailed commentaries on the physiological facts of hanging are rare" (*Suspended Animation*, 26).

39. Lisa McClain, *Lest We Be Damned: Practical Innovation and Lived Experience Among Catholics in Protestant England, 1559–1642* (New York:

Routledge, 2003), 163–165; Constance Classen, *The Deepest Sense: A Cultural History of Touch* (Champaign, IL: University of Illinois Press, 2012), 35.

40. Linebaugh, "The Tyburn Riot," 109–111.

41. Mitchell Merback, *The Thief, the Cross, and the Wheel: Pain and the Spectacle of Punishment in Medieval and Renaissance Europe* (Chicago: University of Chicago Press, 1999), 141.

42. C. V. Calvert, "A Brief Account of Criminal Procedure in Germany in the Middle Ages," *A Hangman's Diary*, ed. Albrecht Keller (New York: D. Appleton and Company, 1928), 56.

43. Merback, *The Thief, the Cross, and the Wheel*, 142.

44. Esther Cohen, *The Crossroads of Justice: Law and Culture in Late Medieval France* (New York: E. J. Brill, 1993), 93.

45. Peter Linebaugh, *The London Hanged: Crime and Civil Society in the Eighteenth Century* (New York: Cambridge University Press, 1992), 53.

46. Merback, *The Thief, the Cross, and the Wheel*, 68.

47. Cohen, *Crossroads of Justice*, 150.

48. Esther Cohen, "Symbols of Culpability and the Universal Language of Justice: The Ritual of Public Executions in Late Medieval Europe," *History of European Ideas* 11 (1989): 404–416, 409.

49. Cohen, *Crossroads of Justice*, 152.

50. Cohen, "Symbols of Culpability," 407

51. Michel Foucault, *Discipline and Punish: The Birth of the Prison*, trans. Alan Sheridan (New York: Vintage Books, 1995), 48.

52. Ibid., 57–58.

53. Dante Alighieri, *The Divine Comedy: Volume 1, Inferno*, trans. Mark Musa (New York: Penguin, 1984), 381 (Canto XXXIV: 61–63).

54. Ibid., 383 (Canto XXXIV: 136–139).

CHAPTER 4

1. Steven Wilf, *Law's Imagined Republic: Popular Politics and Criminal Justice in Revolutionary America* (New York: Cambridge, 2010), 139–146.

2. Clifford M. Lewis and Albert J. Loomie, *The Spanish Jesuit Mission in Virginia, 1570–1572* (Chapel Hill: University of North Carolina Press, 1953). The first execution in the British colonies, though not a hanging, was that of Captain George Kendall by firing squad for mutiny.

3. Toni Morrison, *A Mercy* (New York: Alfred A. Knopf, 2008), 75.

4. Ira Berlin, *Many Thousands Gone: The First Two Centuries of Slavery in North America* (Cambridge, Massachusetts: The Belknap Press of Harvard University Press, 1998), 53–54.

5. Graham Russell Hodges, *Root and Branch: African Americans in New York and East Jersey, 1613–1863* (Chapel Hill: University of North Carolina Press, 1999), 14.

6. Berlin, *Many Thousands Gone*, 51; Hodges, *Root and Branch*, 32.

7. Hodges, *Root and Branch*, 36.

8. Berlin, *Many Thousands Gone*, 187.

9. Ibid., 47.

10. Ibid., 49.

11. Hodges, *Root and Branch*, 78.

12. Berlin, *Many Thousands Gone*, 58.

13. Jerome R. Reich, *Colonial America* (Upper Saddle River, NJ: Prentice Hall, 1998), 191. Some streets were mostly dark at night though on some streets lanterns were hung after every seventh house.

14. Hodges, *Root and Branch*, 89.

15. Berlin, *Many Thousands Gone*, 59.

16. Hodges, *Root and Branch*, 65; Kenneth Scott, "The Slave Insurrection in New York in 1712," *New York Historical Society Quarterly* 45 (1961), 47.

17. Edgar J. McManus, *A History of Negro Slavery in New York* (Syracuse, NY: Syracuse University Press, 1966), 95; Scott, "The Slave Insurrection," 45.

18. *Boston News-Letter*, April 7–14, 1712.

19. Jill Lepore, "The Tightening Vise: Slavery and Freedom in British New York," *Slavery in New York*, eds. Ira Berlin and Leslie M. Harris (New York: New Press, 2005), 79. For more on trial outcomes, see Scott, "The Slave Insurrection," 62–69.

20. David Freeman Hawke, *Everyday Life in Early America* (New York: Harper and Row, 1989), 109; Reich, *Colonial America*, 192–193.

21. Stuart Banner, *The Death Penalty: An American History* (Cambridge, MA: Harvard University Press, 2002), 10.

22. Ibid.

23. Ibid., 6; See William Bradford, *Of Plymouth Plantation* (1642).

24. David D. Hall, *Worlds of Wonder, Days of Judgment* (New York: Alfred A. Knopf, 1989), 168.

25. Banner, *The Death Penalty*, 25.

26. Joshua Hempstead, *Diary of Joshua Hempstead of New London, Connecticut* (New London, CT: New London County Historical Society, 1901), 616–619.

27. Banner, *The Death Penalty*, 24.

28. Ibid., 27–28.

29. See, for example, Increase Mather, "The Folly of Sinning" (1698). For more on this genre see Ronald A. Bosco, "Lectures at the Pillory: The Early American Execution Sermon," *American Quarterly* 30 (1978), or Wayne C. Minnick, "The New England Execution Sermon," *Speech Monographs* 35 (1968).

30. Banner, *The Death Penalty*, 26.

31. Ibid., 22.

32. Ibid., 13.

33. Daniel E. Williams, "Rogues, Rascals, and Scoundrels: The Underworld Literature of Early America," *American Studies* 24, no. 2 (Fall 1983), 6.

34. Hall, *Worlds of Wonder*, 181.

35. John Winthrop, "A Modell of Christian Charity," *Heath Anthology of American Literature: A*, ed. Paul Lauter (Boston: Houghton Mifflin, 2009), 341.

36. Louis P. Masur, *Rites of Execution: Capital Punishment and the Transformation of American Culture, 1776–1865* (New York: Oxford University Press, 1989), 39.

37. Banner, *The Death Penalty*, 8–9.

38. Winthrop Jordan, *White Over Black: American Attitudes Toward the Negro, 1550–1812* (Chapel Hill: University of North Carolina Press, 1968), 112.

39. "Executions in the U.S. 1608–2002: The ESPY File," Death Penalty Information Center, www.deathpenaltyinfo.org/executions-us-1608-2002-espy-file.

40. Jill Lepore's *New York Burning* (New York: Vintage, 2005) offers a thorough examination of this event and exceptional tables of data analysis, xii and 246–259. See also Daniel Horsmanden, *The New York Conspiracy*, ed. Thomas J. Davis (Boston: Beacon Press, 1971), 467–473.

41. This is right where Church becomes Trinity Place.

42. Horsmanden, *New York Conspiracy*, 18–20.

43. Ibid., 15.

44. Ibid., 27.

45. Ibid., 26–31.

46. *New York Weekly Journal*, April 27, 1741.

47. Ibid.

48. Horsmanden, *New York Conspiracy*, 39–42.

49. Lepore, "The Tightening Vise," 60.

50. Michael Kammen, *Colonial New York: A History* (New York: Charles Scribner's Sons, 1975), 213–214.

51. Horsmanden, *New York Conspiracy*, 57.

52. Peter Linebaugh and Marcus Rediker, *The Many-Headed Hydra* (Boston: Beacon Press, 2001), 177.

53. *Boston Weekly News-Letter*, June 4–11, 1741; Lepore, *New York Burning*, 104–106.

54. *Boston Weekly News-Letter*, June 18–25, 1741.

55. Charles Peter Hoffer, *The Great New York Conspiracy of 1741* (Lawrence: University of Kansas Press, 2003), 160.

56. Horsmanden, *New York Conspiracy*, 165.

57. John Laurence, *A History of Capital Punishment* (New York: Citadel Press, 1960), 44.

58. Banner, *The Death Penalty*, 47.

59. Ibid., 37.

60. Horsmanden, *New York Conspiracy*, 273.

61. Ibid., 276.

62. Ibid., 274.

63. *New York Weekly Journal*, June 22, 1741.

64. *Boston Weekly News-Letter*, July 16–23, 1741.

65. Horsmanden, *New York Conspiracy*, 325.

66. *New York Weekly Journal*, July 20, 1741.

67. *American Weekly Mercury*, August 13–20, 1741.

68. *New York Weekly Journal*, August 17, 1741.

69. *New York Weekly Journal*, June 29, 1741.

70. Lepore, *New York Burning*, 196.

71. Lepore and Horsmanden write that his execution was on the 29th, though Hoffer says the 15th.

72. *Boston Weekly News-Letter*, September 3–10, 1741.

73. *Boston Evening-Post*, October 5, 1741.

74. *Boston Weekly News-Letter*, September 3–10, 1741.

75. Lepore, *New York Burning*, 201–202.

76. Quoted in ibid., 205.

77. Hoffer, *Great New York Conspiracy*, 153.

78. See, for example, Herbert Aptheker, *American Negro Slave Revolts* (New York: International Publishers, 1993), 192–195.

79. Linebaugh and Rediker, *Many-Headed Hydra*, 193.

80. Ibid., 176.

81. Ibid., 206.

82. Ibid., 207.

83. Jordan, *White Over Black*, 116–118.

84. Philip D. Morgan, "Conspiracy Scares," *William and Mary Quarterly* 59, no. 1 (January 2002), 166.

85. Andy Doolen, "Reading and Writing Terror: The New York Conspiracy Trials of 1741," *American Literary History* 16, no. 3 (September 2004), 382.

86. Berlin, *Many Thousands Gone*, 1.

87. Horsmanden, *New York Conspiracy*, 105–106.

88. Ibid., 168.

89. Natalie Zemon Davis, *Society and Culture in Early Modern France* (Stanford, CA: Stanford University Press, 1975), 187.

90. "Geert Wilders Speech at New York's Ground Zero Mosque (11/09 /2010)," Youtube.com.

91. Rocco Parascandola, "Noose Found Hanging in World Trade Center," *New York Daily News*, December 29, 2011.

CHAPTER 5

1. Quoted in Laurence M. Hauptman, "The Pequot War and Its Legacies," *The Pequots in Southern New England: The Fall and Rise of an American Indian Nation*, eds. Laurence M. Hauptman and James D. Wherry (Norman: University of Oklahoma Press, 1990), 73.

2. Ibid., 76–77.

3. Ron Eyerman, *Cultural Trauma: Slavery and the Formation of African American Identity* (New York: Cambridge University Press, 2001), 2.

4. See Henry Channing, *God Admonishing His People of Their Duty, as Parents and Masters: A Sermon, Preached at New-London, December 20th, 1786, Occasioned by the . . .* (New London, CT: Timothy Green, 1787); Nancy H. Steenburg, "Murder and Minors: Changing Standards in the Criminal Law of Connecticut, 1650–1853," *Murder on Trial: 1620–2002*, eds. Robert Asher, Lawrence B. Goodheart, and Alan Rogers (Albany: State University of New York Press, 2005), 119.

5. Channing, *God Admonishing His People*, 29.

6. Ibid., 29.

7. Ibid.

8. See Ruth Wallis Herndon and Ella Wilcox Sekatu, "Colonizing the Children: Indian Youngsters in Servitude in Early Rhode Island," *Reinterpreting New England Indians and the Colonial Experience*, eds. Colin G. Calloway and Neal Salisbury (Boston: Colonial Society of Massachusetts, 2003).

9. *Connecticut Courant*, July 28, 1786.

10. Jan Schenk Grosskopf, *"For Mischief Done"* (Niantic, CT: Andres and Blanton, 2012), 250; Channing, *God Admonishing His People*, 29.

11. Channing, *God Admonishing His People*, 29–30.

12. Ibid., 30.

13. Ibid.

14. Ibid.

15. Steenburg, "Murder and Minors," 119.

16. Ibid., 119–120.

17. Channing, *God Admonishing His People*, 29.

18. Victor L. Streib, *Death Penalty for Juveniles* (Bloomington: Indiana University Press, 1987), 75.

19. *Connecticut Courant*, October 9, 1786.

20. Quoted in Streib, *Death Penalty for Juveniles*, 75.

21. Channing, *God Admonishing His People*, 31.

22. Steenburg, "Murder and Minors," 120–121.

23. *Connecticut Courant*, December 25, 1786; Channing, *God Admonishing His People*, 31.

24. Steven Pinker, *The Better Angels of Our Nature: Why Violence Has Declined* (New York: Viking, 2011), 133.

25. Lynn Hunt, *Inventing Human Rights: A History* (New York: Norton, 2007), 33.

26. Hauptman, "The Pequot War and Its Legacies," 45.

27. V. A. C. Gattrell, *The Hanging Tree: Execution and the English People 1770–1868* (New York: Oxford University Press, 1994), 52.

28. *Gentleman's Magazine*, December 1783, 990.

29. Hunt, *Inventing Human Rights*, 103.

30. Cesare Beccaria, *On Crimes and Punishments and Other Writings*, trans. Richard Davies (New York: Cambridge University Press, 2003), 39, 31.

31. Ibid., 66–67.

32. Ibid., 70.

33. Ibid., 71.

34. Louis P. Masur, *Rites of Execution: Capital Punishment and the Transformation of American Culture, 1776–1865* (New York: Oxford University Press, 1989), 54.

35. Ibid., 58.

36. Ibid., 61.

37. Thank you to Denison University student Mimi Mendes DeLeon for pointing this out.

38. Channing, *God Admonishing His People*, 5.

39. Ibid.

40. Ibid., 6.

41. Ibid., 9–10.

42. Ibid., 11–12.

43. Ibid., 17.

44. Ibid., 19.

45. Ibid., 26.

46. Ibid., 27.

47. Katherine Grandjean, "'Our *Fellow-Creatures* and Our *Fellow-Christians*': Race and Religion in Eighteenth-Century Narratives of Indian Crime," *American Quarterly* 62, no. 4 (December 2010): 925–50, 927.

48. Channing, *God Admonishing His People*, 23.

49. Grandjean, "'Our *Fellow-Creatures*'," 942.

50. Thomas Jefferson, *Notes on the State of Virginia* (New York: Penguin Books, 1999), 146.

51. Ibid., 151.

52. Daniel E. Williams, "Rogues, Rascals, and Scoundrels: The Underworld Literature of Early America," *American Studies* 24, no. 2 (Fall 1983): 5–19, 6; Sara Crosby, "Early American Crime Writing," *The Cambridge Companion to American Crime Fiction*, ed. Catharine Ross Nickerson (New York: Cambridge University Press, 2010), 6.

53. Crosby, "Early American Crime Writing," 9.

54. Richard Slotkin, "Narratives of Negro Crime in New England, 1675–1800," *American Quarterly* 25, no. 1 (March 1973): 3–31, 4. For examples of this phenomenon, see Samuel Danforth, "The Woeful Effects of Drunkenness . . ." (Boston: B. Green, 1710); John Grimes, "The Last Speech, Confession, Birth, Parentage and Education of John Grimes, John Fagan, and John Johnson . . ." (Woodbridge, NJ: James Parker, 1765); Aaron Hutchinson, "Iniquity Purged by Mercy and Truth" (Boston: Thomas and John Fleet, 1769); and Samson Occom, "A Sermon Preached at the Execution of Moses Paul, an Indian" (Boston: John Boyle, 1773).

55. Jeannine Marie Lombard, *In the Shadow of the Gallows: Race, Crime, and American Civic Identity* (Philadelphia: University of Pennsylvania Press, 2012), 4–5.

56. Ibid., 19.

57. John Joyce, "Confession of John Joyce" (Philadelphia: Printed . . . for the benefit of Bethel Church, 1808), documenting the American South, http://docsouth.unc.edu.

58. Jenn Williamson, "John Joyce, 1784 (ca.)–1808 and Peter Matthias, ca. 1782–1808 Summary," Documenting the American South, http://docsouth .unc.edu.

59. Grandjean, "'Our *Fellow-Creatures*,'" 945.

60. *Connecticut Courant*, December 25, 1786.

61. Ibid.

62. Benjamin Rush, *An Enquiry into the Effects of Public Punishments upon Criminals and upon Society* (Philadelphia: Joseph James, 1787), 4.

63. Ibid., 6–7.

64. Ibid., 7.

65. Ibid., 13.

66. Ibid., 14.

67. Ibid., 18.

68. Masur, *Rites of Execution,* 71.

69. Ibid., 96

70. James L. Payne, *A History of Force* (Sandpoint, ID: Lytton, 2004), 130.

71. Thank you to my Denison colleague, psychology professor Erin Henshaw, for walking me through this research.

72. Catherine Lebel, Florence Roussotte, and Elizabeth R. Sowell, "Imaging the Impact of Prenatal Alcohol Exposure on the Structure of the Developing Human Brain," *Neuropsychology Review* 21, no. 2 (2011): 102–118.

73. A. Painter, A. D. Williams, and L. Burd, "Fetal Alcohol Spectrum Disorders—Implications for Child Neurology, Part 1: Prenatal Exposure and Dosimetry," *Journal of Child Neurology* 27, no. 2 (February 2012): 258–263.

74. Dana K. Smith, Amber B. Johnson, Katherine C. Pears, Philip A. Fisher, and David S. DeGarmo, "Child Maltreatment and Foster Care: Un-

packing the Effects of Prenatal and Postnatal Parental Substance Abuse," *Child Maltreatment* 12, no. 2 (May 2007): 120–160.

75. Svetlana Popova, Shannon Lange, Dennis Bekmuradov, Alanna Mihic, and Jürgen Rehm, "Fetal Alcohol Spectrum Disorder Prevalence Estimates in Correctional Systems: A Systematic Literature Review," *Canadian Journal of Public Health* 102, no. 5 (September/October 2011): 336–340.

76. David Collins, "Five Connecticut Inmates Challenging Death Penalty," Associated Press, September 5, 2012.

CHAPTER 6

1. Louis P. Masur, *Rites of Execution: Capital Punishment and the Transformation of American Culture, 1776–1865* (New York: Oxford University Press, 1989), 115.

2. Jack Kenny Williams, *Vogues in Villainy: Crime and Retribution in Ante-Bellum South Carolina* (Columbia: University of South Carolina Press, 1959): 102.

3. Edward L. Ayers, *Vengeance and Justice: Crime and Punishment in the Nineteenth-Century American South*, (New York: Oxford University Press, 1984), 136.

4. Williams, *Vogues in Villainy*, 102.

5. Ayers, *Vengeance and Justice*, 136.

6. Charles Ball, *Slavery in the United States* (New York: John S. Taylor, 1837), 375.

7. Ibid., 376.

8. Ibid., 378.

9. In a strange confluence of events 1800 was a most auspicious year: John Brown and Nat Turner were born, Denmark Vesey bought his freedom, and a Gabriel Prosser's revolt conspiracy was uncovered in Virginia.

10. James Sidbury, *Ploughshares into Swords: Race, Rebellion, and Identity in Gabriel's Virginia, 1730–1810* (New York: Cambridge University Press, 1997), 6.

11. Douglas R. Egerton, *Gabriel's Rebellion: The Virginia Slave Conspiracies of 1800 and 1802* (Chapel Hill: University of North Carolina Press, 1993), 111.

12. Ibid., 187.

13. Ibid., 188.

14. Kenneth Greenberg, ed., *The Confessions of Nat Turner and Related Documents* (Boston: Bedford/St. Martin's, 1996), 120.

15. Ibid., 120.

16. Harriet Jacobs, *Incidents in the Life of a Slave Girl* (Mineola, NY: Dover, 2001), 56, 58.

17. John W. Cromwell, "The Aftermath of Nat Turner's Insurrection," in *The Nat Turner Rebellion: The Historical Event and the Modern Controversy*,

eds. John B. Duff and Peter M. Mitchell (New York: Harper and Row, 1971), 101. See also Greenberg, *Confessions of Nat Turner*, 19–20.

18. "Confession Made by John, the Slave of W. Enslow the Cooper, of Participation in Vesey Revolt," Henry Ravenel Papers, South Carolina Historical Society (SCHS).

19. Ibid.

20. Bernard F. Powers, Jr., *Black Charlestonians: A Social History, 1822–1885* (Fayetteville: University of Arkansas Press, 1994), 34.

21. Douglas R. Egerton, *He Shall Go Out Free: The Lives of Denmark Vesey* (Madison, WI: Madison House, 1999), 54.

22. Peter Linebaugh and Marcus Rediker, *The Many-Headed Hydra* (Boston: Beacon Press, 2001), 299.

23. Egerton, *He Shall Go Out Free*, 32–33.

24. See Michael Johnson, "Denmark Vesey and His Co-Conspirators," *William and Mary Quarterly*, 58, no. 4 (October 2001): 915–976. Johnson writes that "historians have been wrong about the conspiracy. . . . In general, I argue that almost all historians have failed to exercise due caution in reading the testimony of witnesses recorded by the conspiracy court, thereby becoming unwitting co-conspirators with the court in the making of the Vesey conspiracy; that the court, for its own reasons, colluded with a handful of intimidated witnesses to collect testimony about an insurrection that, in fact, was not about to happen; that Denmark Vesey and the other men sentenced to hang or to be sold into exile were not guilty of organizing an insurrection; that, rather than revealing a portrait of thwarted insurrection, witnesses' testimony discloses glimpses of ways that reading and rumors transmuted white orthodoxies into black heresies." See also Richard C. Wade, "The Vesey Plot: A Reconsideration," *Journal of Southern History* 30, no. 2 (May 1964): 143–161.

25. Egerton, *He Shall Go Out Free*, 200.

26. John B. Adger, *My Life and Times, 1810–1899* (Richmond, VA: Presbyterian Committee of Publication, 1899), 52.

27. David Robertson, *Denmark Vesey* (New York: Alfred A. Knopf, 1999), 103; Egerton, *He Shall Go Out Free*, 190.

28. Nic Butler, e-mail message to author, September 24, 2012. Charleston librarian and historian Nic Butler told me that he's heard locals refer to a tree that was once in the middle of Ashley Avenue as the site of Vesey's hanging but that he's not sure of the authenticity of the story. He noted that in 1822 that site would have been part of an old fortification and "on farmland belonging to one Mr. Horsey. Thus the oak tree site is much too far west to be considered part of the 'Blake lands.'"

29. Robertson, *Denmark Vesey*, 104.

30. Mary Lamboll Beach to Elizabeth Gilchrist, July 27, 1822, Lamboll Thomas Beach Papers, SCHS.

31. Adger, *My Life and Times*, 52.

32. Ibid., 53.

33. Egerton, *He Shall Go Out Free*, 196.

34. Quoted in John Peyre Thomas, *The History of the South Carolina Military Academy* (Charleston, SC: Walker, Evans and Cogswell Company, 1893), 18.

35. Mary Lamboll Beach to Elizabeth Gilchrist, July 23, 1822, Lamboll Thomas Beach Papers, SCHS.

36. Ibid.

37. Ibid.

38. Bertram Wyatt-Brown, *Honor and Violence in the Old South* (New York: Oxford University Press, 1986), 154–155.

39. Ibid., 58.

40. Ibid., 70.

41. "Brown's Interview with Mason, Vallandigham, and Others," reprinted in Louis Ruchames, ed., *John Brown: The Making of a Revolutionary* (New York: University Library, Grosset and Dunlap, 1969), 132.

42. "Last Address of John Brown to Virginia Court, November 2, 1859," reprinted in Zoe Trodd and John Stauffer, *Meteor of War: The John Brown Story* (Maplecrest, NY: Brandywine Press, 2004), 132.

43. "Death Warrant of John Brown," November 2, 1859, John Brown Papers, Jefferson County Circuit Clerk's Office.

44. "John Brown to Brother Jeremiah, Nov. 12, 1859," Ruchames, *John Brown*, 142.

45. There are a number of accounts for Brown's execution. I relied on the following: *New York Daily Tribune*, December 3 and 5, 1859; *Perrysburg Journal* (Perrysburg, OH), December 8, 1859; David Hunter Strother, "The Hanging of John Brown," ed. Boyd B. Stutler, *American Heritage* VI (February 1955), 6–9; Thomas J. Jackson to his Wife, Mary Anna Jackson, December 2, 1859, and John T. L. Preston to Margaret Junkin Preston, December 2, 1859, reprinted in Elizabeth Preston Allen, *The Life and Letters of Margaret Junkin Preston* (Boston: Houghton Mifflin, 1903), 111–117; "The Execution of Captain Brown," *Liberator*, December 9, 1859; S. K. Donovan, *John Brown at Harper's Ferry and Charlestown: A Lecture* (Columbus, OH: F. J. Heer Printing, 1924), Ohio State Historical Society; and *New York Times*, December 3, 1859.

46. James Redpath, *The Public Life of Capt. John Brown* (Boston: Thayer and Eldridge, 1860), 392; Boyd B. Stutler to Barrie Stavis, March 10, 1969, Boyd B. Stutler Collection of John Brown (BBS).

47. Zeb Ward to Governor Henry Wise, November 23, 1859, Library of Virginia. Some believe the rope was made at a ropeworks in nearby Hagerstown,

Maryland. Historian and blogger Tim Talbot writes that "since he mentions that the rope was made in Frankfort, it was most likely made at the state penitentiary. Ward was the former keeper of the facility, and one of their major prisoner manufacturing operations there during the antebellum era was rope making." See Tim Talbot, "John Brown Hanged with Kentucky Hemp," March 3, 2010, Random Thoughts on History, randomthoughtsonhistory .blogspot.com.

48. *Perrysburg Journal* (Perrysburg, OH), December 8, 1859.

49. *New York Daily Tribune*, December 3, 1859.

50. Strother, "The Hanging of John Brown," 7.

51. Donovan, *John Brown at Harper's Ferry*.

52. *Boston Daily Advertiser*, Friday, December 2, 1859, reprinted in Stauffer, *Meteor of War*, 163.

53. Barrie Stavis, *John Brown: The Sword and the Word* (South Brunswick and New York: A.S. Barnes, 1970), 169; Tony Horwitz, *Midnight Rising: John Brown and the Raid That Sparked the Civil War* (New York: Henry Holt, 2011), 254.

54. John Brown to Reverend James W. McFarland of Wooster, Ohio, November 23, 1859, reprinted in Ruchames, *John Brown*, 154.

55. John Brown to Mrs. George Stearns, November 29, 1859, reprinted in Ruchames, *John Brown*, 142.

56. Elijah Avey, *The Capture and Execution of John Brown: A Tale of Martyrdom* (Elgin, IL: Brethren Publishing, 1906), 43, Jefferson County Museum (JCM).

57. Thomas J. Jackson to his wife, Mary Anna Jackson, December 2, 1859, *Life and Letters of Thomas J. Jackson*, ed. Mary Anna Jackson (New York: Harper, 1892), 130–132.

58. Katherine Mayo, "Execution of Old John Brown," 1909, BBS.

59. Strother, "The Hanging of John Brown," 8.

60. Cleon Moore, *Epitome of the Life of Ossawatomie John Brown, Including the Story of His Attack on Harpers Ferry and His Capture, Trial, and Execution, as Related by Cleon Moore Esq., of Charles-Town WV* (Point Pleasant, WV: Mrs. Livia-Simpson Poffenbarger, editor and publisher, 1904), 15, OHS.

61. Douglas P. Perks, "'The Old Wagon Will Make a Fine Exhibit . . . ,'" *The Magazine of the Jefferson County Historical Society John Brown Raid Issue, 1859–2009*, 111–122, JCM.

62. Boyd B. Stutler, as quoted in Perks, "'The Old Wagon Will Make a Fine Exhibit,'" 119–120.

63. This much-commented-on conversation has been cited in a number of ways. I rely here on Thomas Drew, *John Brown Invasion; An Authentic History of the Harper's Ferry Tragedy* (Boston: James Campbell, 1860), BBS; Barrie Stavis, *John Brown: The Sword and the Word* (South Brunswick and

New York: A. S. Barnes and Company, 1970); Redpath, *The Public Life of Capt. John Brown*; and the *New York Daily Tribune*, December 5, 1859.

64. John T. L. Preston to Margaret Junkin Preston, December 2, 1859. In Elizabeth Preston Allan, *The Life and Letters of Margaret Junkin Preston* (Boston: Houghton Mifflin, 1903), 111–117.

65. Avey, *The Capture and Execution of John Brown*, 40.

66. Edmund Ruffin, *The Diary of Edmund Ruffin: Volume 1*, ed. William Kaufmann Scarborough (Baton Rouge: Louisiana State University Press, 1972), 588.

67. Ibid., 369.

68. Parke Poindexter to His Sister Eliza C. Perkins, *John Brown Pamphlets*, vol. 4, BBS.

69. Louis A. DeCaro Jr., *"Fire from the Midst of You": A Religious Life of John Brown* (New York: New York University Press, 2002), 278.

70. Thomas Gordon Pollock, "Eye-Witness Account of the Hanging of John Brown," *The Magazine of the Jefferson County Historical Society*, vol. LIV (December 1988), 113, JCM.

71. John Brown to His Children at North Elba, November 22, 1859, reprinted in Ruchames, *John Brown*, 150–151.

72. Ruffin, *The Diary of Edmund Ruffin*, 369–370.

73. Avey, *The Capture and Execution of John Brown*, 40.

74. Ruffin, *The Diary of Edmund Ruffin*, 370; Strother, "The Hanging of John Brown," 9.

75. Strother, "The Hanging of John Brown," 9.

76. Thomas J. Jackson ("Stonewall") to his wife, Mary Anna Jackson, December 2, 1859, *Life and Letters of Thomas J. Jackson*, edited by Mary Anna Jackson (New York: Harper, 1892).

77. *New York Daily Tribune*, December 3, 1859.

78. Strother, "The Hanging of John Brown," 9.

79. Ruffin, *The Diary of Edmund Ruffin*, 370; Thomas J. Jackson to his wife, Mary Anna Jackson, December 2, 1859, *Life and Letters of Thomas J. Jackson*.

80. *New York Daily Tribune*, December 3, 1859.

81. John T. L. Preston to Margaret Junkin Preston, December 2, 1859, in Allan, *The Life and Letters of Margaret Junkin Preston*.

82. Ruchames, *John Brown*, 189.

83. *New York Daily Tribune*, December 3, 1859.

84. John T. L. Preston to Margaret Junkin Preston, *The Life and Letters of Margaret Junkin Preston*, 115.

85. *New York Herald*, December 3, 1859.

86. Quoted in David Karsner, *John Brown: Terrible Saint* (New York: Dodd, Mead, and Company, 1934), 331, OHS.

87. "Execution of John Brown," *Register* (Raleigh, NC), December 3, 1859, Secession Era Editorials Project, Furman University Department of History, http://history.furman.edu/editorials/see.py.

88. Mayo, "Execution of Old John Brown."

89. Joseph Barry, *The Strange Story of John Brown* (Martinsburg, WV: Thompson Brothers, 1903), 85, JCM.

90. Massachusetts Historical Society Artifact no. 0544, length of rope with noose, supposedly used to hang John Brown, 1859.

91. Pieces of the rope can be found in the Warren Rifles Confederate, Front Royal, Virginia, as well as in the Historic Sandusky Historic Site and Civil War Museum, Lynchburg, Virginia.

92. "Brown Rope Is Given Stutler on Birthday," *Charleston Gazette*, July 14, 1929.

93. Stella I. Brown to Boyd B. Stutler, September 17, 1933, BBS.

94. Louisa Williamson to Jebidiah Williamson, December 8, 1859, BBS.

95. Boyd B. Stutler, "Notes on John Brown Hanging Rope," BBS. Stutler cites an excerpt from a letter by Theodore Tilton (no date given) and from the library of the late Frederick S. Wait that was sold at auction in New York City in 1900. Tilton apparently accompanied the body from Philadelphia to New York City.

96. Horwitz, *Midnight Rising*, 181–182.

97. Henry David Thoreau, "The Last Days of John Brown," in *Collected Essays and Poems* (New York: Library of America, 2001), 427.

98. Ralph Waldo Emerson, "Courage," lecture at the Boston Music Hall (November 8, 1859), reprinted in *New-York Daily Tribune*, November 24, 1859, Chronicling America, Library of Congress (LOC).

99. Quoted in David S. Reynolds, *John Brown, Abolitionist* (New York: Alfred A. Knopf, 2005), 339.

100. Ibid., 340.

101. Ibid., 343.

102. Henry David Thoreau, "A Plea for John Brown," in *Collected Essays and Poems*, 416.

103. John Brown to His Wife and Children, November 8, 1859, reprinted in Ruchames, *John Brown*, 140.

104. John Brown to Rev. H. L. Vaill, November 15, 1859, reprinted in Ruchames, *John Brown*, 143. See also John Brown to Thomas B. Musgrave Jr., November 17, 1859, reprinted in Ruchames, *John Brown*, 147.

105. John Brown to Rev. Luther Humphrey, November 19, 1859, reprinted in Ruchames, *John Brown*, 148.

106. John Brown to J. B. Musgrave, November 17, 1859, reprinted in Ruchames, *John Brown*, 147.

107. John Brown to Wife, Sons, and Daughters, November 30, 1859, reprinted in Ruchames, *John Brown*, 164–166. In this last letter to his wife and family on November 30 he implores them to live as Christians and to not be ashamed that he is about to die on the gallows and to follow the golden rule, which means to abhor, above all else, slavery, the "sum of all villainies."

108. John Brown to Rev. James W. McFarland, November 23, 1859, reprinted in Ruchames, *John Brown*, 154.

109. "John Brown Dead," *New York Daily Tribune*, December 3, 1859.

110. Trodd and Stauffer, *Meteor of War*, 163.

111. Laurence Greene, *The Raid: A Biography of Harpers Ferry* (New York: Henry Holt, 1953), 205. See also Extract from a letter to Burton from Mauzy, December 1859, BBS, and Boyd B. Stutler to Samuel Ha. Miller, April 15, 1961, BBS.

112. Bluford Adams, *E Pluribus Barnum: The Great Showman and the Making of U.S. Popular Culture* (Minneapolis: University of Minnesota Press, 1997), 157.

113. Barry, *The Strange Story of John Brown*, 85–86.

114. "John Brown's Scaffold," *New York Times*, February 26, 1884; "In John Brown's Land," *New York Tribune*, May 25, 1884; and Susan Collins, "Given in Evidence," *Magazine of the Jefferson County Historical Society: John Brown Raid Issue, 1859–2009*, 97. The land on which Brown was hanged was bought in 1891 by Colonel John Thomas Gibson. He was among the first to respond to Harpers Ferry with his 55th Regiment of the Virginia Militia and was on hand when Brown was arrested.

115. A note in the papers of Oswald Garrison Villard from an unidentified newspaper claimed that the scaffold was owned by Messrs. John M. Coyle & Co. and that they planned to publish a pamphlet proving the origins of the scaffold and then carve it up into "watch charms, chains, finger rings, earrings" and sell them. Oswald Garrison Villard John Brown Manuscripts, Box 3, Rare Book and Manuscript Library, Columbia University in the City of New York.

116. Herman Melville, "The Portent," in *Tales, Poems, and Other Writings*, ed. John Bryant (New York: Modern Library, 2001), 337.

CHAPTER 7

1. The name is spelled variously Chaskay, Chaske, or Caske (it is pronounced Chas-kay). Typically among Dakota "Caske" is the public name of the first-born son (and Winona is the public name of the first-born daughter).

2. Gwen Westerman and Bruce White, *Mni Sota Makoce: The Land of the Dakota* (St. Paul: Minnesota Historical Society Press, 2012), 15, 19; Waziyatawin, *What Does Justice Look Like?: The Struggle for Liberation in the Dakota Homeland* (St. Paul, MN: Living Justice Press, 2008), 21.

3. Westerman and White, *Mni Sota Makoce*, 134: "Both the Dakota people and the Europeans have an intense and intimate relationship with the land, but that relationship springs from strikingly different sources of understanding. Dakota people view the land as their homeland, their relative, their mother; the Europeans see it as a possession."

4. David A. Nichols, *Lincoln and the Indians* (St. Paul: Minnesota Historical Society Press, 2012), 11–12.

5. Ibid., 20.

6. Ibid., 18.

7. Ibid., 23–24.

8. George E. H. Day to President Lincoln, January 1, 1862, Abraham Lincoln Papers, Manuscript Division, Library of Congress (LOC).

9. Bishop Henry B. Whipple to Abraham Lincoln, March 6, 1862, reprinted in Bishop Henry Whipple, *Lights and Shadows of a Long Episcopate* (New York: Macmillan, 1899), 510–514.

10. Mary Lethert Wingerd, *North Country: The Making of Minnesota* (Minneapolis: University of Minnesota Press, 2010), 304.

11. H. L. Gordon, *The Feast of the Virgins and Other Poems* (Chicago: Laird and Lee, 1891), 343–344.

12. Wingerd, *North Country*, 307.

13. Samuel J. Brown, "Samuel J. Brown's Recollections," *Through Dakota Eyes: Narrative Accounts of the Minnesota Indian War of 1862*, ed. Gary Clayton Anderson and Alan R. Woolworth (St. Paul: Minnesota Historical Society Press), 227.

14. Carol Chomsky, "The United States-Dakota War Trials: A Study in Military Injustice," *Stanford Law Review* 13, no. 1 (November 1990), 91.

15. In Dakota, Wicaŋhpi Wastedaŋpi (Little Good Stars). Carrie Zeman explained in an e-mail exchange (October 18, 2012), "In the modern Dakota orthography it [his Dakota name] is written Wicaŋhpi Wastedaŋpi. In English, it is spelled 'Wicanpi Wastedanpi,' which translates as Little Good Stars." Caske's 1862 War Trial Record (Case #21). Transcription from National Archives microfilm and compared to holograph in the National Archives, by Walt Bachman Walt and Elizabeth Bachman via Carrie Zeman. Thank you, Carrie Zeman, for sharing this valuable resource with me.

16. Caske's 1862 War Trial Record (Case #21).

17. Chomsky, "The United States-Dakota War Trials," 34.

18. Richard Mott Jackson, "Rescue of White Girl Captives from Indians: An Incident of the Minnesota Massacre of 1862," Minnesota Historical Society (MHS).

19. Carl Sandburg, *Abraham Lincoln: The Prairie Years and the War Years* (New York: Harcourt, Brace, 1954), 90–91.

20. Nichols, *Lincoln and the Indians*, 5–6.

21. Bethany Schneider, "Abraham Lincoln and the American Indians," *The Cambridge Companion to Abraham Lincoln*, ed. Shirley Samuels (New York: Cambridge University Press, 2012), 93.

22. *Mankato Daily Review*, December 26, 1896.

23. Henry L. Mills and Family Papers, 1851–1894, MHS.

24. Chomsky, "The United States-Dakota War Trials," 33–34.

25. *St. Paul Press*, December 28, 1863.

26. *New York Times*, January 11, 1863.

27. *St. Paul Press*, December 28, 1863.

28. Ibid.; Eli K. Pickett Correspondence, 1861–1865, MHS.

29. *St. Paul Press*, December 28, 1863.

30. Chomsky, "The United States-Dakota War Trials," 36.

31. *New York Times*, January 11, 1863.

32. Ibid.

33. Ibid.

34. Henry L. Mills and Family Papers, 1851–1894, MHS.

35. *St. Paul Press*, December 28, 1863.

36. Ibid.

37. In the same issue of *Harper's Weekly* (January 17, 1863) that published Lincoln's Emancipation Proclamation is an image from the Mankato execution. Thank you to Mark Noonan for bringing this to my attention.

38. *New York Times*, January 11, 1863. The translations I have used are from "Names of the Condemned Dakota Men," *American Indian Quarterly* 28, no. 1/2 (Winter-Spring 2004): 175–183.

39. J. K. Arnold to J. Fletcher Williams, July 26, 1869, MHS.

40. For more on this ceremony, see George Blue Bird, "Wicozani Wakan Ota Akupi (Bringing Back Many Sacred Healings)," *American Indian Quarterly* 28, no. 1/2 (Winter-Spring 2004): 252–257. George Blue Bird explains, "This ceremony is very important because it unites the spirits of our dead relatives and lets them pass on to the world up above. In this ceremony we gather the family and the relatives of those who are deceased, and we release the dead through prayer, memorial songs, food, tobacco, and crying," 255.

41. Carrie Reber Zeman, "A Veiled Cabinet of Curiosities: A Preliminary Report on Minnesota's 1862 Gallow's Artifacts," http://athrillingnarrative.files .wordpress.com/2012/04/execution-artifacts-report.pdf.

42. Ibid.

43. "Cane from Mankato," MHS, Collections Online, http://collections.mnhs .org.

44. Carrie Reber Zeman, e-mail message to author, August 26, 2013.

45. Ian Lilligran, e-mail message to author, November 2, 2012. The Barnum museum subsequently burnt down.

46. Tim Khron, "Wood Believed to Be from 1862 Gallows Stashed Away," *Mankato Free Press*, February 4, 2012.

47. "The Timber History Mystery," Blue Earth County Historical Society, www.bechshistory.com/timber.

48. Scott W. Berg, *38 Nooses* (New York: Pantheon, 2012), 299.

49. Chomsky, "The United States-Dakota War Trials," 43–46.

50. "Execution of Two Indians at Fort Snelling, Minnesota," *Cleveland Plain Dealer*, November 17, 1865.

51. Ibid.

52. Rick Lybeck's analysis of the ways Minnesota has and has not remembered the war shaped how I wrote this chapter. I am grateful for his assistance.

53. For a recent example of the issues facing some Dakota communities, see "Abandoned in Indian Country," *New York Times*, July 23, 2013, www.nytimes.com/2013/07/24/opinion/abandoned-in-indian-country .html?_r=0.

54. From "Black Elk Speaks," reprinted in *Masterpieces of American Indian Literature*, ed. Willis G. Regier (Lincoln: University of Nebraska Press, 2005), 466–477.

CHAPTER 8

1. This initial version of the story relies on "Lynched at Lyndrum: Acquitted Lawfully but Hung," *Spartanburg Herald*, November 23, 1894. This story was reproduced in the *Greenville Mountaineer* (Greenville, SC), November 28, 1894, vol. LXX, no. 25, Microfilm (Reel 4, January 1893–Marce 30, 1895) and in the *Laurens Advertiser* in Laurens, South Carolina. A truncated version was published in *The State* (Columbia, SC). However, there was no mention of the Dick Wofford lynching in other local papers in Pickens, Edgefield, Walhalla, or Abbeville, South Carolina. Nor was it reported in any other North Carolina newspaper that I could uncover.

2. From roughly July 16, 1894, to July 26, 1894, rain and cooler temperatures prevailed across the region. See "The Weather," *Charlotte Daily Observer*, July 19, 1894, and "Heavy Rains," *Charlotte Daily Observer*, July 26, 1894.

3. For the State: James Frank Henderson, E. J. Foster, and J. G. Waldrop. For the Defense: Slick Balin, Eunice Booker, Eli Shehan, Una Raines, and the defendant himself (his employer did not testify on his behalf). Eli Shehan was a thirty-year-old white male farm laborer, married, with two sons.

4. *Spartanburg Herald*, November 23, 1894.

5. Edward Ayers, *Vengeance and Justice: Crime and Punishment in the 19th Century American South* (New York: Oxford University Press, 1984), 155.

6. Stewart E. Tolnay and E. M. Beck, *A Festival of Violence: An Analysis of Southern Lynchings, 1882–1930* (Urbana: University of Illinois Press, 1995), 57.

7. See Eric Foner, *Reconstruction: America's Unfinished Revolution, 1863–1877* (New York: Harper Row, 1988), 425–429. The Ku Klux Klan's disguises and rituals were a great mechanism for reasserting white power in the wake of the Civil War. Foner notes that in western North Carolina's Rutherford County (Polk's neighbor to the east) the Klan went after white Republicans as well as those who had supported keeping the Union. They also attacked black-led institutions: churches, schools—anything that reeked of "black autonomy." They attacked literate black people and black people who had been financially successful. The Klan's actions had significant social and political implications. The federal government began to crack down on the Klan in the early 1870s, but federal as well as locally organized African American responses to the Klan could not undo the damage this group had wrought. Republicans, both black and white, had been pushed out of office and the party itself made virtually impotent in most of the South. With Democrats in charge by the late 1870s, states began enacting a white supremacist agenda.

8. Philip Dray, *At the Hands of Persons Unknown: The Lynching of Black America* (New York: Random House, 2002), vii.

9. Vann R. Newkirk, *Lynching in North Carolina: A History, 1865–1941* (Jefferson, NC: McFarland and Company, 2009), 1.

10. Tolnay and Beck, *A Festival of Violence*, ix.

11. Ibid.

12. Daniel T. Williams, *Amid the Gathering Multitude: The Story of Lynching in America, A Classified Listing* (Unpublished: Tuskegee University, 1968).

13. NAACP, *Thirty Years of Lynching in the United States, 1889–1918* (New York: NAACP, 1919), 29.

14. Manfred Berg, *Popular Justice: A History of Lynching in America* (Chicago: Iva R. Dee, 2011), 117.

15. Christopher Waldrep, *The Many Faces of Judge Lynch: Extralegal Violence and Punishment in America* (New York: Palgrave Macmillan, 2002), 13–25.

16. Catharine Van Cortlandt Mathews, *Andrew Ellicott: His Life and Letters* (New York: Grafton Press, 1908), 221.

17. For example, on March 2, 1819, the Norfolk-based *American Beacon* published a story regarding a group of Charleston, South Carolina, citizens who ran a "gang of desperadoes" out of town by burning down the buildings they were using as hideouts. The article claims they acted under "Lynch's Law." The term "Lynch Law" appeared as the title for a brief article in the *New York Evening Post* on December 1, 1826, describing the beating death

of a man in Baton Rouge, Louisiana. The man fell victim to "Lynch's Law" and eventually died.

18. "Origin of Lynch Law," *Baltimore Gazette and Daily Advertiser*, January 10, 1827.

19. Washington Irving, *A Tour on the Prairies* (Paris: Baudry's European Library, 1835), 33–34.

20. W. J. Cash, *The Mind of the South* (New York: Random House, 1969), 43.

21. Waldrep, *The Many Faces of Judge Lynch*, 2. Waldrep notes that the "NAACP definition," which the organization never actually agreed upon, added that the killing must have been committed in order to serve "justice or tradition." See my Preface above.

22. Leon F. Litwack, *Trouble in Mind: Black Southerners in the Age of Jim Crow* (New York: Vintage, 1999), 294.

23. *Memphis Commercial*, July 23, 1892.

24. Edward Ayers, *The Promise of the New South: Life after Reconstruction* (New York: Oxford University Press, 1992), 156.

25. Ibid., 156–157.

26. Jack Bass and Jack Nelson, *The Orangeburg Massacre* (Macon, GA: Mercer University Press, 2002), 161.

27. I can only speculate as to how Dick Wofford's murder qualifies as a lynching based on the definition mentioned above, but there is evidence he was killed illegally, likely by several people, based on reports it was a posse and because his murder follows a court decision setting a black man free after the alleged rape of a white woman.

28. In Ida B. Wells-Barnett's *The Red Record: Tabulated Statistics and Alleged Cause of Lynchings in the United States* (1895 Chicago: Donohue & Henneberry, 1895), she lists his death under those lynched for "Unknown Offenses": "Nov. 23, unknown, Landrum, S.C." In 1919 the NAACP reported his death as follows: "Nov. 29 . . . Unknown Negro . . . Landrum, Spartanburg Co . . . Cause Unknown" (*Thirty Years of Lynching*, 89). More recent scholars like Tolnay and Beck (*A Festival of Violence*) as well as Newkirk (*Lynching in North Carolina*) correctly identify Wofford.

29. Anna Pack Conner, *Tryon: An Illustrated History* (Spartanburg, SC: Reprint Company, 2008), 14.

30. Ibid., 20.

31. "Polk County and Slavery," *For the Record: A Journal of Polk County History and Genealogy* (Fall 1982), 76.

32. Ibid., 77. For example, Reuban Jordan owned thirty slaves, and Daniel Harvey, fourteen.

33. Ibid., 78.

34. 1880 US Federal Census.

35. Thank you to Susan Thoms of the Spartanburg County Library for helping me with this.

36. General Index to Criminal Minutes Books, Polk County, NC, Defendants, 63. In Spring 1894 Court Minutes Dick Wofford appears in a list of defendants.

37. William S. Powell, *North Carolina through Four Centuries* (Chapel Hill: University of North Carolina Press, 1989), 376.

38. Litwack, *Trouble in Mind*, 304.

39. Ibid., 302.

40. Ida B. Wells-Barnett, *Southern Horrors: Lynch Law in All Its Phases* (New York: New York Age Print, 1892).

41. Ibid.

42. Ibid.

43. Wells-Barnett, *Red Record*.

44. NAACP, *Thirty Years of Lynching*, 10. Of African American victims, "35.8 per cent were accused of murder; 28.4 per cent of rape and 'attacks upon women'" during the period of their research, 1889 to 1918.

45. Ayers, *Vengeance and Justice*, 241.

46. Elizabeth Henderson Michaels, *The Hannon Family of Polk County, North Carolina*, 3rd ed. (Morganton, NC: self-published, 2008), 82–83.

47. Ibid., 107.

48. Ayers, *Vengeance and Justice*, 242.

49. The *Spartanburg Herald* had another suggestion, that Dick Wofford was found innocent because of local politics. They claim "that care was taken by the counsel for the defendant that all the jurymen be of one political opinion. . . . The judge and lawyers and everybody were surprised [by the verdict], for all who heard the evidence in the case were unanimous in the opinion that he was proven guilty beyond a reasonable doubt and universal indignation prevailed at the finding of the jury."

50. Michaels, *The Hannon Family*, 83.

51. Ibid., 84.

52. Newkirk, *Lynching in North Carolina*, 4–5; Tolnay and Beck, *A Festival of Violence*, 72, 257.

53. Ayers, *Vengeance and Justice*, 250.

54. Tolnay and Beck, *A Festival of Violence*, 149.

55. Foner, *Reconstruction*, 12.

56. Milton Ready, *The Tar Heel State: A History of North Carolina* (Columbia: University of South Carolina Press, 2005), 253.

57. Newkirk, *Lynching in North Carolina*, 170.

58. Ibid., 4.

59. Stephen West, *From Yeoman to Redneck in the South Carolina Upcountry, 1850–1915* (Charlottesville: University of Virginia Press, 2008), 137.

60. Quoted in W. J. Megginson, *African American Life in the South Carolina Upper Piedmont* (Columbia: University of South Carolina Press, 2006), 386.

61. Stephen Kantrowitz, *Ben Tillman and the Reconstruction of White Supremacy* (Chapel Hill: University of North Carolina Press, 2000), 167–168.

62. Ibid., 157.

63. West, *From Yeoman to Redneck*, 134–135.

64. Ibid., 135.

65. Newkirk, *Lynching in North Carolina*, 169.

66. Ayers, *Promise of the New South*, 137–140. By the 1880s the legal structures of Jim Crow were not completely in place across the South (the word "segregation" was not part of common usage until the twentieth century), but the attitudes were already there. Those attitudes were best observed on the railroads, an especially contested site for race relations in the late nineteenth century. Black people were often forced to sit in the dirty, smoky, second-class cars. Those who could afford first-class tickets were often sent to the second-class car anyway. By the late 1880s southern states began making laws require separate cars. In 1892 a light-skinned African American man named Homer Adolph Plessy contested these laws by taking a seat in the white car on the East Louisiana Railroad and refused to leave. The case made its way to the Supreme Court, and the idea of "equal accommodations" or "separate but equal" was born.

67. Ibid., 136.

68. D. William Bennett, ed., *Polk County, North Carolina History* (Spartanburg, SC: Reprint Company, 2006), 9.

69. Conner, *Tryon*, 15.

70. Ibid., 15.

71. Nina Simone, *I Put a Spell on You* (New York: Da Capo, 2003), 1.

72. Ibid.

CHAPTER 9

1. For example, James Elbert Cutler's *Lynch Law* (New York: Longman's, Green, and Co., 1905); Walter White's *Rope and Faggot: A Biography of Judge Lynch* (New York: Alfred A. Knopf, 1929); and the NAACP's *Thirty Years of Lynching in the United States, 1889–1918* (New York: NAACP, 1919). Add to this countless reports written by often anonymous NAACP investigators. Though first published in 1962, Ralph Ginzburg's *100 Years of Lynching* (Baltimore, MD: Black Classic Press, 1988) offers a useful compendium of newspaper articles that cover the lynching years.

2. Report of the Secretary for the April Meeting of the Board, April 4, 1937, Papers of the NAACP, Microfilm, part I, reel 6.

3. Tolnay and Beck, *A Festival of Violence*, 203–204.

4. Thank you to Glenn Dickey for his help with reading this photograph.

5. Sherwood Anderson, *Winesburg, Ohio* (New York: Viking Press, 1919), 28.

6. Ibid., 32.

7. Ibid., 33.

8. Table 13: State Population, US Census Bureau, www.census.gov/compendia /statab/2011/tables/11s0013.pdf.

9. NAACP, *Thirty Years of Lynching*.

10. Sloane Gordon, "Booze, Boodle, and Bloodshed in the Middle West," *Cosmopolitan*, November 1910, 765.

11. Ibid., 766.

12. Ray Stannard Baker, "The Thin Crust of Civilization: A Study of the Liquor Traffic in a Modern American City," *American Magazine* (April 1911), 691.

13. "Blind Pig Raider Lynched by Mob," *Oregonian*, July 9, 1910.

14. According to local historian Chris Evans, Etherington's gravesite in Willisburg, Kentucky, indicates that Etherington was seventeen years old when he was lynched in Newark. US Marine Corps, Discharge, November 2009.

15. William T. Utter, *Granville: The Story of an Ohio Village* (Granville, OH: Granville Historical Society and Denison University, 1956), 284.

16. Hubert Howe Bancroft, *Popular Tribunals, vol. 1* (San Francisco: History Company, 1887), 8.

17. Chris Evans, interview with author, August 1, 2011.

18. Ray Stannard Baker, "The Thin Crust of Civilization: A Study of the Liquor Traffic in a Modern American City," *American Magazine* (April 1911): 691–704.

19. Evans, interview with author.

20. "Detective Lynched by Ohio Mob at Jail," *New York Times*, July 9, 1910.

21. Evans, interview with author.

22. *Newark Advocate*, July 9, 1910.

23. "Detective Lynched by Ohio Mob at Jail."

24. Baker, "The Thin Crust of Civilization," 692.

25. "Detective Lynched by Ohio Mob at Jail."

26. Wayne B. Wheeler, *The Newark Lynching: Its Causes and Results* (Westerville, OH: American Issue Publishing, 1910), 19.

27. "Blind Pig Raider Lynched by Mob."

28. Ibid.

29. Wheeler, *The Newark Lynching*, 19.

30. "Murder—Mob—Lynching," *Johnstown Independent*, July 14, 1910.

31. Ibid.

32. *Newark Advocate*, July 9, 1910.

33. Baker, "The Thin Crust of Civilization," 692.

34. "Blind Pig Raider Lynched by Mob."

35. Gordon, "Booze, Boodle, and Bloodshed," 769.

36. "Scent of Riot," *Newark Advocate*, July 9, 1910.

37. "Blame Sheriff for Lynching," *New York Times*, July 10, 1910.

38. "Newark Must Clean House," *Newark Advocate*, July 11, 2010.

39. See Wheeler, *The Newark Lynching*.

40. Paul Thompson, *A Most Stirring and Significant Episode: Religion and the Rise and Fall of Prohibition in Black Atlanta, 1865–1887* (Dekalb: Northern Illinois University Press, 2013), 129–134, 166–170.

41. "Cause of the Lynching," *Newark American Tribune*, July 14, 1910. See also "A Northern Lynching," *Outlook*, July 23, 1910: 597–598. Another interesting source is Alonzo B. Shaw's *Trails in Shadow Land: Stories of a Detective* (Columbus, OH: Hahn and Adair, 1910).

42. Gordon, "Booze, Boodle, and Bloodshed," 775.

43. "Blame Sheriff for Lynching."

44. Katy Klettinger, "County Records Shed Fresh Light on Historic Crime," *Newark Advocate*, July 24, 2012.

45. Bertillon Cards with Photographs, 1888–1919, and State Bertillon Cards with Photographs, 1913–1982, Ohio State Historical Society (OSHS).

46. *Marion Daily Star* (Ohio), July 11, 1910.

47. Hartwell Etherington Certificate of Death, June 25, 1912, Commonwealth of Kentucky, State Board of Health, Bureau of Vital Statistics.

48. See comments after Anna Sudar, "100 Years Ago, Newark's Streets were Lawless," *Newark Advocate*, July 12, 2010.

49. "Lynch Replay Draws Wrath," *Newark Advocate*, March 15, 1972.

50. Baker, "The Thin Crust of Civilization," 692.

51. Gordon, "Booze, Boodle, and Bloodshed," 762.

52. Sherwood Anderson, "This Lynching," An Art Commentary on Lynching, Arthur U. Newton Galleries, 1935.

53. Bertram Wyatt-Brown, *Honor and Violence in the Old South* (New York: Oxford University Press, 1986), 212.

CHAPTER 10

1. James H. Madison, *A Lynching in the Heartland: Race and Memory in America* (New York: Palgrave, 2001), 113.

2. Ibid., 115.

3. Quoted in Ed Breen, "Aug. 7, 1930, Returns to Haunt Us," *Chronicle Tribune* (Marion, IN), April 3, 1988.

4. Madison, *Lynching in the Heartland*, 115.

5. *100 Photographs That Changed the World* (New York: Life Books, 2011), 56.

6. Alistair Cooke, *Allistair Cooke's America* (New York: Alfred A Knopf, 1973), 311–313.

7. Breen, "Aug. 7, 1930, Returns to Haunt Us."

8. Madison, *Lynching in the Heartland*, 112.

9. James H. Madison, *Indiana Way: A State History* (Bloomington: Indiana University Press; Indianapolis: Indiana Historical Society, 1986), 122.

10. Madison, *Lynching in the Heartland*, 29.

11. Ibid.

12. Wyn Craig Wade, *The Fiery Cross: The Ku Klux Klan in America* (New York: Simon and Schuster, 1987), 138.

13. See Kenneth Jackson, *The Ku Klux Klan in the City* (New York: Oxford University Press, 1967).

14. Allen Safianow, "The Klan Comes to Tipton," *Indiana Magazine of History* 95, no. 3 (September 1999), 203.

15. Madison, *Lynching in the Heartland*, 40.

16. William Munn, interview with author, August 6, 2011.

17. Madison, *Lynching in the Heartland*, 6.

18. National Association for the Advancement of Colored People, "Report of the Acting Secretary for the September Meeting of the Board," September 1930, Papers of the NAACP Microfilm, part 1, reel 5. The sheriff told this to Walter White of the NAACP.

19. From "Strange Fruit: Anniversary of a Lynching," *All Things Considered*, National Public Radio, August 6, 2010.

20. James Cameron, *A Time of Terror* (Baltimore, MD: Black Classic Press, 1994), 9.

21. Ibid., 10

22. Ibid., 54.

23. Ibid., 73–74.

24. "Strange Fruit: Anniversary of a Lynching."

25. Original Depositions of the Lynching in Marion, Indiana, August 13–15, 1930, Marion Public Library (MPL). Tellingly, a man who must have known many of the community's residents, Sheriff Campbell, says he couldn't identify any particular persons.

26. Paul Laurence Dunbar, "The Haunted Oak," in *The Collected Words of Paul Laurence Dunbar*, ed. Joanne M. Braxton (Charlottesville: University Press of Virginia, 1993), 219–220.

CHAPTER 11

1. "Hickock and Smith Die Early Today at K.S.P.," *Leavenworth Times*, April 14, 1965.

2. *Kansas City Star*, April 13, 1965.

3. Truman Capote, *In Cold Blood: A True Account of a Multiple Murder and Its Consequences* (New York: Random House, 1965), 337.

4. Capote's physical descriptions of the gallows and warehouse seem to match those of other reporters. See "Pair Meet Death on KSP Gallows," *Garden City Telegram*, April 14, 1965, and "Two Die on Gallows for Kansas Killings," *New York Times*, April 14, 1965.

5. Capote, *In Cold Blood*, 337–338.

6. "Hickock and Smith Die."

7. Capote, *In Cold Blood*, 338.

8. "Hickock and Smith Die"; Capote, *In Cold Blood*, 338.

9. Capote, *In Cold Blood*, 338.

10. Ibid., 339. "Hickock and Smith Die" reported his words as, "I don't have any hard feelings. You're sending me to a better place."

11. "Hickock and Smith Die."

12. Capote, *In Cold Blood*, 339.

13. Ibid., 340.

14. There's a dispute about what he said. "Hickock and Smith Die" reported it as such: "'I think it's a hell of a thing that a life has to be taken in this manner. . . . I think capital punishment is legally and morally wrong.' Commenting that apologies for what he had done were meaningless, Smith climbed the gallows at 1 A.M."

15. *Kansas City Star*, April 14, 1965.

16. Quoted in *Kansas City Star*, April 14, 1965.

17. Their bodies were exhumed as part of an investigation into the December 1959 murder of Cliff and Christine Walker and their two children in Osprey, Florida. Hickock and Smith had long been suspects in the case because they had fled to Florida around the same time and had been in the area where the murders occurred, among other things. DNA testing was inconclusive and failed to link the two to the grizzly murders, but it also failed to rule them out.

18. In an interview, Michael McKnight told me, "That was the first thing I thought of. It's almost like I could see myself hanging from that particular rope. When I saw it I had a vision—like I was in a movie and I saw myself hanging from a tree. Seriously! Me hanging from a tree."

19. There are so many of these I couldn't begin to discuss them all. More recently the video for Toby Keith's song "Beer for my Horses" plays with this genre.

20. The most recent and well-known film hanging with a hangman's knot was in Steve McQueen's adaptation of Solomon Northrup's *Twelve Years a Slave* (2013).

21. Samuel Haughton, "On Hanging Considered from a Mechanical and Physiological Point of View," *The London, Edinburgh, and Dublin Philosophical Magazine and Journal of Science* 32 (1866), 29.

22. Anthony Stokes, *Pit of Shame: The Real Ballad of Reading Gaol* (Sherfield on Loddon: Waterside Press, 2007), 54.

23. Edward J. Akins, e-mail message to author, July 30, 2013; Jerry Akins, *Hangin' Times in Fort Smith: A History of Executions in Judge Parker's Court* (Little Rock, AK: Butler Center Books, 2012).

24. Department of the Army, Pamphlet No. 27–4, Procedure for Military Executions, Department of the Army, December, 1947. The inclusion of the drop table may have been due to what many believed were "botched" executions at Nuremberg, though there is evidence to suggest that those hanging executions were just as violent as hanging executions had always been. Nonetheless, it appears the military wanted to make hangings seem more precise than they had been in the past:

120 lbs or less	8'1"	170 lbs	6'0"
125 lbs	7'10"	175 lbs	5'11"
130 lbs	7'7"	180 lbs	5'9"
135 lbs	7'4"	185 lbs	5'7"
140 lbs	7'1"	190 lbs	5'6"
145 lbs	6'9"	195 lbs	5'5"
150 lbs	6'7"	200 lbs	5'4"
155 lbs	6'6"	205 lbs	5'2"
160 lbs	6'4"	210 lbs	5'1"
165 lbs	6'2"	220 lbs and over	5'0"

25. Quoted in *Campbell v. Wood*, 18 F.3d 662 (9th Cir. 1994), 21.

26. Quoted in *Campbell v. Wood*, 27.

27. "Executions by Method, 1608–2002," Death Penalty, Pro-Con.org.

28. According to the Espy file a black male named John Marshall was hung in chains in McDowell County, West Virginia, on April 4, 1913, but I have had trouble confirming this information. See M. Watt Espy and John Ortiz Smykla, "Executions in the U.S.: The Espy File," Death Penalty Information Center, www.deathpenaltyinfo.org/documents/ESPYyear.pdf.

29. "Coroner Concludes Murderer Felt Little Pain When Hanged," *New York Times*, January 10, 1993.

30. Ibid.

31. Timothy Egan, "For First Time Since '65, a State Uses Its Gallows," *New York Times*, January 6, 1993.

32. Quoted in Egan, "For First Time Since '65."

33. "Coroner Concludes Murderer Felt Little Pain."

34. *Campbell v. Wood*, 21–22.

35. Ibid. 22.

36. Ibid., 14, 23.

37. Ibid., 29.

38. Ibid., 39.

39. Ibid., 41.

40. Ibid., 25.

41. Ibid., 28.

42. Ibid.

43. Ibid.

44. "Washington Hangs Murderer; Texas Executed Officer Killer," *New York Times*, May 28, 1994.

45. "Charles Campbell Execution by Hanging and Press Conference Afterward—Parts 11–14," *King 5 Television News*, Youtube.com.

46. Bob Faw, "Death Penalty: Hanging," *NBC Evening News*, Wednesday, January 24, 1996.

47. Ibid.

48. Quoted in Richard Clark, "Billy Bailey—Delaware, January 25, 1996," *Capital Punishment UK*, www.capitalpunishment.uk/bailey.

49. Faw, "Death Penalty: Hanging."

50. Clark, "Billy Bailey."

51. Gary Tuchman, "Death Penalty—Delaware Hanging," *CNN Evening News*, January 1, 2007.

52. "Killer of Two Is Hanged in Delaware as Kin of Victims Watch," *New York Times*, January 26, 1996; Rich Heidorn Jr., "Bailey Is Hanged in Delaware," *Philadelphia Inquirer*, January 25, 1996; Tuchman, "Death Penalty."

53. Tuchman, "Death Penalty."

54. Heidorn, "Bailey Is Hanged in Delaware."

55. Tuchman, "Death Penalty."

56. Clark, "Billy Bailey."

57. On February 11, 2014, Washington state Governor Jay Inslee declared a moratorium on the state's death penalty.

58. "Delaware Gallows the Victim at Final Public Spectacle," *Baltimore Sun*, July 9, 2003. In California a prisoner snuck into the execution chamber and destroyed the gallows with a crowbar; see Clinton T. Duffy, *The San Quentin Story* (Garden City, NY: Doubleday, 1950), 84.

CHAPTER 12

1. Greg Sowinski, "Cops Explain Third St. Drug Investigation," *Lima News*, May 31, 2008.

2. Jennifer Feehan, "Lima Police Pressed for Racial Fairness," *Toledo Blade*, January 27, 2008.

3. Tom Walton, "Racial Harmony in Lima Still a Work in Progress," *Toledo Blade*, June 23, 2008.

4. 2010 US Federal Census, www.census.gov.

5. Walton, "Racial Harmony in Lima."

6. 2010 United States Federal Census.

7. Sowinski, "Cops Explain Third St. Drug Investigation."

8. He was sentenced under USC, Section 3553(a).

9. Transcript of the Sentencing Proceedings Before the Honorable David A. Katz, US District Judge, *USA vs. Daniel Lee Jones*, Case No. 3:09cr0441, Toledo, Ohio, November 8, 2010, 6.

10. Transcript, *USA vs. Daniel Lee Jones*, 7.

11. Ibid., 7.

12. Ibid., 8.

13. Ibid., 11; see also Greg Sowinski, "Prison for Noose," *Lima News*, November 9, 2010.

14. Transcript, *USA vs. Daniel Lee Jones*, 15.

15. "Oregon Man Sentenced for Threatening Lima, Ohio, Civil Rights Leader by Mailing Noose," Department of Justice, Office of Public Affairs, November 8, 2010, http://www.justice.gov/opa/pr/2010/November /10-crt-1265.html. I made repeated attempts to interview Jones, to no avail.

16. Daniel T. Williams, *Amid the Gathering Multitude: The Story of Lynching in America, A Classified Listing* (Unpublished, Tuskegee University, 1968).

17. Another interesting example is when George Haley found a noose hanging from the ceiling of his room while attending law school at the University of Arkansas in the early 1950s.

18. Quoted in Michael Newton, *The Invisible Empire: The Ku Klux Klan in Florida* (Gainesville: University Press of Florida, 2001), 83.

19. Newton, *The Invisible Empire*, 83.

20. See "Hangman's Noose," *Hate on Display: A Visual Database of Extremist Symbols, Logos, and Tattoos*, Anti-Defamation League, http://archive.adl .org/hate_symbols/racist_noose.asp. See also the black baby doll with noose around its neck at 4:07 minutes in the History Channel–produced documentary *The Ku Klux Klan: A Secret History* (1998).

21. "No Negroes at Early Classes in Texarkana," *Del Rio News Herald*, September 11, 1956.

22. "Artist to Lynch Confederate Flag," *USA Today*, August 27, 2004, http://usatoday30.usatoday.com/life/2004–08–27-confederate-flag_x.htm.

23. See Timothy Clark, "Lynching in Another America: Race, Class, and Gender in Brazil, 1980–2003," in *Globalizing Lynching History*, eds. Manfred Berg and Simon Wendt (New York: Palgrave MacMillan, 2011).

24. "Ruston, Louisiana, Man Sentenced for Federal Hate Crime," Department of Justice, Public Affairs, November 5, 2010, www.justice.gov/opa /pr/2010/November/10-crt-1259.html.

25. Abbey Doyle, "Employee in Elwood Factory Noose Incident Speaks Out," *Herald Tribune*, September 13, 2010, www.newsandtribune.com/statenews /x204465677/Employee-in-Elwood-factory-noose-incident-speaks-out/print.

26. "Family Claims Noose Found in Front Yard," RTV6, October 2, 2010, www.theindychannel.com/news/family-claims-noose-found-in-front -yard.

27. Zellie Pollon, "African American Soldier Says Noose Strung Outside Barracks," *Reuters*, June 7, 2011, www.reuters.com/article/2011/06/07 /us-soldier-racism-new-mexico-idUSTRE75674C20110607.

28. Erica Lovely, "Race Tensions Build at Capitol Architect's Office," *Politico*, October 21, 2010, www.politico.com/news/stories/1010/43933.html.

29. "Noose Found on Tree Limb Outside Varina High School," *Richmond Times-Dispatch*, May 17, 2012, www.timesdispatch.com/news /noose-found-on-tree-limb-outside-varina-high-school/article_01473b0a -cb4e-5dac-8e35–8fc2374bb1ec.html?mode=jqm; "Student Admits Placing Noose Outside Varina High," *Richmond Times-Dispatch*, May 17, 2012, www .timesdispatch.com/news/student-admits-placing-noose-outside-varina-high /article_d15f6162-dd03–5c84-b4b1–4b5bdc366988.html?mode=jqm_com.

30. Drew Karedes, "Interracial Couple Overwhelmed with Support After Racist Vandalism," KHOU, June 7, 2012, www.khou.com/news/Interracial -couple-overwhelmed-with-support-after-racist-vandalism-157993535.html.

31. "FBI Joins Investigation into Noose Found Outside Business," WAPT, April 26, 2013, http://www.wapt.com/news/mississippi/fbi-joins-investigation -into-noose-found-outside-business/19910390; "Noose Hung at Mayoral Candidate's Office," *Clarion-Ledger*, April 29, 2013.

32. "Clyburn: Racist Faxes, Image of Noose Were Sent to Office," *Huffington Post*, March 23, 2010, www.huffingtonpost.com/2010/03/23/clyburn -racist-faxes-imag_n_509365.html.

33. "State Senator Leland Yee Receiving Hateful, Racist and Threatening Emails," *Los Angeles Times*, April 20, 2010.

34. Arlene Johns, "Text Message Is Hate Crime, Parent Says," *Tribune-Democrat* (Johnstown, PA), September 8, 2010.

35. Toya Graham, "School Bus Driver Loses Job over Noose in Text Message," *Post and Courier* (Charleston, SC), www.postandcourier.com /article/20110211/PC1602/302119983.

36. "Halloween Noose Sparks Controversy," *10 News Tampa Bay*, September 27, 2012, www.wtsp.com/news/article/275700/19/Halloween -noose-decoration-sparks-controversy; "Racially-Driven Halloween Display Removed at Sheriff's Request," KFVS 12, October 20, 2010, www.kfvs12 .com/story/13358148/halloween-display-of-black-man-in-tree-kkk-member -causes-stir.

37. "Halloween Billboard Stirs Controversy on North Side," CBS Pittsburgh, October 14, 2011, http://pittsburgh.cbslocal.com/2011/10/14 /halloween-billboard-stirs-controversy-on-north-side/.

38. "Idaho Snowman Shaped Like KKK Member Appalls Local Residents," *Huffington Post*, December 2, 2010, www.huffingtonpost.com/2010/12/03 /idaho-kkk-snowman-_n_791939.html.

39. Robert Kahn, "Liars or Cowards?" *Courthouse News Service*, October 15, 2010, www.courthousenews.com/2010/10/15/31111.htm.

40. Ed Kemmick, "Members of the Tea Party Spewing Hate," *Billings Gazette*, September 11, 2010, http://billingsgazette.com/news/opinion/blogs /city-lights/city-lights-members-of-tea-party-spewing-hate/article_dd99052c -be17–11df-817f-001cc4c002e0.html.

41. "Noose, Watermelons on Anti-Obama Display Called Racist," *Morgan Hill-Times*, October 10, 2012, www.morganhilltimes.com/articles_from _gilroy/noose-watermelons-on-anti-obama-display-called-racist/article_ c884adeb-55c2–57e3-ace3–7896c5c95616.html?mode=image&photo=0; Lisa Edge, "Noose on Empty Chair Display Causes Concern in Horry County," *Carolina Live*, October 29, 2012, www.carolinalive.com/news/story.aspx ?id=818861.

42. "Italy: Nooses Protest Over First Black Minister," *Sky News*, July 15, 2013, http://news.sky.com/story/1116068/italy-nooses-protest-over -first-black-minister.

43. Barbara Perry, *In the Name of Hate: Understanding Hate Crimes* (New York: Routledge, 2001), 3.

44. US Department of Justice, "Hate Crime Victimization Report, 2003– 2011," US Department of Justice, Office of Justice Programs, Bureau of Justice Statistics, March 2013, www.bjs.gov/content/pub/pdf/hcv0311.pdf.

45. Jeannine Bell, "The Hangman's Noose and the Lynch Mob: Hate Speech and the Jena Six," *Harvard Civil Rights-Civil Liberties Law Review* 44 (2009): 329–359, 342.

46. Ibid., 343.

47. Ibid., 350.

48. Allison Barger, "Changing State Laws to Prohibit the Display of Hangman's Nooses: Tightening the Knot Around the First Amendment?" *William and Mary Bill of Rights Journal* 17, no. 1 (2008): 263–292.

49. "Senate Passes Bill to Make It a Felony to Display a Noose on Public or Private Property," *US States News*, October 22, 2007. One of the most well-known noose incidents from this period was the discovery of a noose on the door of former Columbia University Teacher's College professor Madonna Constantine.

50. Bell, "The Hangman's Noose," 352.

51. Ibid., 354.

52. Ibid., 358.

53. Ibid., 359.

54. My description of what happened in Jena is based on interviews with Alan Bean as well as accounts from local and national newspapers including Craig Franklin, "Media Myths About the Jena 6," *Christian Science Monitor*, October 24, 2007, www.csmonitor.com/2007/1024/p09s01-coop.html; and various articles from the *New York Times* including Richard G. Jones's "In Louisiana, a Tree, a Fight, and a Question of Justice" (September 19, 2007) and "Louisiana Protest Echoes the Civil Rights Era" (September 21, 2007); and a report prepared by Alan Bean for Friends of Justice entitled, "Responding to the Crisis in Jena, Louisiana: The Jena Case in Brief."

55. Alan Bean, interview with author, October 27, 2011.

56. Quoted in Alan Bean, "Challenging the New Jim Crow: Part 3," Friends of Justice, November 29, 2010, http://friendsofjustice.wordpress .com/2010/11/29/challenging-the-new-jim-crow-part-3/.

57. Franklin, "Media Myths About the Jena 6."

58. Craig Franklin, "DA/School Officials Grant Exclusive Interviews." *Jena Times*, October 3, 2007.

59. Ibid.

60. Ibid.

61. For example, Tom Mangold, "'Stealth Racism' Stalks Deep South," *BBC News*, September 21, 2007, http://news.bbc.co.uk/2/hi/programmes /this_world/6685441.stm.

62. Anonymous, phone interview with author, September 2011.

63. "Committee to Examine Race Relations in Jena," Associated Press, November 14, 2007. I was unable to track down further evidence that this committee still exists.

64. Alan Bean noted that Jena is not a typical southern town. In 1990 Jena's LaSalle Parish was the strongest supporter of former Klansman David Duke in Louisiana. "He got 70 percent of the vote and roughly 15 percent of the Parish is African American," Bean said. District Attorney Reed Walters was Speedy Long's protégée; Speedy Long once sought Klan support and was a Dixiecrat Congressman in 1973. "So," Bean said, "they would have been taking a major risk if they'd said it was a hate crime—and they probably didn't see it as a hate crime. The problem is that the leadership in that community was incapable of responding to a hate crime, they didn't have the language for it." See Alan Bean, "Challenging the New Jim Crow: Part 3."

65. Bennett Wall et al., *Louisiana: A History*, 3rd ed. (Wheeling, IL: Harlan Davidson, 1997), 237. I cite this source because it is often used as a textbook.

66. See, for example, Terry Jones, *The Louisiana Journey* (Layton, UT: Gibbs Smith, 2007). This book is geared toward seventh and eighth graders.

67. "Social Studies Grade-Level Expectations," Louisiana Department of Education, www.doe.state.la.us/lde/uploads/3948.pdf.

68. During the Jim Crow years some young people were educated about lynching in very vivid ways. A friend of mine remembers a story he heard in the 1980s from his great-grandmother. She had grown up in rural Mississippi, and sometime around the First World War some men came into her elementary classroom and led all the students to a tree in a nearby field from which a black man was hanging. The men told them he had been lynched. I have no way of proving or disproving this story.

69. Mangold, "'Stealth Racism' Stalks Deep South."

70. "Nooses Result in Jail Time," Associated Press, August 16, 2008, http://query.nytimes.com/gst/fullpage.html?res=9C03E3D91F38F935A2 575BC0A96E9C8B63.

71. Daryl Fears, "La. Town Fells 'White Tree,' But Tension Runs Deep," *Washington Post*, August 4, 2007, www.washingtonpost.com/wp-dyn/content /article/2007/08/03/AR2007080302098.html. See also James H. Cone, *The Cross and the Lynching Tree* (Maryknoll, NY: Orbis, 2011).

72. "F.B.I. Expert Ties Blood to Jasper Defendant," *New York Times*, February 20, 1999, www.nytimes.com/1999/02/20/us/fbi-expert-ties-blood -to-jasper-defendant.html; Rick Lyman, "Man Guilty of Murder in Texas Dragging Death," *New York Times*, February 24, 1999, www.nytimes.com /1999/02/24/us/man-guilty-of-murder-in-texas-dragging-death.html.

73. B. J. Hollers, *Thirteen Loops: Race, Violence, and the Last Lynching in America* (Tuscaloosa: University of Alabama Press, 2011).

74. *State v. Cox*, no. cc-87–2143, ALA 1987, 1059–1071, Alabama Supreme Court and State Law Library, Heflin-Torbert Judicial Building, Montgomery, Alabama.

75. "Espy File: 1608–2002," Death Penalty Information Center, http:// dpic.org; "Searchable Execution Database," Death Penalty Information Center.

76. "US Executions from 1608–2002: A Demographic Breakdown of the Executed Population," Death Penalty, Pro-Con.org, http://deathpenalty .procon.org/view.resource.php?resourceID=004087.

77. "Top 20 Occupations of the Executed, 1608–2002," Death Penalty Pro-Con, http://deathpenalty.procon.org/view.resource.php?resource ID=004087#II.

78. Robert Penn Warren, *Legacy of the Civil War* (Lincoln: University of Nebraska Press, 1998), 60.

CHAPTER 13

1. "Abolitionist and Retentionist Countries," Death Penalty Information Center, www.deathpenaltyinfo.org/abolitionist-and-retentionist-countries ?scid=30&did=140#all%20crimes.

2. Amnesty International, *Death Sentences and Executions: 2013* (London: Amnesty International, March 2013).

3. J. L. Payne, *A History of Force* (Sandpoint, ID: Lytton, 2004), 129.

4. "US Executions from 1608–2002: A Demographic Breakdown of the Executed Population," Death Penalty. Pro-Con.Org, http://deathpenalty.procon.org/view.resource.php?resourceID=004087.

5. "Executions by Year Since 1976," Death Penalty Information Center, http://www.deathpenaltyinfo.org/executions-year.

6. John J. Donohue, "Capital Punishment in Connecticut, 1973–2007: A Comprehensive Evaluation from 4686 Murders to One Execution," Stanford Law School, National Bureau of Economic Research, October 15, 2011.

7. National Research Council, *Deterrence and the Death Penalty*, eds. Daniel S. Nagin and John V. Pepper (Washington, DC: National Academies Press, 2012); Justin F. Marceau and Hollis A. Whitson, "The Cost of Colorado's Death Penalty," *University of Denver Criminal Law Review* 3 (2013): 145–163; "Creating More Victims: How Executions Hurt the Families Left Behind," Murder Victim's Families for Human Rights, 2006, www.mvfhr.org/sites/default/files/pdf/MVFHReport.pdf.

8. "The Innocence List," Death Penalty Information Center, www.deathpenaltyinfo.org/innocence-list-those-freed-death-row.

9. Michael Lipka, "Support for Death Penalty Drops Among Americans," Pew Research Center, February 12, 2014, www.pewresearch.org/fact-tank/2014/02/12/support-for-death-penalty-drops-among-americans/.

10. Amnesty International, *Death Sentences and Executions: 2013* (London: Amnesty International, March 2013). According to Amnesty International there are no accurate numbers for China, Iran had 369+, Iraq 169+, and Saudi Arabia 79+.

11. "Annual Report, 2012," Dui Hua Foundation, http://duihua.org/wp/wp-content/uploads/2013/05/AR2012/2012AR_Eng_web.pdf. The Dui Hua Foundation estimated 4,000 in 2011 and less than that in 2012.

12. "Searchable Execution Database," Death Penalty Information Center, http://www.deathpenaltyinfo.org/views-executions. I counted executions occurring between September 1, 2011, and February 12, 2013.

13. Marc Santora, "On the Gallows, Curses for U.S. and 'Traitors,'" *New York Times*, December 31, 2006, www.nytimes.com/2006/12/31/world/middleeast/31gallows.html?_r=2&oref=slogin&.

14. Ibid.

15. Ibid.

16. Ibid.

17. Ibid.

18. Ibid.

19. John F. Burns and Marc Santora, "U.S. Questioned Iraq on the Rush to Hang Saddam," *New York Times*, January 1, 2007, www.nytimes.com/2007/01/01/world/middleeast/01iraq.html?pagewanted=all.

20. Ibid.

21. "The Ugly Death of Saddam Hussein," *New York Times*, January 4, 2007, www.nytimes.com/2007/01/04/opinion/04thur1.html.

22. Quoted in Hassan Fattaj, "Images of Hanging Make Hussein a Martyr to Many," *New York Times*, January 6, 2007, www.nytimes.com/2007/01/06/world/middleeast/06arabs.html?pagewanted=all.

23. "Saddam Hanging Sets Off Copy-Cat Deaths of Boys," Associated Press, January 15, 2007.

24. John F. Burns, "Two Hussein Allies Are Hanged; One Is Decapitated," *New York Times*, January 15, 2007, www.nytimes.com/2007/01/15/world/middleeast/16iraqcnd.html?pagewanted=all.

25. Dora Apel, "Torture Culture: Lynching Photographs and the Images of Abu Ghraib," *Art Journal* 64, no. 2 (Summer 2005), 91.

26. See Phong Bui, "In Conversation: Richard Serra with Phong Bui," *Brooklyn Rail*, June 12, 2006, www.brooklynrail.org/2011/07/art/richard-serra-with-phong-bui-july11.

27. Apel, "Torture Culture," 89.

28. Ibid., 89.

29. Ibid., 91.

30. Ibid., 93.

31. Haitham Eid, "Noose," mixed media, 71" x 45," 2008. The painting was displayed at the Eighth Annual Martin Luther King Exhibit at New Orleans African American Museum of Art, Culture and History and at the New Orleans Jazz and Heritage Foundation Art Gallery.

32. Robert Mills, *Suspended Animation: Pain, Pleasure, and Punishment in Medieval Culture* (London: Reaktion Books, 2005), 13.

33. Ensemble Contre la Peine de Mort and Iran Human Rights, "Annual Report on the Death Penalty in Iran, 2012," Ensemble Contre la Peine de Mort and Iran Human Rights, www.abolition.fr/sites/default/files/rapport_iran_2012-gb-270313-mdb.pdf, 2; Ahmed Shaheed, "Stop the Executions," UN Special Rapporteur on Human Rights in Iran, January 22, 2014, http://shaheedoniran.org/english/dr-shaheeds-work/press-releases/stop-the-executions-un-rights-experts-alarmed-at-the-sharp-increase-in-hangings-in-iran/. Shaheed notes that at least forty people were executed in Iran during the first two weeks of January 2014. Because many executions are held in secret, Amnesty International claims the total executed in 2013 could be as high as 704. See "Death Sentences and Executions 2013," Amnesty International, 2014.

34. Ensemble Contre la Peine de Mort, "Annual Report," 3.

35. Shaheed, "Stop the Executions."

36. Human Rights Watch, "Iran," *World Report 2013*, Human Rights Watch, www.hrw.org/world-report/2013/country-chapters/iran.

37. Ahmed Shaheed, "The Special Rapporteur's March 2013 Report on the Situation of Human Rights in the Islamic Republic of Iran," Human Rights Council Twenty-Second Session, Agenda Item 4, February 28, 2013; "IHRDC Chart of Executions by the Islamic Republic of Iran, 2013," Iran Human Rights Documentation Center, www.iranhrdc.org/english/publications /1000000225-ihrdc-chart-of-executions-by-the-islamic-republic-of -iran-2013.html.

38. Bryan Walsh, "What Should Social-Media Sites Do About Syria's Savage War Videos?" *Time*, May 27, 2013, http://content.time.com/time /magazine/article/0,9171,2143567,00.html.

39. "Execution in Iran," Youtube.com, www.youtube.com/watch?v=K8y 7VNL-FhU. A similar execution occurs on the television series *Homeland*, "The Star," season 3.

40. "Rapist Hanged in Public in the Town of Pakdasht," Youtube.com, www.youtube.com/watch?v=y6bKT7q5yBg.

41. "Political Executions in Iran," Youtube.com, www.youtube.com/watch ?v=CO4br72yOBo.

42. "Iranian Authorities Hang an Accused Rapist Off the Back of a Pick-up Truck," Youtube.com, www.youtube.com/watch?v=Wb4hx80tYT0.

43. "Saving People Being Executed in Iran by People," Youtube.com, www.youtube.com/watch?v=ylWYNCJ9aVY.

44. "Iranian Asks to Be Spared After Surviving Hanging," *Orlando Sentinel*, July 5, 1996, http://articles.orlandosentinel.com/1996–07–05/news/9607040701 _1_hanging-iranian-newspaper-survived.

45. Quoted in Richard Clark, "Hanged by the Neck Until Dead! The Processes and Physiology of Judicial Hanging." Capital Punishment UK, www.capitalpunishment.uk/hanging2.

46. Elaine Scarry, *The Body in Pain: The Making and Unmaking of the World* (New York: Oxford University Press, 1985), 5.

47. Ibid., 172.

48. John Conroy, *Unspeakable Acts, Ordinary People: The Dynamics of Torture* (New York: Knopf, 2000).

49. Orpingalik, "Songs are Thoughts . . . ," in *Poems for the New Millennium*, vol. 1, eds. Jerome Rothenberg and Pierre Joris (Berkeley: University of California Press, 1995), 735.

Sources

ARCHIVES

Alabama Supreme Court and State Law Library, Heflin-Torbert Judicial Building, Montgomery, Alabama.

Autry National Center, Los Angeles, California (ANC).

Boyd B. Stutler Collection of John Brown. West Virginia Archives and History (BBS).

Carolina First South Carolina Room at Greenville Public Library, Greenville, South Carolina (CFSC).

Columbia University Rare Book and Manuscript Library. New York, New York (CRB).

Jefferson County Museum. Charles Town, West Virginia (JCM).

Kansas Historical Society, Topeka, Kansas (KHS).

Library of Congress, Washington, DC (LOC).

Marion Public Library, Marion, Indiana (MPL).

Minnesota Historical Society Library, St. Paul, Minnesota (MHS).

The Morgan Library and Museum, New York, New York (MLM).

New York City Historical Society. New York, New York (NYCHS).

North Carolina Collection at Pack Memorial Library, Asheville, North Carolina (NCC).

North Carolina State Archives, Raleigh, North Carolina (NCSA).

Ohio State Historical Society. Columbus, Ohio (OSHS).

Polk County Historical Society, Columbus, North Carolina (PCHS).

South Carolina Historical Society. Charleston, South Carolina (SCHS).

Tryon Room at Isothermal Community College Library, Spindale, North Carolina (TR).

United States Army War College Library, Carlisle, Pennsylvania (AWCL).

United States Naval War College Library, Newport, Rhode Island (NWCL).

Washington State Library, Olympia, Washington (WSL).

INTERVIEWS

Ainslie, Ricardo. October 7, 2012.
Armbrust, Crys. June 7, 2011.
Baer, Elizabeth. October 6, 2012.
Bean, Alan. October 27, 2011.

Burgess, James. August 6, 2011.

Burrhus, Don. May 11, 2013

Conner, Anna. June 6, 2011.

Counts, Fred. June 10, 2011.

Dickey, Glenn. March 18, 2011.

Eid, Haitham. June 10, 2013.

Evans, E. Chris. August 1, 2011.

Forman, Cyrus. May 19, 2011.

Fox, David. June 25, 2012.

Fox, Joseph. June 17, 2011.

Geshick, Sandy. October 6 and November 27, 2012.

Gessner, Ben. October 5, 2012.

Ghaemi, Hadi. May 7 and July 26, 2013.

Gregersen, Markil. April 2, 2013

Henshaw, Erin. October 11, 2012.

Leonard, Ben. October 7, 2012.

Lybeck, Rick. October 5 and November 5, 2012.

McKnight, Michael. August 6, 2011.

Miller, Jerry. August 15, 2011.

Munn, William. August 6, 2011.

Nielson, Ole. March 17, 2013.

Philpott, Lindsey. May 12, 2013

Potok, Mark. February 11, 2011

Steenburg, Nancy. July 30, 2013.

Tarr, Blair. August 13, 2013.

Tompkins, Bernice. September 20, 2012.

Upthegrove, Jason. October 15, 2011.

Weston, J. B. October 7, 2012.

Wolfchild, Sheldon. October 6, 2012.

Zeman, Carrie Reber. October 24, 2012.

Zwierzyna, John. January 28, 2013.

Selected Bibliography

Adger, John B. *My Life and Times, 1810–1899*. Richmond, VA: Presbyterian Committee of Publication, 1899.

Akins, Jerry. *Hangin' Times in Fort Smith: A History of Executions in Judge Parker's Court*. Little Rock, AK: Butler Center Books, 2012.

Alighieri, Dante. *The Divine Comedy: Volume 1, Inferno*. Translated by Mark Musa. New York: Penguin, 1984.

Allen, James, and John Littlefield. *Without Sanctuary: Lynching Photography in America*. www.withoutsanctuary.org.

Anderson, Eric. *Race and Politics in North Carolina, 1872–1901: The Black Second*. Baton Rouge: Louisiana State University Press, 1981.

Anderson, Sherwood. "This Lynching." An Art Commentary on Lynching. Arthur U. Newton Galleries, 1935.

_____. *Winesburg, Ohio*. New York: Viking Press, 1919.

Apel, Dora. "Torture Culture: Lynching Photographs and the Images of Abu Ghraib." *Art Journal* 64, no. 2 (Summer 2005): 88–100.

Aptheker, Herbert. *American Negro Slave Revolts*. New York: International Publishers, 1993. [1943].

Ashley, Clifford J. *Ashley's Book of Knots*. New York: Doubleday, 1944.

Atwood, Margaret. *The Penelopiad*. New York: Canongate, 2005.

Augustine. *City of God*. Translated by Marcus Dods. *Nicene and Post-Nicene Fathers, First Series, vol. 2*. Edited by Philip Schaff. Buffalo, NY: Christian Literature Publishing, 1887.

Avey, Elijah. *The Capture and Execution of John Brown: A Tale of Martyrdom*. Elgin, IL: Brethren Publishing, 1906. JCM.

Ayers, Edward L. *The Promise of the New South: Life after Reconstruction*. New York: Oxford University Press, 1992.

_____. *Vengeance and Justice: Crime and Punishment in the Nineteenth-Century American South*. New York: Oxford University Press, 1984.

Baker, Ray Stannard. "The Thin Crust of Civilization: A Study of the Liquor Traffic in a Modern American City." *American Magazine* (April 1911): 691–704.

Ball, Charles. *Slavery in the United States*. New York: John S. Taylor, 1837. University of North Carolina-Chapel Hill, Documenting the American South.

Banner, Stuart. *The Death Penalty: An American History.* Cambridge, MA: Harvard University Press, 2002.

Barry, Joseph. *The Strange Story of John Brown.* Martinsburg, WV: Thompson Brothers, 1903. JCM.

Bartlett, Robert. *The Hanged Man: A Story of Miracle, Memory, and Colonialism in the Middle Ages.* Princeton, NJ: Princeton University Press, 2006.

Bauman, Richard A. *Crime and Punishment in Ancient Rome.* New York: Routledge, 1996.

Beccaria, Cesare. *On Crimes and Punishments and Other Writings.* Translated by Richard Davies. New York: Cambridge University Press, 2003.

Bede, The Venerable. *Commentary on the Acts of the Apostles.* Translated by Lawrence T. Martin. Kalamazoo, MI: Cistercian Publications, 1989.

Bell, Jeannine. "The Hangman's Noose and the Lynch Mob: Hate Speech and the Jena Six." *Harvard Civil Rights-Civil Liberties Law Review* 44 (2009): 329–359.

Benjamin, Walter. "The Work of Art in the Age of Mechanical Reproduction." In *The Critical Tradition: Classic Texts and Contemporary Trends,* edited by David H. Richter. Boston: Bedford, 1998.

Berlin, Ira. *Many Thousands Gone: The First Two Centuries of Slavery in North America.* Cambridge, MA: Belknap Press of Harvard University Press, 1998.

Boghossian, Elie, Renaud Clement, Margaret Redpath, and Anny Sauvageau. "Respiratory, Circulatory, and Neurological Responses to Hanging: A Review of Animal Models." *Journal of Forensic Sciences* 55, no. 5 (September 2010): 1272–1277.

Breen, Ed. "Aug. 7, 1930, Returns to Haunt Us." *Chronicle Tribune* (Marion, Indiana). April 3, 1988.

Budworth, Geoffrey. "Bog Body." *Knotting Matters: The Magazine of the International Guild of Knot Tyers.* September 2009.

Cameron, James. *A Time of Terror.* Baltimore, MD: Black Classic Press, 1994.

Campbell v. Wood, 18 F.3d 662 (9th Cir. 1994). LexisNexis.

Cantarella, Eva. "Dangling Virgins: Myth, Ritual, and the Place of Women in Ancient Greece." *Poetics Today* 6, no. 1/2. *The Female Body in Western Culture: Semiotic Perspectives* (1985): 91–101.

Capote, Truman. *In Cold Blood: A True Account of a Multiple Murder and Its Consequences.* New York: Random House, 1965.

Cash, W. J. *The Mind of the South.* New York: Random House, 1969.

Caske's 1862 War Trial Record (Case #21). Transcription from National Archives microfilm and compared to holograph in the National Archives, by Walt Bachman Walt and Elizabeth Bachman.

Chisnall, Robert. "Basic Principles of Forensic Knot Analysis: A Qualitative Study of Tying Behaviour." *Investigative Sciences Journal* 2, no. 3 (November 2010): 33–44.

Channing, Henry. *God Admonishing His People of Their Duty, as Parents and Masters: A Sermon, Preached at New-London, December 20th, 1786, occasioned by the.* . . . New-London, CT: Timothy Green, 1787.

Chomsky, Carol, "The United States-Dakota War Trials: A Study in Military Injustice." *Stanford Law Review* 13 (1990): 13–98.

Clark, Richard. "Billy Bailey—Delaware, January 25, 1996." Capital Punishment UK. www.capitalpunishment.uk/bailey.

_____. "Hanged by the Neck Until Dead! The Processes and Physiology of Judicial Hanging." Capital Punishment UK. www.capitalpunishment .uk/hanging2.

Cohen, Daniel A. "In Defense of the Gallows: Justifications of Capital Punishment in New England Execution Sermons, 1674–1825." *American Quarterly* 40, no. 2 (June 1988): 147–164.

_____. *Pillars of Salt, Monuments of Grace: New England Crime Literature and the Origins of American Popular Culture, 1674–1860.* Amherst: University of Massachusetts Press, 1993.

_____. "Social Injustice, Sexual Violence, Spiritual Transcendence: Constructions of Interracial Rape in Early American Crime Literature, 1767–1817." *William and Mary Quarterly* 56, no. 3 (July 1999): 481–526.

Cohen, Esther. *The Crossroads of Justice: Law and Culture in Late Medieval France.* New York: E. J. Brill, 1993.

_____. "Symbols of Culpability and the Universal Language of Justice: The Ritual of Public Executions in Late Medieval Europe." *History of European Ideas* 11 (1989): 407–416.

Cone, James H. *The Cross and the Lynching Tree.* Maryknoll, NY: Orbis, 2011.

"Confession Made by John, the Slave of W. Enslow the Cooper, of Participation in Vesey Revolt." Henry Ravenel Papers. SCHS.

Conner, Anna Pack. *Tryon: An Illustrated History.* Spartanburg, SC: Reprint Company, 2008.

Crosby, Sara. "Early American Crime Writing." *The Cambridge Companion to American Crime Fiction.* Edited by Catharine Ross Nickerson. New York: Cambridge University Press, 2010.

Davis, Natalie Zemon. *Society and Culture in Early Modern France.* Stanford, CA: Stanford University Press, 1975.

Davis, T. J. *A Rumor of Revolt: The 'Great Negro Plot' in Colonial New York.* Amherst: University of Massachusetts Press, 1985.

Day, Cyrus L. "Knots and Knot Lore." *Western Folklore* 9, no. 3 (1950): 229–526.

Day, George E. H. George E. H Day to President Lincoln., January 1, 1862. Abraham Lincoln Papers, Manuscript Division, LOC.

DeCaro, Louis A. Jr. *"Fire from the Midst of You": A Religious Life of John Brown.* New York: New York University Press, 2002.

Department of the Army. Pamphlet No. 27–4. Procedure for Military Executions. Department of the Army, December 9, 1947.

Donovan, S. K. *John Brown at Harper's Ferry and Charlestown: A Lecture.* Columbus, OH: F. J. Heer Printing, 1924. OSHS.

Doolen, Andy. "Reading and Writing Terror: The New York Conspiracy Trials of 1741." *American Literary History* 16, no. 3 (2004): 377–406.

Dray, Philip. *At the Hands of Persons Unknown: The Lynching of Black America.* New York: Random House, 2002.

Drew, Thomas. *John Brown Invasion: An Authentic History of the Harper's Ferry Tragedy.* Boston: James Campbell, 1860. BBS.

Egerton, Douglas R. *He Shall Go Out Free: The Lives of Denmark Vesey.* Madison, WI: Madison House, 1999.

_____. *Gabriel's Rebellion: The Virginia Slave Conspiracies of 1800 and 1802.* Chapel Hill: University of North Carolina Press, 1993.

Emerson, Ralph Waldo. "Courage," Lecture at the Boston Music Hall, November 8, 1859. Reproduced in *New-York Daily Tribune*, November 24, 1859.

Ensemble Contre la Peine de Mort and Iran Human Rights. "Annual Report on the Death Penalty in Iran, 2012." www.abolition.fr/sites/default /files/rapport_iran_2014-gb-030314-bd-e.pdf.

Esmaeli, Kouross, Rick Rowley, and Jacqueline Soohen (directors). *The Jena 6* (Part 2). Big Noise Films, 2008.

Executive Documents of the State of Minnesota for the Year 1862. St. Paul, MN: Wm. R. Marshall, State Printer, 1863. MHS.

Eyerman, Ron. *Cultural Trauma: Slavery and the Formation of African American Identity.* New York: Cambridge University Press, 2001.

Faw, Bob. "Death Penalty: Hanging." *NBC Evening News.* January 24, 1996.

Fennell, Christopher G. "Group Identity, Individual Creativity, and Symbolic Generation in a BaKongo Diaspora." *International Journal of Historical Archaeology* 7, no. 1 (March 2003): 1–31.

Fischer, Christian. *Tollund Man: Gift to the Gods.* Stroud, Gloucestershire: History Press, 2012.

Foner, Eric. *Reconstruction: America's Unfinished Revolution, 1863–1877.* New York: Harper Row, 1988.

Foucault, Michel. *Discipline and Punish: The Birth of the Prison.* Translated by Alan Sheridan. New York: Vintage Books, 1995.

Franklin, Craig. "DA/School Officials Grant Exclusive Interviews." *Jena Times.* October 3, 2007.

_____. "Media Myths About the Jena 6." *Christian Science Monitor*, October 24, 2007. www.csmonitor.com/2007/1024/p09s01-coop.html.

Frazer, James George. *The Golden Bough: A Study in Magic and Religion*, vol. 1, part 1. New York: Macmillan, 1922.

Ginzberg, Louis. "Ahithophel." *The Jewish Encyclopedia, vol. 1.* Edited by Isidore Singer et al. New York: Funk and Wagnall, 1901.

Glob, P. V. *The Bog People: Iron-Age Man Preserved.* Translated by Rupert Bruce-Mitford. Ithaca, NY: Cornell University Press, 1969.

Goodheart, Lawrence B. *The Solemn Sentence of Death: Capital Punishment in Connecticut.* Amherst: University of Massachusetts Press, 2011.

Gordon, Sloane. "Booze, Boodle, and Bloodshed in the Middle West." *Cosmopolitan.* November 1910: 761–775.

Grandjean, Katherine. "'Our *Fellow-Creatures* & our *Fellow-Christians*': Race and Religion in Eighteenth-Century Narratives of Indian Crime." *American Quarterly* 62, no. 4 (December 2010): 925–950.

Graumont, Raoul. *Handbook of Knots.* Centreville, MD: Cornell Maritime Press, 1945.

Greenberg, Kenneth, ed. *The Confessions of Nat Turner and Related Documents.* Boston: Bedford/St. Martin's, 1996.

Grosskopf, Jan Schenk. "*For Mischief Done.*" Niantic, CT: Andres and Blanton, 2012.

Gubar, Susan. *Judas: A Biography.* New York: Norton, 2009.

Hall, David D. *Worlds of Wonder, Days of Judgment.* New York: Alfred A. Knopf, 1989.

Halley, H. H. *Halley's Bible Handbook.* Grand Rapids, MI: Zondervan, 1965.

Haughton, Samuel. "On Hanging Considered from a Mechanical and Physiological Point of View." *London, Edinburgh, and Dublin Philosophical Magazine and Journal of Science* 32 (1866).

Hauptman, Laurence M. "The Pequot War and Its Legacies." *The Pequots in Southern New England: The Fall and Rise of an American Indian Nation.* Edited by Laurence M. Hauptman and James D. Wherry. Norman: University of Oklahoma Press, 1990.

Hawke, David Freeman. *Everyday Life in Early America.* New York: Harper and Row, 1989.

Hawthorne, Nathaniel. "My Kinsman Major Molineaux." In *Heath Anthology of American Literature: B.* Edited by Paul Lauter. Boston: Houghton Mifflin, 2009.

Herndon, Ruth Wallis, and Ella Wilcox Sekatu. "Colonizing the Children: Indian Youngsters in Servitude in Early Rhode Island." *Reinterpreting New England Indians and the Colonial Experience.* Edited by Colin G. Calloway and Neal Salisbury. Boston: Colonial Society of Massachusetts, 2003.

Herzfeld, Chris, and Dominique Lestel. "Knot Tying in Great Apes: Etho-Ethnology of an Unusual Tool Behavior." *Social Science Information* 44, no. 4 (2005): 621–653.

Hillman, Harold. "The Possible Pain Experienced During Executions by Different Methods." *Perception* 22 (1993): 745–753.

Hodges, Graham Russell. *Root and Branch: African Americans in New York and East Jersey, 1613–1863*. Chapel Hill: University of North Carolina Press, 1999.

Hoffer, Charles Peter. *The Great New York Conspiracy of 1741*. Lawrence: University of Kansas Press, 2003.

Homer. *The Odyssey*. Translated by Robert Fitzgerald. New York: Vintage, 1990.

Horsmanden, Daniel. *The New York Conspiracy*. Edited by Thomas J. Davis. Boston: Beacon Press, 1971.

Horwitz, Tony. *Midnight Rising: John Brown and the Raid That Sparked the Civil War*. New York: Henry Holt and Company, 2011.

Human Rights Watch. "Iran." *World Report 2013*. Human Rights Watch. www.hrw.org/world-report/2013/country-chapters/iran.

Hunt, Lynne. *Inventing Human Rights*. New York: W. W. Norton, 2007.

Ide, Roger. "Knots Under the Microscope: Part 1." *Knotting Matters* no. 103 (2009): 24–27.

Ingold, Tim. *The Perception of the Environment: Essays in Livelihood, Dwelling and Skill*. New York: Routledge, 2000.

International Federation for Human Rights. "Iran: Death Penalty—A State Terror Policy." International Federation for Human Rights. April 2009. www.fidh.org/IMG/pdf/Rapport_Iran_final.pdf.

Irving, Washington. *A Tour on the Prairies*. Paris: Baudry's European Library, 1835.

————. "Rip Van Winkle." In *Heath Anthology of American Literature: B*. Edited by Paul Lauter. Boston: Houghton Mifflin, 2009.

Jackson, Richard Mott. "Rescue of White Girl Captives from Indians: An Incident of the Minnesota Massacre of 1862." MHS.

Jefferson, Thomas. *Notes on the State of Virginia*. New York: Penguin Books, 1999.

John T. L. Preston to Margaret Junkin Preston, December 2, 1859. In Allan, Elizabeth Preston. *The Life and Letters of Margaret Junkin Preston*. Boston: Houghton Mifflin, 1903.

Jordan, Winthrop. *White Over Black: American Attitudes Toward the Negro, 1550–1812*. Chapel Hill: University of North Carolina Press, 1968.

Juran, Nathan (director). *Good Day for a Hanging* (film). 1959.

Kammen, Michael. *Colonial New York: A History*. New York: Charles Scribner's Sons, 1975.

Laskin, Sheldon H. "Jena: A Missed Opportunity for Healing." *Tikkun*, Nov/Dec 2007.

Lepore, Jill. *New York Burning: Liberty, Slavery, and Conspiracy in Eighteenth-Century Manhattan*. New York: Vintage, 2005.

_____. "The Tightening Vise: Slavery and Freedom in British New York." In *Slavery in New York*. Edited by Ira Berlin and Leslie M. Harris, 57–89. New York: New Press, 2005.

Lieberknecht, Otfried. "Death and Retribution: Medieval Visions of the End of Judas the Traitor." Saint John's University. Collegeville, Minnesota. May 13, 1997.

Linebaugh, Peter. *The London Hanged: Crime and Civil Society in the Eighteenth Century*. New York: Cambridge University Press, 1992.

_____. "The Tyburn Riot Against the Surgeons." In *Albion's Fatal Tree: Crime and Society in Eighteenth-Century England*. Edited by Douglas Hay, Peter Linebaugh, John G. Rule, E. P. Thompson, and Cal Winlow. New York: Pantheon, 1975.

Linebaugh, Peter, and Marcus Rediker. *The Many-Headed Hydra: Sailors, Slaves, Commoners, and the Hidden History of the Revolutionary Atlantic*. Boston: Beacon Press, 2001.

Litwack, Leon F. *Trouble in Mind: Black Southerners in the Age of Jim Crow*. New York: Vintage, 1999.

Lombard, Jeannine Marie. *In the Shadow of the Gallows: Race Crime, and American Civic Identity*. Philadelphia: University of Pennsylvania Press, 2012.

Madison, James H. *A Lynching in the Heartland: Race and Memory in America*. New York: Palgrave, 2001.

_____. *The Indiana Way: A State History*. Bloomington: Indiana University Press, 1986.

Masur, Louis P. *Rites of Execution: Capital Punishment and the Transformation of American Culture, 1776–1865*. New York: Oxford University Press, 1989.

Mather, Increase. "The Folly of Sinning. . . ." Boston: B. Green and J. Allen, 1699.

McManus, Edgar J. *A History of Negro Slavery in New York*. Syracuse, NY: Syracuse University Press, 1966.

Merback, Mitchell. *The Thief, the Cross, and the Wheel: Pain and the Spectacle of Punishment in Medieval and Renaissance Europe*. Chicago: University of Chicago Press, 1999.

Meyer, Marvin. *Judas: The Definitive Collection of Gospels and Legends about Infamous Apostle of Jesus*. New York: Harper, 2007.

Michaels, Elizabeth Henderson. *The Hannon Family of Polk County, North Carolina*, 3rd ed. Morganton, NC: self-published, 2008.

Mills, Robert. *Suspended Animation: Pain, Pleasure, and Punishment in Medieval Culture*. London: Reaktion Books, 2005.

Morrison, Toni. *A Mercy*. New York: Alfred A. Knopf, 2008.

NAACP. *Thirty Years of Lynching, 1889–1918.* New York: NAACP, 1919.

Nash, Gary B. *The Urban Crucible: The Northern Seaports and the Origins of the American Revolution.* Cambridge, MA: Harvard University Press, 1986.

Newkirk, Vann R. *Lynching in North Carolina: A History, 1865–1941.* Jefferson, NC: McFarland and Company, 2009.

Newton, Michael. *The Invisible Empire: The Ku Klux Klan in Florida.* Gainesville: University Press of Florida, 2001.

Nichols, David A. *Lincoln and the Indians.* St. Paul: Minnesota Historical Society Press, 2012.

Payne, J. L. *A History of Force.* Sandpoint, ID: Lytton, 2004.

Perks, P. Douglas. "'The Old Wagon Will Make a Fine Exhibit. . . .'" *Magazine of the Jefferson County Historical Society John Brown Raid Issue, 1859–2009:* 111–122. JCM.

Perry, Barbara. *In the Name of Hate: Understanding Hate Crimes.* New York: Routledge, 2001.

Pickett, Eli K. Eli K. Pickett Correspondence, 1861–1865. MHS.

Pinker, Steven. *The Better Angels of Our Nature: Why Violence Has Declined.* New York: Viking, 2011.

"Polk County and Slavery." *For the Record: A Journal of Polk County History and Genealogy* (Fall 1982). Columbus, North Carolina.

Polk County Index to Civil Action, Defendant. North Carolina State Archives, Raleigh, North Carolina. Microfilm. NCSA.

Polk County Superior Court Minutes, 1847–1848, 1855–1897, 4 vols. North Carolina State Archives, Raleigh, North Carolina. Microfilm. NCSA.

Powell, William S. *North Carolina Through Four Centuries.* Chapel Hill: University of North Carolina Press, 1989.

Powers, Bernard E. Jr. *Black Charlestonians: A Social History, 1822–1885.* Fayetteville: University of Arkansas Press, 1994.

Ravn, Morten. "Burials in Bogs: Bronze and Early Iron Age Bog Bodies from Denmark." *Acta Archaeologica* 81 (2010): 112–123.

Redpath, James. *The Public Life of Capt. John Brown.* Boston: Thayer and Eldridge, 1860.

Reich, Jerome R. *Colonial America.* Upper Saddle River, NJ: Prentice Hall, 1998.

Reynolds, David S. *John Brown, Abolitionist.* New York: Alfred A. Knopf, 2005.

Robertson, David. *Denmark Vesey.* New York: Alfred A. Knopf, 1999.

Ruchames, Louis, ed. *John Brown: The Making of a Revolutionary.* New York: University Library, Grosset and Dunlap, 1969.

Ruffin, Edmund. *The Diary of Edmund Ruffin: Volume 1.* Edited by William Kaufmann Scarborough. Baton Rouge: Louisiana State University Press, 1972.

Rush, Benjamin. *Considerations on the Injustice and Impolicy of Punishing Murder by Death, Extracted from the American Museum.* Philadelphia: 1792.

_____. *An Enquiry into the Effects of Public Punishments upon Criminals and upon Society.* London: 1787.

Ryan, Donald P., and David H. Hansen. *A Study of Ancient Egyptian Cordage.* British Museum, 1987.

Sauvageau, Anny, and Stephanie Racette. "Agonal Sequences in a Filmed Suicidal Hanging: Analysis of Respiratory and Movement Responses to Asphyxia by Hanging." *Journal of Forensic Sciences* 52, no. 4 (July 2007): 957–959.

Scarry, Elaine. *The Body in Pain: The Making and Unmaking of the World.* New York: Oxford University Press, 1985.

Scott, Kenneth. "The Slave Insurrection in New York in 1712." *New York Historical Society Quarterly* 45 (1961): 43–74.

Sewall, Samuel. *Diary of Samuel Sewall: 1674–1729, Volume 2; Collections of the Massachusetts Historical Society, Volume 6.* Cambridge, MA: John Wilson and Son, 1878.

Slotkin, Richard. "Narratives of Negro Crime in New England, 1675–1800." *American Quarterly* 25, no. 1 (March 1973): 3–31.

Sontag, Susan. *Regarding the Pain of Others.* New York: Picador, 2003.

Sophocles. *Sophocles I: Oedipus the King, Oedipus at Colonus, and Antigone.* Translated by David Greene. Chicago: University of Chicago Press, 1991.

Stavis, Barrie. *John Brown: The Sword and the Word.* South Brunswick and New York: A. S. Barnes and Company, 1970.

Steenburg, Nancy H. "Murder and Minors: Changing Standards in the Criminal Law of Connecticut, 1650–1853." *Murder on Trial: 1620–2002.* Edited by Robert Asher, Lawrence B. Goodheart, and Alan Rogers. Albany: State University of New York Press, 2005.

Streib, Victor L. *Death Penalty for Juveniles.* Bloomington: Indiana University Press, 1987.

Strother, David Hunter. "The Hanging of John Brown." Edited by Boyd B. Stutler. *American Heritage* VI (February 1955): 6–9.

Sullivan, Lee R. "The Hanging of Judas: Medieval Iconography and the German Peasants' War." *Essays in Medieval Studies* 15 (1998): 93–102.

Tacitus, Cornelius. *The Germany and the Agricola of Tacitus: The Oxford Translation Revised, with Notes, With an Introduction by Edward Brooks, Jr.* Philadelphia: David McKay, 1897.

Taylor, Archer. "The Gallows of Judas Iscariot." *Washington University Studies* 9, no. 2 (1922): 135–156.

Thomas J. Jackson ("Stonewall") to his wife, Mary Anna Jackson, December 2, 1859. *Life and Letters of Thomas J. Jackson.* Edited by Mary Anna Jackson. New York: Harper, 1892.

Thomas Lamboll Beach Papers. SCHS.

Thoreau, Henry David. *Collected Essays and Poems.* New York: Library of America, 2001.

Tilles, Stanley, and Jeff Denhart. *By the Neck Until Dead: The Gallows at Nuremburg.* Bedford, Indiana: JoNa Books, 1999.

Tolnay, Stewart E., and E. M. Beck. *A Festival of Violence: An Analysis of Southern Lynchings, 1882–1930.* Urbana: University of Illinois Press, 1995.

Trodd, Zoe, and John Stauffer. *Meteor of War: The John Brown Story.* Maplecrest, NY: Brandywine Press, 2004.

Tuchman, Gary. "Death Penalty—Delaware Hanging." *CNN Evening News,* January 1, 2007.

Tuskegee Institute News Clippings File. Tuskegee Institute, Alabama: Division of Behavioral Science Research, Carver Research Foundation, Tuskegee Institute. Sanford, NC: Microfilming Corporation of America, 1976. Microfilm. Reels 221 and 226.

US Army, Military Commission. Sioux War Trials 1862. Trial Transcripts. File P1423. MHS.

van der Sanden, W. *Through Nature to Eternity: The Bog Bodies of Northwest Europe.* Amsterdam: Batavian Lion International, 1996.

Waldrep, Christopher. *The Many Faces of Judge Lynch: Extralegal Violence and Punishment in America.* New York: Palgrave Macmillan, 2002.

_____. "Prologue." In *Lynching in America: A History in Documents.* Edited by Christopher Waldrep. New York: New York University Press, 2006.

Walsham, Alexandra. "Introduction: Relics and Remains." *Relics and Remains.* Edited by Alexandra Walsham. New York: Oxford University Press, 2010.

War Department. Pamphlet No. 27–4. Procedure for Military Executions. War Department, June 12, 1944.

Weisberg, Jacob. "This Is Your Death." *New Republic.* July 1, 1991.

Weitzmann, Kurt. "Age of Spirituality: Late Antique and Early Christian Art, Third to Seventh Century." *Metropolitan Museum of Art Bulletin* 35, no. 2 (Autumn 1979).

Wells-Barnett, Ida B. "Lynch Law in Georgia." Chicago: Chicago Colored Citizens, 1899.

_____. *The Red Record: Tabulated Statistics and Alleged Cause of Lynchings in the United States.* Chicago: Donohue and Henneberry, 1895. www.gutenberg.org/files/14977/14977-h/14977-h.htm.

_____. *Southern Horrors: Lynch Law in All Its Phases*. New York: New York Age Print, 1892.

West, Stephen A. *From Yeoman to Redneck in the South Carolina Upcountry, 1850–1915*. Charlottesville: University of Virginia Press, 2008.

Westerman, Gwen, and Bruce White. *Mni Sota Makoce: The Land of the Dakota*. St. Paul: Minnesota Historical Society Press, 2012.

Wheeler, Wayne B. *The Newark Lynching: Its Causes and Results*. Westerville, OH: American Issue Publishing, 1910.

Whipple, Bishop Henry. *Lights and Shadows of a Long Episcopate*. New York: Macmillan, 1899.

White, Lynn Jr. "The Legacy of the Middle Ages in the American Wild West." *Speculum* 40, no. 2 (April 1965): 191–202.

Whitney R. Harris to Justice Robert H. Jackson. In Douglas O. Linder, "Nuremberg Trials (1945–1949)" *Famous Trials*. University of Missouri-Kansas City, School of Law. 2012. http://law2.umkc.edu/faculty/projects/ftrials/ftrials.htm.

Williams, Daniel E. "'Behold a Tragic Scene Strangely Changed into a Theater of Mercy': The Structure and Significance of Criminal Conversion Narratives in Early New England." *American Quarterly* 38, no. 5 (Winter 1986): 827–847.

_____. *Pillars of Salt: An Anthology of Early American Criminal Narratives*. Madison, WI: Madison House, 1993.

_____. "Rogues, Rascals, and Scoundrels: The Underworld Literature of Early America." *American Studies* 24, no. 2 (Fall 1983): 5–19.

Williams, Daniel T. *Amid the Gathering Multitude: The Story of Lynching in America, A Classified Listing*. Unpublished, Tuskegee University, 1968.

Williams, Jack Kenny. *Vogues in Villainy: Crime and Retribution in Ante-Bellum South Carolina*. Columbia: University of South Carolina Press, 1959.

Wilson, Angela Cavender. *What Does Justice Look Like?: The Struggle for Liberation in the Dakota Homeland*. St. Paul, MN: Living Justice Press, 2008.

Wingerd, Mary Lethert. *North Country: The Making of Minnesota*. Minneapolis: University of Minnesota Press, 2010.

Wyatt, Jonathan, Tom Squires, Guy Norfolk, and Jason Payne-James. *Oxford Handbook of Forensic Medicine*. New York: Oxford University Press, 2011.

Wyatt-Brown, Bertram. *Honor and Violence in the Old South*. New York: Oxford University Press, 1986.

Zeman, Carrie Reber. "A Veiled Cabinet of Curiosities: A Preliminary Report on Minnesota's 1862 Gallow's Artifacts." http://athrillingnarrative.files.wordpress.com/2012/04/execution-artifacts-report.pdf.

Index

Abu Ghraib scandal, 271–272
Acme News Service, 202
Adger, John, 103–104
African Americans, 168, 240
  negative texts on, 92–93
  New York burial ground, 77–79
  noose symbolization for, 2
  racial category of, 92
  violence against, after
    Reconstruction, 161–162
  See also Black rape; Slave
    rebellion; Slavery; Slaves
African Burial Ground National
  Monument, 77–79
Age of Enlightenment, 85–86
  literacy during, 86
  racial categories, 92
Ahithophel hanging, in Bible,
  43–44
Alistair Cooke's America, 202
Allen, James, 184
American art, on noose, 248–249
American Historical Association,
  117
American Indian and Fine Arts
  Collections, at MHS, 142–143
American Weekly Mercury, 69
Ames, Levi, 68 (photo)
Amnesty International, 86
Anderson, Sherwood, 186–187, 199
Anonymity, of communications
  technology, 252–253
Anti-Defamation League, 255
Anti-Saloon League, 188, 189, 193

Apel, Dora, 271, 272
Arnold, Benedict, 95
Arnold, J. K., 143
Artifacts
  of Dakota tribe, 151
  of US-Dakota War, at MHS,
    142–147
Ashley, Clifford, 18, 19
Ashley Book of Knots (Ashley), 18
Asphyxiation, 24, 25
Association of Southern Women for
  the Prevention of Lynching,
  183
Assyrians, hanging among, 42–44
Atherton, Herbert, 191, 193,
  194–195
Atlantic Slave Trade, organizations
  against, 86
Avery, William H., 221
Avis, John, 110
Ayers, Edward, 172
Ayers, Stephen, 251

Bailey, Billy, 229, 231–233, 268
Bailey, Robert, 257, 259–260
Bailey, Flossie, 209, 212
Baker, David, 265
Baker, Ray Stannard, 189
Ball, Charles, 100
Ball, Mary, 209, 215–216
Ban
  of capital punishment, in 1794
    Pennsylvania, 96
  of crucifixion, in Middle Ages, 49

Rachel Dobbelaer

JACK SHULER holds the John and Christine Warner Chair at Denison University, where he is an associate professor teaching American literature and Black Studies. He is the author of two books on the nexus of race and violence in America, *Calling Out Liberty* and *Blood and Bone*. Shuler's criticism, interviews, reviews, and poems have appeared in the *Columbia Journal of American Studies, Journal of Southern History, South Carolina Review, Southern Studies,* and *Failbetter,* among others. He lives in Ohio.

PublicAffairs is a publishing house founded in 1997. It is a tribute to the standards, values, and flair of three persons who have served as mentors to countless reporters, writers, editors, and book people of all kinds, including me.

I. F. STONE, proprietor of *I. F. Stone's Weekly*, combined a commitment to the First Amendment with entrepreneurial zeal and reporting skill and became one of the great independent journalists in American history. At the age of eighty, Izzy published *The Trial of Socrates*, which was a national bestseller. He wrote the book after he taught himself ancient Greek.

BENJAMIN C. BRADLEE was for nearly thirty years the charismatic editorial leader of *The Washington Post*. It was Ben who gave the *Post* the range and courage to pursue such historic issues as Watergate. He supported his reporters with a tenacity that made them fearless and it is no accident that so many became authors of influential, best-selling books.

ROBERT L. BERNSTEIN, the chief executive of Random House for more than a quarter century, guided one of the nation's premier publishing houses. Bob was personally responsible for many books of political dissent and argument that challenged tyranny around the globe. He is also the founder and longtime chair of Human Rights Watch, one of the most respected human rights organizations in the world.

·   ·   ·

For fifty years, the banner of Public Affairs Press was carried by its owner Morris B. Schnapper, who published Gandhi, Nasser, Toynbee, Truman, and about 1,500 other authors. In 1983, Schnapper was described by *The Washington Post* as "a redoubtable gadfly." His legacy will endure in the books to come.

Peter Osnos, *Founder and Editor-at-Large*